2nd Workshop on Computational Modeling of People's Opinions, Personality, and Emotions in Social Media (PEOPLES 2018)

New Orleans, Louisiana, USA
6 June 2018

ISBN: 978-1-5108-6360-6

NAACL HLT 2018

Computational Modeling of PEople's Opinions, PersonaLity, and Emotions in Social media

Proceedings of the Second Workshop

June 6, 2018
New Orleans, USA

Preface

Welcome to the second edition of PEOPLES (Workshop on Computational Modeling of People's Opinions, Personality and Emotions in Social Media), co-located with the 16th Annual Conference of the North American Chapter of the Association for Computational Linguistics: Human Language Technologies. The first edition was held at the 26th International Conference on Computational Linguistics (COLING 2016) in Osaka, Japan.

The idea of organizing PEOPLES stemmed from two related observations, namely the availability of large amounts of spontaneous data covering a range of personal aspects and the fact that such aspects are usually studied in isolation. Social media users nowadays freely express what is on their mind at any moment in time, at any location, and about virtually anything. These large amounts of spontaneously produced texts open up a unique opportunity to learn more about such users, e.g., predicting demographic variables (age, gender), but also personality types, as well as emotions and opinion expressions. This observation is not new, of course, and this opportunity has largely been exploited in the recent years, with abundant works on sentiment analysis, emotion detection, and personality. However, such traits of human personality and behavior have indeed attracted a substantial amount of attention but have been mostly studied *in isolation*, often in different - but related - communities, such as NLP, CL, AI. Therefore, we thought that the time was ripe to bring these communities a step closer to study people's traits and expressions jointly and in their interplay on such large volumes of available data.

The communities' response, with 25 received submissions coming from 11 different countries and going well beyond typical NLP topics, proves again this year that there is wide interest at this intersection, and we are happy to be able to provide a context for exchanging ideas.

Following the reviewers's advice, 14 papers were selected for inclusion in the proceedings. They cover a wide range of topics related to the three main PEOPLES themes (personality, emotion and opinion), their interaction and the impact of their modeling on social aspects like well-being, political preferences, humor and language use.

To further enrich this volume, we additionally invited our keynote speakers to submit position papers that accompany their talks, and are excited that both of our keynotes submitted excellent papers touching upon issues of making NLP models more demographically aware and how researchers from related fields such as demography can benefit from NLP techniques.

We hope that this is just the second edition of what will become series of workshops bringing together researchers in Computational Linguistics, Natural Language Processing and Computational Social Science, who share an interest in personality, opinion and emotion detection, and especially in researching the intertwining of such traits and expressions.

We would like to thank our program committee consisting of 33 researchers from a variety of backgrounds for their insightful and constructive reviews. Without their support, this workshop would not have been possible. In addition, we thank all authors for submitting papers and making PEOPLES a big success. Also thanks to our two invited speakers, Dirk Hovy and Letizia Mencarini (Bocconi University, Italy), for having accepted to come to the workshop and share their expertise and ideas on PEOPLES' topics. We thank NAACL for hosting us, and in particular the local organizers for their support. Lastly, we are extremely grateful to our sponsors, CELI Language Technologies, and the Computational Linguistics group of the University of Groningen for their financial support, without which this workshop would not have gone through.

We look forward to welcoming you all at PEOPLES 2018 in New Orleans!

Malvina, Viviana, Barbara, Claudia

PEOPLES: https://peopleswksh.github.io/

Organisers

Malvina Nissim, University of Groningen, The Netherlands

Viviana Patti, University of Turin, Italy

Barbara Plank, IT University of Copenhagen, Denmark

Claudia Wagner, Claudia Wagner, University of Koblenz and GESIS - Köln

Programme Committee

Nikolaos Aletras, Sheffield University, UK
Pierpaolo Basile, University of Bari, Italy
Valerio Basile, INRIA Sophia Antipolis Méditerranée, France
Arnim Bleier, GESIS Leibniz Institute for the Social Sciences, Germany
Gosse Bouma, University of Groningen, The Netherlands
Erik Cambria, Nanyang Technological University, Singapore
Fabio Celli, University of Trento, Italy
Chloé Clavel, LTCI-CNRS, Telecom-ParisTech, France
Franco Cutugno, University of Naples Federico II, Italy
Walter Daelemans, University of Antwerp, Belgium
David Garcia, Complexity Science Hub Vienna and Medical University of Vienna, Austria
Ancsa Hannak, Central European University, Hungary
Dan Hardt, Copenhagen Business School, Denmark
Dirk Hovy, Bocconi University, Italy
Richard Johansson, University of Gothenburg, Sweden
David Jurgens, Stanford University, US
Svetlana Kiritchenko, NRC-Canada, Canada
Florian Kuhnemann, Radboud Universiteit Nijmegen, The Netherlands
Fei Liu, Melbourne University, Australia
Nikola Ljubešić, Jožef Stefan Institute, Slovenia
Kim Luyckx, Biomina Research Group, Belgium
Eric Malmi, Aalto University, Finland
Héctor Martínez Alonso, Thomson Reuters, CA
Rada Mihalcea, University of Michigan, US
Saif Mohammad, NRC-Canada, Canada
Dong Nguyen, University of Twente, The Netherlands
Scott Nowson, Accenture Centre for Innovation, Dublin, Ireland
Massimo Poesio, Queen Mary University, UK
Martin Potthast, Leipzig University, Germany
Daniel Preotiuc-Pietro, University of Pennsylvania, US
Paolo Rosso, Technical University of Valencia, Spain
Hassan Saif, Knowledge Media Institute, UK
Ingmar Weber, QCRI, Qatar

Sponsors

PEOPLES 2018 is organized with the support of CELI Language Technology (https://www.celi.it/en/) and the Computational Linguistics group of CLCG (http://www.rug.nl/research/clcg/), University of Groningen.

Table of Contents

Conference Program

Thursday, June 6, 2018

8:50–9:00   *Opening Remarks*

Session 1

9:00–09:20   *What makes us laugh? Investigations into Automatic Humor Classification*
Vikram Ahuja, Taradheesh Bali and Navjyoti Singh

9:20–09:40   *Social and Emotional Correlates of Capitalization on Twitter*
Sophia Chan and Alona Fyshe

9:40–10:00   *Building an annotated dataset of app store reviews with Appraisal features in English and Spanish*
Natalia Mora and Julia Lavid-López

10:00–10:15   *Enabling Deep Learning of Emotion With First-Person Seed Expressions*
Hassan Alhuzali, Muhammad Abdul-Mageed and Lyle Ungar

10:15–10:30   *A Dataset of Hindi-English Code-Mixed Social Media Text for Hate Speech Detection*
Aditya Bohra, Deepanshu Vijay, Vinay Singh, Syed Sarfaraz Akhtar and Manish Shrivastava

10:30–11:00   *Coffee*

Session 2

11:00–12:00   **Keynote:** *The Social and the Neural Network: How to Make Natural Language Processing about People again*
Dirk Hovy

12:00–12:15   *Observational Comparison of Geo-tagged and Randomly-drawn Tweets*
Tom Lippincott and Annabelle Carrell

12:15–12:30   *Johns Hopkins or johnny-hopkins: Classifying Individuals versus Organizations on Twitter*
Zach Wood-Doughty, Praateek Mahajan and Mark Dredze

12:30–14:00   *Lunch*

What makes us laugh? Investigations into Automatic Humor Classification

Taradheesh Bali *
International Institute of
Information Technology
Hyderabad, India
taradheesh.bali
@research.iiit.ac.in

Vikram Ahuja *
International Institute of
Information Technology
Hyderabad, India
vikram.ahuja
@research.iiit.ac.in

Late Prof. Navjyoti Singh
International Institute of
Information Technology
Hyderabad, India
navjyoti@iiit.ac.in

Abstract

Most scholarly works in the field of computational detection of humour derive their inspiration from the incongruity theory. Incongruity is an indispensable facet in drawing a line between humorous and non-humorous occurrences but is immensely inadequate in shedding light on what actually made the particular occurrence a funny one. Classical theories like Script-based Semantic Theory of Humour and General Verbal Theory of Humour try and achieve this feat to an adequate extent. In this paper we adhere to a more holistic approach towards classification of humour based on these classical theories with a few improvements and revisions. Through experiments based on our linear approach and performed on large data-sets of jokes, we are able to demonstrate the adaptability and show componentizability of our model, and that a host of classification techniques can be used to overcome the challenging problem of distinguishing between various categories and sub-categories of jokes.

1 Introduction

Humor is the tendency of particular cognitive experiences to provoke laughter and provide amusement. Humor is an essential element of all verbal communication. Natural language systems should be able to handle humor as it will improve user-friendliness and human-computer interaction. Humour has been studied for a number of years in computational linguistics in terms of both humour generation (Ritchie and Masthoff, 2011), (Stock and Strapparava, 2006) and detection, but no such work has been done to create a classification of humor. Humor Detection has been approached as a classification problem by (Mihalcea and Strapparava, 2005). Classification of humour is a very dif-

ficult task because even theoretically there is not much consensus among theorists regarding what exactly humour is? Even if there were a specific theory as to what are the categories of humor, the sense of humour varies from person to person and therefore giving its types is even more difficult. Consensus is yet to be achieved regarding the categorization of humour (Attardo et al., 1994). To achieve this difficult feat of classification we try to answer the most basic question of Why do we laugh on a joke?. What factors motivate us. This is the most novel thing that only we are trying to achieve as of now. First of all the possible types of humor can be virtually infinite. Some researchers reduce humor to just one, or a few types, for example, incongruity (Ruch and Carrell, 1998). Since there are infinite possible types, there is a continued lack of any generally accepted taxonomy of humor, thus it may be classified according to different purposes. These classifications may often overlap. For instance the joke: A clean desk is a sign of a cluttered desk drawer can be labeled as a sarcastic joke as well as a wordplay joke/pun(antonyms).

We are trying to formulate the problem of determining different types of humor as a traditional classification task by feeding positive and negative datasets to a classifier. The data-set consists of one liners jokes of different types collected from many jokes websites, multiple subreddits and multiple twitter handles.

In short, our contributions can be summarized as follows:

- We present a theoretical framework which also provides the base for the task of computational classification of a vast array of types of jokes into categories and sub-categories

- We present a comparative study of a wide range of topic detection methods on large

---

* Both authors have contributed equally towards the paper (names in lexicographic sequence).

1

Proceedings of the Second Workshop on Computational Modeling of People's Opinions, Personality, and Emotions in Social Media, pages 1–9
New Orleans, Louisiana, June 6, 2018. ©2018 Association for Computational Linguistics

data sets of one-liner jokes.

- We analyze jokes based on the theme that they expresses and the emotion that they evoke.

The remainder of the paper is structured as follows. Section 2 provides an overview of related work and their shortcomings. Section 3 presents the framework proposed. Section 4 presents the dataset along with some pre-processing steps. Section 5 presents the various experiments conducted on the data set. Section 6 discusses the results, while Section 7 concludes the paper.

2 Related Work

Research in humour is a field of interest pertaining not only to linguistics and literature but neuroscience and evolutionary psychology as well. Research in humor has been done to understand the psychological and physiological effects, both positive and negative, on a person or groups of people. Research in humor has revealed many different theories of humor and many different kinds of humor including their functions and effects personally, in relationships, and in society.

Historically, humour has been synonymous with laughter but major empirical findings suggest that laughter and humour do not always have a one-to-one association. For example, Non-Duchenne laughter (Gervais and Wilson, 2005). At the same point of time it is also well documented that even though humour might not have a direct correlation with laughter it certainly has an influence in evoking certain emotions as a reaction to something that is considered humorous (Samson and Gross, 2012). Through the ages there have been many theories of humour which attempt to explain what humor is, what social functions it serves, and what would be considered humorous. Though among the three main rival theories of humour, incongruity theory is the more widely accepted as compared to relief[1] and superiority[2] theories, it is necessary but not sufficient in containing the scope of what constitutes humour.

[1] Relief theory maintains that laughter is a homeostatic mechanism by which psychological tension is reduced.(2018)

[2] The general idea behind Superiority Theory is that a person laughs about either misfortunes of others (so called schadenfreude) as laughter expresses feelings of superiority over them or over a former state of ourselves.(2016)

Script Semantic Theory of Humour (SSTH): In his book Raskin (Raskin, 2012) divulges the concept of semantic scripts. Each concept expressed by a word which is internalized by the native speaker of a language, is related to a semantic script via some cognitive architecture to all the surrounding pieces of information. Thereafter, he posits that in order to produce the humor of a verbal joke, the following 2 conditions must be met

- "The text is compatible, fully or in part, with two different (semantic) scripts

- The two scripts with which the text is compatible are opposite. The two scripts with which the text is compatible are said to overlap fully or in part on this text."

Humor is evoked when a trigger at the end of the joke, the punch line, causes the audience to abruptly shift its understanding from the primary (or more obvious) script to the secondary, opposing script.

General Verbal Theory of Humour (GVTH): The key idea behind GVTH are the 6 levels of independent Knowledge Resources (KRs) defined by (Attardo and Raskin, 1991). These KRs could be used to model individual jokes and act as the distinguishing factors in order to determine the similarity or differences between types of jokes. The KRs are ranked below in the order of their ability to '*determine*'/restrict the options available for the instantiation of the parameters below them:

1. Script Opposition (SO)

2. Logical Mechanism (LM)

3. Situation (SI)

4. Target (TA)

5. Narrative Strategy (NS)

6. Language (LA)

Owing to the use of Knowledge Resources GVTH has a much higher coverage as a theory of humour as compared to SSTH, but there still are a few aspects where GVTH comes up short. In prior sections we have established that humour has a direct correlation with the emotions that it evokes. In a similar manner emotions also act as a trigger to a humorous event. In such said events because the reason for inception of the humorous content lies with the post-facto realization/resolution of the incongruity caused by the emotion rather than the event itself applying script opposition is out of line. For example, fear, a negative emotion that can stem as a result of some incongruity in the expected behaviour of our surroundings. Our primary emotion to such a situation is fear. Even so, the result of this incongruity caused in our emotional state, which incipiently was caused by the incongruity in our physical surroundings, can lead to humour. It must be noted that the trigger here is neither the situation nor any LM or script opposition, but the emotional incongruity.

Correspondingly, humour can also prompt itself in form of meta-humour just as emotions do. For example, one way to appreciate a bad joke can be the poorness of the joke. Another major point of contention in GVTH is Logical Mechanism. Here, logical does not stand for deductive logic or strict formal logicality but rather should be understood in some looser quotidian sense rational thinking and acting or even ontological possibility.

In his paper (Krikmann, 2006) correctly points out that in SSTH and GVTH both, Raskins concept of script is merely a loose and coarse approximation, borrowed from cognitive psychology which attempts to explain what actually happens in human consciousness. Such scripts encapsulate not only direct word meanings, but also semantic information presupposed by linguistic units as well as the encyclopaedic knowledge associated to them. Even so, in order to explain certain instances where direct or indirect script opposition is missing we need to inject an inference mechanism and a script elaborator to the current cognitive model, which would work off of the pre-existing script and ones that are newly formed through the inference mechanism. These two features become indispensable as, it is not always the case that opposing scripts are readily available to us.

3 Proposed Framework

Having Script Opposition as the only derivative bedrock behind the start of a humorous event proves deleterious in SSTH and GVTHs ability to be able to adapt to different kinds of incongruities. Further, due to the inability of GVTH to accommodate emotions at any level, uncertainty surrounding Logical Mechanism with its really vague identity, and the order of the Knowledge resources instigate us to diverge from SSTH and GVTH as the foundation for our computational setup. Rather, in order to address such shortcomings we have kept the structure of our theory to be much more consequence driven.

Having an approach solely derived from the existing types of humour, would be subject to changes and alterations with the addition of every new type of humor and will add the limitation of the model being either too rigid, which might lead to overfitting while performing computational analysis or can lead to a model which becomes unstable as it is unable to sustain new types after more and more changes. In preference to this we proceed with caution keeping in mind the scope of this problem, drawing from the successes of the previous theories such as SSTH and GVTH with a more holistic approach in mind.

From the outset, Attardo and Raskin (Script theory revis(it)ed: joke similarity and joke representation model) had their features focused towards recognizing the distinguishing parameters of various degrees of similarity among jokes. In a similar manner we recognize three major marked characteristics which are reflected across all types of jokes, viz.

1. **Mode (*Modus Operandi*) :** Each joke whether verbal, textual or graphic has a way in which it is put across to the respective audience. This *mode* of delivery of a joke can be (but not always) decided upon by the performer of the humorous act. The mode can be a matter of conscious choice or the spontaneous culmination of a dialogue. Different situations might warrant for different modes of delivery leading to varied effects after the humour behind the joke is resolved. For example, the delivery of joke can be sarcastic, where the speaker might want to retort to someone in a conversation or it can be deadpan, where the triviality of speakers reaction becomes the source of humour. As compared to SSTH and GVTH which investigate the reason behind the incongruity (incongruity being the single source of humour) in the scripts or situations in such scenarios, we embrace incongruity as one of the many mechanisms that can be possible and keep the scope open for all categories which encompass far greater types of humour including and not being limited to juxtaposition of opposing scripts.Thus, the tools that are at the

disposal to bring about variations in the mode become more than mere language based artifacts like puns, alliterations etc. The mode can be based on the phonetics of the words such as in a limerick.

Two unique sub-categories that can be addressed here which would otherwise cause problems in SSTH and GVTH, due to their structure of logical mechanism are Anti-Humour and Non-Sequitur. Both are unconventional forms of humour and posit a stringent challenge to such theories. Non-Sequitur is difficult to accommodate even for GVTH due to its reliance on Logical Mechanisms. While all the jokes which follow any sort of logical structure could have been classified according to GVTH due to LM, Non-Sequitur does not follow any logical structure whatsoever. The entire point of a non-sequitur is that it is *absurd* in its reason and it also makes *no sense* according to semantics or meaning. The case with anti-humour could not be more different as it is not a play on the logical structure of the normal conversation but on that of the joke. Hence, as we have also mentioned in the criticisms section, there does not exist a mechanism in the previous theories to deal with such second order humour and meta-jokes.

2. **Theme :** Each joke through the use of its language and the subject matter conveys a feeling or an emotion along with it. As we have discussed at lengths in the previous sections emotion plays a very important role in a humorous event. It can by itself spur a new thread for a joke as well as act as the conclusive feeling that we get along with the humorous effect. For example, the feeling of disgust on hearing a joke about a gross situation or thing. Hence, the function that the *'theme'* of a joke can serve is, as a pointer towards the overall affect the joke has during its delivery and after its resolution. In this way we are able to tackle the aspects of a humorous event which are content and language dependent.

3. **Topic :** Most jokes have some central element, which can be regarded as the butt of the joke. This element is the key concept around which the joke revolves. It can be based on

stereotypes, such as in blonde jokes or can be based off of a situation such as '__walks into a bar'. As can be observed in the latter case it is mostly but not always the case that the central element be single object or a person. The '__walks into a bar' might further lead to a topic or a situation which ends up with the punchline being on the *'dumb blonde'* stereotype. Hence, a single joke can therefore, without such restrictions on its definition can have multiple topics at the same time. Also by not restricting ourselves to only stereotypes about things, situations and beings we can also play with cases where the topic is the stereotype of a particular type of joke itself, leading to humour about stereotypes of humour. For example, a joke about a bad knock knock joke.

On inspection of the aforementioned categories we can clearly observe that unlike GVTH giving a hierarchical structure to these metrics is unsustainable. This works in our favour as we get rid of establishing problematic dependencies like ontological superiority for each category. Instead, we provide a flatter approach where a joke can be bred out of various combinations from each category and belong to multiple sub-categories at the same time.

The culmination of our work towards creating computationally detectable entities leads us to recognizing a sub-set in each of the categories that we have defined above. In the coming sections we venture towards testing our theoretical framework in real-life scenarios extracted through various social-media. Table 1 provides a catalogue of the sub-categories that we detect in each category.

4 Dataset

- **Topic Detection :** For the task of topic detection in Jokes we mined many jokes websites and collected their tags and considered those our topics. We have restricted our Jokes to the following categories: Animal, Blonde, Fat, Food, Profession, Kids, Marriage, Money, Nationality, Sports, News/politics, Police/military , Technology, Height, Men/Women, Celebrities/Pop Culture, Travel, Doctor, Lawyer, God/religion, Pick up lines, school, party, Walks into a bar, Yo-mama. Most of the

Table 1: Computationally Detectable Characteristics

Categories	Sub-Categories
Mode	Sarcastic
	Exaggeration/Hyperbole
	Phonetics Assisted
	Semantic Opposites
	Secondary Meaning
Theme	Dark Joke
	Gross Joke
	Adult/Sexual Joke
	Insults
Topics	Animal, Blonde, Fat, Food, Profession, Kids, Marriage, Money, Nationality, Sports, News/politics, Police/military, Technology,Height,Men/ Women, Celebrities, Pop Culture, Travel, Doctor, Lawyer, God/religion, Pick up lines, School, Parties, Walks into a bar, Yo-mama

jokes websites had the above topics as common topics. We mined nearly 40,000 one liners jokes belonging to these 25 categories for the use of Topic Detection. Since they were collected automatically, it is possible to have noise in the dataset.

- **Sarcastic Jokes :** For the task of Sarcasm Detection we mined Sarcastic jokes(positive) from reddit and other jokes websites which had sarcasm tags in it. For negative data we considered data under tags other than Sarcasm and manually verified the jokes. We created a dataset of 5000 jokes with 2500 belonging to the the positive set and and equal amount of negative instances and manually verified them

- **NSFW Jokes :** These are the types of jokes which are most famous on the online media.These types of jokes are mainly associated with heavy nudity, sexual content, heavy profanity and adult slangs. We collected multiple one liner jokes from subreddit /r/dirtyjokes and took jokes from various jokes websites with tags NSFW, dirty, adult and sexual. We created a dataset of 5000 jokes with 2500 belonging to the positive instances and equal number of negative

instances verified manually.

- **Insults :** These kinds of jokes mainly consists mainly of offensive insults directed someone else or towards the speaker itself. (Mendrinos, 2004) Typical targets for insult include individuals in the show's audience, or the subject of a roast. The speaker of an insult joke often maintains a competitive relationship with the listener. We collected multiple jokes from the subreddit /r/roastme and after manual verification we had 2000 jokes of positive instances and for negative instances we manually created a dataset of 2000 one liner jokes.

- **Gross :** A joke having to do with disgusting acts or other things people might find grotesque. We extracted 500 jokes various ous jokes website which had a "gross" category/tag in it. We selected equal number of non gross jokes from the above datatset. After manual verification we had a total of 1000 jokes in this category, 500 belonging to both positive and negative sets.

- **Dark Humor :** It's a form of humor involving a twist or joke making the joke seen as offensive, harsh, horrid, yet the joke is still funny. We collected multiple jokes from subreddit /r/darkjokes as well as as many jokes websites containing the tag Dark Humor. After removing duplicates we had a dataset of 3500 dark jokes. For negative samples we randomly selected 3500 jokes from the jokes websites which did not contain Dark Humor in their tags and manually verified them.

4.1 Data Preprocessing

The content of user created jokes on Twitter and Reddit can be noisy. They could contain elements like @RT, links, dates, ID's, name of users, HTML Tags and hashtags to name a few. To reduce the amount of noise before the classification task , the data is subjected to the following pre processing tasks.

- **Tokenization :** In a raw post, terms can be combined with any sort of punctuation and hyphenation and can contain abbreviations, typos, or conventional word variations. We use the NLTK tokenizer package to extract tokens from the joke by removing stop words,

5

Table 2: My caption

Sarcastic Joke	I asked my North Korean friend how it was there? He said he couldn't complain.
Exaggeration/Hyperbole	You know what, we need a huge spoon to take care of this. Guy who invented shovels
Phonetics Assisted	Coca Cola went to town, Diet Pepsi shot him down. Dr. Pepper fixed him up, Now we are drinking 7up.
Semantic Opposites	Humpty Dumpty had a great fall - and a pretty good spring and summer , too .
Secondary Meaning	Those who like the sport fishing can really get hooked
Dark Jokes	Why don't black people go on cruises? They are not falling for that one.
Gross Joke	Q: Why did the skeleton burp? A: It didn't have the guts to fart.
Adult/Sexual Joke	Does time fly when you're having sex or was it really just one minute?
Insults	You are proof that evolution can go in reverse.

punctuation, extra white space and hashtags and removing mentions, i.e., IDs or names of other users included in the joke and converting to lowercase.

- **Stemming :** Stemming is the process of reducing words to their root (or stem), so that related words map to the same stem or root form. This process naturally reduces the number of words associated with each document, thus simplifying the feature space. We used the NLTK Porter stemmer in our experiments.

5 Experiment

We performed various experiments on our dataset. For the evaluation we randomly divided our dataset into 90% training and 10% testing. All the experiments were conducted 10 fold and the final performance is reported by averaging the result.

- **Topic Detection :** There are a wide variety of methods and variables and they greatly affect the quality of results. We compare results from three topic detection methods on our dataset to detect topics of these jokes. We use LDA, Naive Bayes and SVM along with lexical and Pragmatic features and compared their results. We also augment the used approaches by boosting proper nouns and then, recalculating the experiment results on the same dataset. The boosting techniques that we have used are duplication proper nouns. This boosting technique was chosen keeping in mind the need to give priority to the tweet semantic.

- **Sarcastic :** We treat sarcasm detection as a classification problem. After pre-processing the data we extracted n-grams more precisely, unigrams and bigrams from the dataset and then were added to the feature dictionary. Along with this we used brown clustering which helped us to put similar kinds of words in same cluster. Along with these features we also took sentiment values of the different parts of joke(here 3) as a feature because there is usually a great difference in sentiment scores in different part of a sarcastic joke or a tweet. Using these lexical as well as pragmatic features as in (González-Ibánez et al., 2011) we train a logistic regression and a SVM to distinguish between sarcastic jokes from non sarcastic jokes.

- **Exaggeration :** These are types of statements that represents something as better or worse than it really is. They can create a comical effect when used appropriately. For eg: In the joke "You grandma is as old as mountains", the intensity of the statement is increased by using phrase like "as old as". We detect such intense phrases in jokes to categorize under this category by getting sentiment score of every token. Individual sentiment score of every token in phase as well the combined sentiment score will be in positive range to generate an exaggeration effect.

- **Antonyms/Semantic Opposites :** An antonym is one of a pair of words with opposite meanings. Each word in the pair is the antithesis of the other. We use the antonym relation in WORDNET among noun, adjectives and verbs and used approach similar to (Mihalcea and Strapparava, 2005)

- **Phonetic Features :** Rhyming words also create a joke. For instance the joke - Coca Cola went to town, Diet Pepsi shot him down. Dr. Pepper fixed him up, Now we are drinking 7up creates a comical effect due the fact that town and down , up and 7up are rhyming words. Similar rhetorical devices play an important role in wordplay jokes, and are often used in. We used CMU Pronunciation Dictionary to detect rhyming words

- **Secondary Meaning :** These are the types of the jokes where we find that there is semantic relation among words in a jokes and that relation could be in a form located in, part of, type of, related to, has, etc. For eg: In the joke "Those who like the sport fishing can really get hooked" comical effect is created due to the relation between "hook" and "fishing". In order to detect these relations in a joke we are using Concept Net (Speer et al., 2017). It is a multilingual knowledge base, representing words and phrases that people use and the common-sense relationships between them. So, using concept net we are able to give a used in relationship between hook and fishing. We are going upto three levels to detect secondary relationship between different terms in a joke.

- **Dark Humor :** It is a comic style that makes light of subject matter that is generally considered taboo, particularly subjects that are normally considered serious or painful to discuss such as death. Some comedians use it as a tool for exploring vulgar issues, thus provoking discomfort and serious thought as well as amusement in their audience. Popular themes of the genre include violence, discrimination, disease, religion and barbarism. Treating it as a classification problem, we extracted unigrams from the dataset. We also

Table 3: Topic Detection

Classifier	Accuracy
LDA	59%
Naive Bayes	63%
SVM	72%
SVM + Proper Noun Boosting	**76%**

Table 4: Sarcastic Jokes

Results	
Features	**Acc.**
Logistic Regression (LR)	68%
LR + (1,2) grams	71%
LR + (1,2) grams + Brown Clustering	71.5%
LR + (1,2) grams + Brown Clustering + Sentiment Scores	75.2%
SVM + Sentiment Scores + N garms	77%

extracted sentiment scores of the sentence because of the hypothesis that dark humor tends to have a very negative sentiment score throughout the joke. We then compared the accuracies of classification techniques such as SVM and Logistic Regression.

- **Adult Slangs/Sexual Jokes :** These types of jokes are most famous on the internet.After pre-processing we extracted unigrams and bigrams. To detect these types of jokes we used a slang dictionary called Slang SD (Wu et al., 2016). It contains over 90,000 slang words/phrases along with their sentiment scores. We used these features and compared accuracies of classification methods such as SVM and Logistic Regression.

- **Gross :** Treating the problem of detecting Gross Jokes as a classification problem, unigrams are extracted after pre-processing. We kept a list of top 100 gross words according to their tf-idf score. This feature indicated the presence of gross words. Along with this we also maintain sentiment scores because of the

Table 5: Dark Jokes

Results	
Features	Accuracy
Logistic Regression (LR)	59%
LR + Sentiment Scores	63%
SVM + Sentiment Scores	64%

Table 6: Adult Slang/Sexual Jokes

Results	
Features	Accuracy
Logistic Regression (LR)	71%
LR + (1,2)grams + Slang SD	85%
SVM + (1,2)grams + Slang SD	88%

Table 7: Gross Jokes

Results	
Features	Accuracy
Logistic Regression (LR)	56%
LR + Common Gross Words + Sentiment	65%
SVM + Common Gross Words + Sentiment	67%

hypothesis that gross jokes tends to have a negative sentiment. Using all these features we compare accuracies using SVM and Logistic Regression.

- **Insults:** After pre-processing we are extracting unigrams and bigrams from the dataset. Along with this we are creating a list of insulting words using top 100 words according to their Tfidf score. Along with this we calculated semantic scores of each of the joke and used these features in a Naive Bayes Classifier and a SVM.

6   Analysis

In Tables 3, 4, 5 ,6 , 7 and 8 we can see results of our classifiers. We see that SVM has a better accuracy in all the cases than Naive Bayes and Logistic Regression. In the case of Topic Detection, Proper noun boosting increases the accuracy furthermore. In the case of sarcasm detection, we see the sentiment scores as well as unigrams and bigrams given to a SVM gave the best possible result. In the case of detection of dark humor we see that there is significant increase in in accuracy as sentiment values are introduced. These maybe because of the fact

Table 8: Insult Jokes

Features	**Accuracy**
Naive Bayes + (1,2) grams	72%
SVM + (1,2) grams	72%
SVM + insulting words sentiment values +(1,2) grams	79%

the sentiment values in the negative instances are opposites to what it is in positive instances. This result is expected because dark jokes tend to have negative sentiment values. In case of adult slang detection we are getting a very good accuracy as soon as a slang dictionary is introduced. In detection of gross jokes, the accuracy is increased as soon as sentiment and common gross words are introduced. In short,we find that sentiment values prove to be a very important feature in detection of various sub categories. We are also able to detect intense phrases which lead to exaggeration as well as jokes in which there is some kind of a semantic relation among different terms. Using these subcategories we have covered a lot in our ground in categorization of jokes. The results that we achieve act as binary indicators for each subcategory in our experiment, thus giving multiple tags according to topic, theme and mode to a joke, making our approach more extensive and unique as compared to our counterparts.

7   Future Work

Given the constraints of the scope of our paper as well as our research we have tried to assimilate as many sub-categories as possible to include as a part of our computational framework, but at the same point of time we also make an ambitious yet modest assumption that it is still possible to add a few more sub-categories. As our model is versatile enough to handle the addition of such subcategories seamlessly, the only impediment would the the feasibility of the effort and availability of the computational tools for them to be integrated. With the addition of more and diverse data the model can be made more robust and accurate as well. In future, the framework can also be extended to distinguish between humorous and non-humorous events, allowing us to use the complete tool on various types of data, such as, movie or television show scripts to detect the occurrences of various types of humour and hence, giving birth to a more holistic classification of said media.

References

Salvatore Attardo, Donalee Hughes Attardo, Paul Baltes, and Marnie Jo Petray. 1994. The linear organization of jokes: analysis of two thousand texts. *Humor-International Journal of Humor Research*, 7(1):27–54.

Salvatore Attardo and Victor Raskin. 1991. Script theory revis (it) ed: Joke similarity and joke representation model. *Humor-International Journal of Humor Research*, 4(3-4):293–348.

Wikipedia contributors. 2018. Theories of humor — wikipedia, the free encyclopedia. [Online; accessed 12-March-2018].

Matthew Gervais and David Sloan Wilson. 2005. The evolution and functions of laughter and humor: A synthetic approach. *The Quarterly review of biology*, 80(4):395–430.

Roberto González-Ibánez, Smaranda Muresan, and Nina Wacholder. 2011. Identifying sarcasm in twitter: a closer look. In *Proceedings of the 49th Annual Meeting of the Association for Computational Linguistics: Human Language Technologies: Short Papers-Volume 2*, pages 581–586. Association for Computational Linguistics.

Arvo Krikmann. 2006. Contemporary linguistic theories of humour. *Folklore*, 33(2006):27–58.

James Mendrinos. 2004. *The Complete Idiot's Guide to Comedy Writing*. Penguin.

Rada Mihalcea and Carlo Strapparava. 2005. Making computers laugh: Investigations in automatic humor recognition. In *Proceedings of the Conference on Human Language Technology and Empirical Methods in Natural Language Processing*, pages 531–538. Association for Computational Linguistics.

John Morreall. 2016. Philosophy of humor. In Edward N. Zalta, editor, *The Stanford Encyclopedia of Philosophy*, winter 2016 edition. Metaphysics Research Lab, Stanford University.

Victor Raskin. 2012. *Semantic mechanisms of humor*, volume 24. Springer Science & Business Media.

Graeme Ritchie and Judith Masthoff. 2011. The standup 2 interactive riddle builder. In *Proceedings of the Second International Conference on Computational Creativity*. Universidad Aut´ onoma Metropolitana, Mexico City.

Willibald Ruch and Amy Carrell. 1998. Trait cheerfulness and the sense of humour. *Personality and Individual Differences*, 24(4):551–558.

Andrea C Samson and James J Gross. 2012. Humour as emotion regulation: The differential consequences of negative versus positive humour. *Cognition & emotion*, 26(2):375–384.

Robert Speer, Joshua Chin, and Catherine Havasi. 2017. Conceptnet 5.5: An open multilingual graph of general knowledge. In *AAAI*, pages 4444–4451.

Oliviero Stock and Carlo Strapparava. 2006. Laughing with hahacronym, a computational humor system. In *PROCEEDINGS OF THE NATIONAL CONFERENCE ON ARTIFICIAL INTELLIGENCE*, volume 21, page 1675. Menlo Park, CA; Cambridge, MA; London; AAAI Press; MIT Press; 1999.

Liang Wu, Fred Morstatter, and Huan Liu. 2016. Slangsd: Building and using a sentiment dictionary of slang words for short-text sentiment classification. *arXiv preprint arXiv:1608.05129*.

Social and Emotional Correlates of Capitalization on Twitter

Sophia Chan
University of Victoria
schan1@uvic.ca

Alona Fyshe
University of Victoria
afyshe@uvic.ca

Abstract

Social media text is replete with unusual capitalization patterns. We posit that capitalizing a token like THIS performs two expressive functions: it marks a person socially, and marks certain parts of an utterance as more salient than others. Focusing on gender and sentiment, we illustrate using a corpus of tweets that capitalization appears in more negative than positive contexts, and is used more by females compared to males. Yet we find that both genders use capitalization in a similar way when expressing sentiment.

1 Introduction

Gender lines divide language use in speech (Eckert and McConnell-Ginet, 2003); in writing (Koppel et al., 2002); and on social media (Koppel et al., 2006; Bamman et al., 2014). Unsurprisingly, genders differ in their use of emotive language as well (Volkova et al., 2013; Hovy, 2015). Volkova et al. (2013) give the example of *weakness*. Whereas females are more likely to use the word in a positive context, as in *chocolate is my weakness*, males are more inclined to use it when speaking negatively.

Orthographic choices in particular, such as lengthening (*coool*) and coda deletion (*walkin*), have been shown to be socially meaningful (Androutsopoulos, 2000; Eisenstein, 2015) and tied to sentiment (Brody and Diakopoulos, 2011). To the best of our knowledge, however, the use of capitalization has not yet been examined in this context.

Social media text is replete with non-standard capitalization. While many agree that capitalization has some communicative function (Vandergriff, 2013; Nebhi et al., 2015), in practice this information is frequently interpreted as noise and removed by text normalization procedures early on in natural language processing (NLP) pipelines (Eisenstein, 2013).

We posit that capitalization (operationalized here as the number of fully capitalized words in a tweet) has two functions. Capitalizing a token like THIS marks a person socially, and marks certain parts of the utterance as more salient than others. Capitalization thus encodes information about the user and their attitude that can be useful for NLP tasks, such as sentiment analysis.

With these suggested functions in mind, we focus on examining how capitalization patterns vary with respect to two variables: the gender of the user and sentiment of the tweet. We are also interested in possible interaction effects.

Our analysis extends existing literature on orthographic variation in social media, filling the research gap in capitalization. We define a meaningfulness criteria to differentiate between when capitalization is used for convention (e.g. in acronyms) and when it is used creatively to add expressive value, since we are only interested in the latter.

The results indicate that capitalization on Twitter does indeed vary with respect to gender and sentiment, and that effects are strengthened when you consider only *meaningfully* capitalized tokens. We find no interaction effects, suggesting that both genders use capitalization in a similar way when it comes to expressing sentiment.

2 Data

For the purpose of training a gender classifier Burger et al. (2011) built a corpus of approximately 213 million tweets from 18.5 million users and annotated them for gender by following links to users' Facebook or MySpace profiles, where self reporting of gender was required. Volkova et al. (2013) later refined the corpus by excluding re-tweets and non-English tweets, and selecting a random, gender-balanced sample of 1 million tweets. We were able to retrieve 85.50% of

Proceedings of the Second Workshop on Computational Modeling of People's Opinions, Personality, and Emotions in Social Media, pages 10–15
New Orleans, Louisiana, June 6, 2018. ©2018 Association for Computational Linguistics

the tweets from this sample using the Twitter API.

Apart from this sample, we collected 1% of all tweets in North America using Twitter's streaming API from January 2017 to July 2017 and randomly sampled a set of 15 million tweets to be used to approximate true frequency distributions.

2.1 Emoticons as sentiment labels

The first step in examining possible interactions between gender and sentiment was to obtain sentiment labels for each tweet. We refrained from relying on text-based features (e.g. "happy" words versus "sad" words) to annotate our gender-labeled dataset for sentiment, as we are interested in examining the distribution of capitalization, a text-based feature itself. Rather, we assumed that the polarity of emoticons found in a tweet is a valid proxy for the sentiment of the tweet.

Table 1: Distribution of gender and sentiment in our dataset of tweets.

	positive		negative	
	count	%	count	%
male	4798	25.06	4569	24.01
female	4746	24.94	4945	26.00

For each tweet that contained at least one emoticon, we determined its sentiment by matching emoticons to human-annotated sentiment labels (positive, negative, or neutral) (Hogenboom et al., 2015). From this set, we retained only positive and negative tweets for which there were no conflicts in emoticon sentiment. In other words, we excluded tweets if they contained both positive and negative emoticons.

This process yielded 75,670 tweets labeled for both gender and sentiment. From these tweets, we obtained a random sample of 19,028 tweets balanced across gender (male or female) and sentiment (positive and negative) groups. The distribution of our dataset is summarized in Table 1.

3 Methodology

3.1 Preprocessing

All tweets were tokenized using Natural Language Toolkit (NLTK)'s TweetTokenizer[1] (Bird et al., 2009). We removed non-alphabetic tokens and tokens that consisting of fewer than three characters.

---

[1] ```nltk.tokenize.TweetTokenizer(
preserve_case=False, reduce_len=True)```

3.2 Identifying meaningful capitalization

While we claim that capitalization has expressive function, this does not apply across the board to all capitalized tokens. Acronyms, for example, are frequently capitalized by convention to signal to the reader that the token is a stand-in for some longer string, as opposed to being a creative language resource that users can draw on to express themselves.

Nonetheless, it is clear that in certain cases capitalizing a word causes a change in interpretation—as in *that's so cool* versus *that's SO cool*—that may serve the purpose of mimicking real-life conversational cues such as intonation or volume (Vandergriff, 2013).

To operationalize this intuition, we set a threshold designed to filter out acronyms from our data. We obtained counts for how often a token appeared in uppercase and non-uppercase (lowercase or title case) forms in the corpus of 15 million tweets, and called a token meaningfully capitalized if it appeared in its uppercase form less than 10% of the time. The definition for *meaningful* capitalization is shown below.

$$\frac{Count(upper)}{Count(upper) + Count(nonupper)} < 0.1$$

3.3 Analysis

We ran two ANOVAs (*gender* $\times$ *sentiment*) on our data, using as response variables (1) the number of uppercase tokens and (2) the number of meaningfully capitalized tokens in each tweet, as identified by the metric described in Section 3.1. Data analysis was performed in R 3.4.2 (R Core Team, 2013).

Within the categories of male, female, positive, and negative, we identified tokens that are most likely to be capitalized by calculating each specific token's probability of being capitalized. For example, if *rip* was capitalized 9 times out of 10 in our corpus, it was assigned a probability of 0.9. To reduce noise in our findings, we only considered tokens that appeared at least 10 times within the category under analysis. We also identified tokens most likely to be *meaningfully* capitalized.

4 Results

The mean number of capitalized tokens and *meaningfully* capitalized tokens for each group are shown in Figures 1a and 1b, respectively. Across

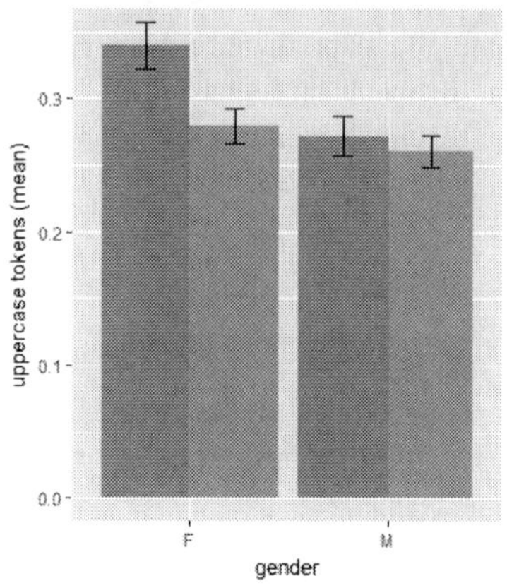

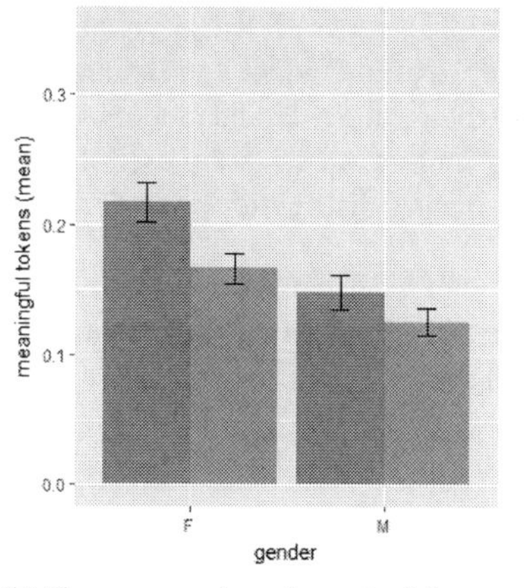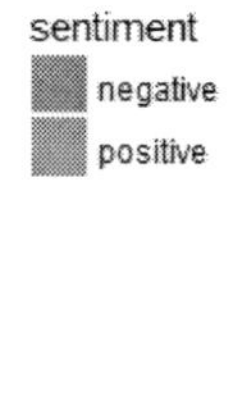

(a) The mean number of capitalized tokens in each tweet (without our meaningfulness criteria applied) across sentiment and gender. Within female tweets, the mean is **0.28** in positive contexts and **0.34** in negative contexts. For male tweets, the mean is **0.26** in positive contexts and **0.27** in negative contexts.

(b) The mean number of *meaningfully* capitalized tokens in each tweet, across sentiment and gender. Within female tweets, the mean is **0.17** in positive contexts and **0.22** in negative contexts. For male tweets, the mean is **0.13** in positive contexts and **0.15** in negative contexts.

both genders, capitalization is employed more in negative contexts.

As shown in Table 2, we find a main effect of both gender ($p < 0.01$) and sentiment ($p < 0.05$) for capitalized tokens, but no interaction. Similarly, Table 3 displays main effects of gender ($p < 0.001$) and sentiment ($p < 0.01$) for meaningfully capitalized tokens and no interaction.

Table 4 shows the 10 tokens most likely to be capitalized, and to be *meaningfully* capitalized within each gender and sentiment category.

5 Discussion and conclusion

Our results in Table 2 show that capitalization varies systematically with respect to gender and sentiment, but that these two factors do not interact. On average, capitalization is used more by females, and used to express negativity as opposed to positivity.

Crucially, the use of capitalization functions as both a marker of identity and a marker of sentiment, following a similar pattern to other types of non-standard orthography, such as lengthening or phonologically-motivated variation (Brody and Diakopoulos, 2011; Eisenstein, 2015).

We also provide an operational definition of meaningful capitalization. A token was considered *meaningfully* capitalized if, in a corpus of 15 million tweets, it was capitalized less than 10% of the time.

The value of our meaningfulness criteria can be seen by comparing capitalized to *meaningfully* capitalized tokens in Table 4. Acronyms such as *rip*, *nyc*, *dvd* are stripped out. Because these tokens are capitalized out of convention, orthography does not reflect user attributes or attitudes.

Several abbreviations appear in the meaningful columns in Table 4, such as *lol*, *lmao*, and *smh*. Our intuition is that people have stopped uppercasing these for the most part, probably due in part to their high frequency. In fact, it has been suggested that the status of *lol* is shifting from abbreviation to discourse marker (Tagliamonte and Denis, 2008; Markman, 2017). Our threshold of 10% appears to filter out most acronyms in our data, but it would be valuable to systematically test different thresholds to quantitatively validate our method. We leave this for future work.

The use of capitalization may serve another function in addition to signaling acronyms and encoding user attitudes. If a token can refer to multiple entities, capitalization can help differentiate one meaning from another, allowing users to refer, say, to the band *TOOL* as opposed to the category of *tools*. While we were not interested in detecting such cases, the insight that capitalization has functions beyond what is discussed here provides future avenues for research.

As shown in Table 3, the effects of gender and sentiment are stronger when we apply our mean-

Table 2: ANOVA table for testing the significance of all capitalized tokens, without our meaningfulness criteria applied. We find a main effect of sentiment and gender, but no interaction. $* = p < 0.05$ and $** = p < 0.01$.

	sum of squares	mean square	F	p
gender	9.0	9.044	8.085	**.003** **
sentiment	6.2	6.616	5.999	**.014** *
gender:sentiment	2.8	2.827	2.755	.097

Table 3: ANOVA table for testing the significance of meaningfully capitalized tokens. We find a main effect of sentiment and gender, but no interaction. Using our meaningfully capitalized token filter increases the margin of significance for gender and sentiment. $** = p < 0.01$ and $*** = p < 0.001$.

	sum of squares	mean square	F	p
gender	14.7	14.686	19.319	**.000** ***
sentiment	6.6	6.587	8.665	**.003** **
gender:sentiment	0.9	0.989	1.222	.269

ingfulness criteria, corroborating our intuition that we need to consider each token separately, taking its capitalization distribution into account in order to differentiate between capitalization as convention, and capitalization as a creative resource.

This study was limited by the availability of Twitter data that are labeled for both gender and sentiment. Alongside, our dataset is composed entirely of tweets that contain emoticons, which may be biasing the sample towards users who are predisposed to use language (including capitalization) in a specific way. By selecting tweets on the basis of whether they contain emoticons, we may be introducing age, gender, and/or sentiment biases. In a study involving blogging data, for example, Rosenthal and McKeown (2011) found that younger users were more likely to use both emoticons and capitalization. In the future, these biases could be mitigated by incorporating human-annotated sentiment labels.

We suspect that capitalization is a type of conversational cue which serves to clarify the meaning of an utterance over text-based communication and help the reader select one of the possible interpretations. According to Vandergriff (2013), these cues are difficult to study because they are often "subtle, highly variable, and relatively infrequent".

Notwithstanding these limitations, our analysis suggests that capitalization encodes information about speaker attributes and attitudes, calling into question the pervasive practice of complete lowercasing in NLP.

Our work displays a computational approach for analyzing the special orthographic characteristics that permeate social media, and positions capitalization as a type of orthographic variation that warrants further, and more detailed analyses in terms of function and distribution. The use of capitalization may be related to other demographic factors, such as age, and may serve different functions depending on the context it appears in.

Acknowledgments

During the course of this work Sophia Chan received support from an NSERC Undergraduate Research Award (USRA).

We would like to thank Alexandra D'Arcy and David Medler for their insightful discussion and feedback, as well as Sam Liu for collecting and sharing with us a large corpus of Twitter data.

References

Jannis K Androutsopoulos. 2000. Non-standard spellings in media texts: The case of german fanzines. *Journal of Sociolinguistics*, 4(4):514–533.

David Bamman, Jacob Eisenstein, and Tyler Schnoebelen. 2014. Gender identity and lexical variation in social media. *Journal of Sociolinguistics*, 18(2):135–160.

Table 4: For each category, we show the 10 tokens most likely to be capitalized (**upper**) compared to the 10 tokens that are most likely to be meaningfully capitalized (**mng-ful**). A token is considered meaningful if it occurs in uppercase less than 10% of the time in a corpus of 15 million tweets.

male		female		positive		negative	
upper	**mng-ful**	**upper**	**mng-ful**	**upper**	**mng-ful**	**upper**	**mng-ful**
rip	tool	nyc	lmao	tool	tool	rip	lmao
tool	nom	dvd	smh	nyc	lol	nyc	smh
omg	lol	omg	lol	dvd	lmao	omg	lol
nom	lmao	huge	goodness	omg	halloween	asap	entire
wtf	thx	hahah	kill	huge	exactly	lmfao	burn
yay	note	wtf	none	lol	heck	gah	concert
lol	fire	lmao	fuck	lmao	damn	wtf	tour
btw	goin	smh	bless	hahahaha	hugs	lmao	none
lmao	joke	lol	nuts	halloween	ice	smh	yikes
thx	idk	hahahaha	jonas	exactly	note	aim	fail

Steven Bird, Ewan Klein, and Edward Loper. 2009. *Natural language processing with Python: analyzing text with the natural language toolkit.* O'Reilly Media, Inc.

Samuel Brody and Nicholas Diakopoulos. 2011. Cooooooooooooooolllllllllllllll!!!!!!!!!!!!!!: using word lengthening to detect sentiment in microblogs. In *Proceedings of the 2011 Conference on Empirical Methods in Natural Language Processing*, pages 562–570. Association for Computational Linguistics.

John D Burger, John Henderson, George Kim, and Guido Zarrella. 2011. Discriminating gender on twitter. In *Proceedings of the 2011 Conference on Empirical Methods in Natural Language Processing*, pages 1301–1309. Association for Computational Linguistics.

Penelope Eckert and Sally McConnell-Ginet. 2003. *Gender and language.* Cambridge: Cambridge University Press.

Jacob Eisenstein. 2013. What to do about bad language on the internet. In *Proceedings of the 2013 Conference of the North American Chapter of the Association for Computational Linguistics*, pages 359–369.

Jacob Eisenstein. 2015. Systematic patterning in phonologically-motivated orthographic variation. *Journal of Sociolinguistics*, 19(2):161–188.

Alexander Hogenboom, Daniella Bal, Flavius Frasincar, Malissa Bal, Franciska De Jong, and Uzay Kaymak. 2015. Exploiting emoticons in polarity classification of text. *J. Web Eng.*, 14(1&2):22–40.

Dirk Hovy. 2015. Demographic factors improve classification performance. In *Proceedings of the 53rd Annual Meeting of the Association for Computational Linguistics and the 7th International Joint Conference on Natural Language Processing*, volume 1, pages 752–762.

Moshe Koppel, Shlomo Argamon, and Anat Rachel Shimoni. 2002. Automatically categorizing written texts by author gender. *Literary and Linguistic Computing*, 17(4):401–412.

Moshe Koppel, Jonathan Schler, Shlomo Argamon, and James Pennebaker. 2006. Effects of age and gender on blogging. In *AAAI 2006 Spring Symposium on Computational Approaches to Analysing Weblogs*, pages 1–7.

Kris M Markman. 2017. Exploring the pragmatic functions of the acronym lol in instant messenger conversations.

Kamel Nebhi, Kalina Bontcheva, and Genevieve Gorrell. 2015. Restoring capitalization in# tweets. In *Proceedings of the 24th International Conference on World Wide Web*, pages 1111–1115. ACM.

R Core Team. 2013. *R: A Language and Environment for Statistical Computing.* R Foundation for Statistical Computing, Vienna, Austria.

Sara Rosenthal and Kathleen McKeown. 2011. Age prediction in blogs: A study of style, content, and online behavior in pre-and post-social media generations. In *Proceedings of the 49th Annual Meeting of the Association for Computational Linguistics: Human Language Technologies-Volume 1*, pages 763–772. Association for Computational Linguistics.

Sali A Tagliamonte and Derek Denis. 2008. Linguistic ruin? lol! instant messaging and teen language. *American speech*, 83(1):3–34.

Ilona Vandergriff. 2013. Emotive communication online: A contextual analysis of computer-mediated communication (cmc) cues. *Journal of Pragmatics*, 51:1–12.

Svitlana Volkova, Theresa Wilson, and David Yarowsky. 2013. Exploring demographic language variations to improve multilingual sentiment analysis in social media. In *Proceedings of the 2013 Conference on Empirical Methods in Natural Language Processing*, pages 1815–1827.

Building an annotated dataset of app store reviews
with Appraisal features in English and Spanish

Natalia Mora and Julia Lavid
Department of English Studies
Complutense University of Madrid

Abstract

This paper describes the creation and annotation of a dataset consisting of 250 English and Spanish app store reviews from Google's Play Store with Appraisal features. This is one of the most influential linguistic frameworks for the analysis of evaluation and opinion in discourse due to its insightful descriptive features. However, it has not been extensively applied in NLP in spite of its potential for the classification of the subjective content of these reviews. We describe the dataset, the annotation scheme and guidelines, the agreement studies, the annotation results and their impact on the characterisation of this genre.

1 Introduction

Application distribution platforms, or app stores have proliferated in the last decade, allowing users to allow users not only to search, buy, and deploy software apps for mobile devices, but also to share their opinion about the app and other app store products (e.g. films, games, music, et.) in text reviews, not only in English but also in other languages such as Spanish. This is the case of Google's Play Store where app and other product reviews are published online. When users write product reviews, they can either encourage or discourage other users to download the item in question, so these reviews may play a key role in making a product a success or a failure. An example of a typical app review is shown in (1) below:

(1) *Love it... But. I really like this app, it is the best task manager I've had, my phone runs bet-*
ter and I am really maximizing my (limited) storage space. I just wish there would be an ad free version.

As illustrated by this app review, these texts differ from traditional reviews found in sites like epinions.com in that: a) users have slightly deviated from valuing the items in polarity terms and turned to describing their performance; b) users address directly application' developers; c) users' comments are limited to 1200 characters and, since comments are usually posted via smartphone, typical elements of the internet and mobile language are included, such as abbreviations and emoticons. In addition, sentences frequently miss subjects and links, since authors try to speed up their writing in their phone's small keyboard. All these features make these reviews particularly interesting not only from the linguistic point of view, but also to drive the development effort of app designers and to improve forthcoming releases of a given product.

NLP work on these reviews has mostly focused on extracting patterns related to the length of the review (Vasa et al., 2012) its content (Khalid, 2013), collocation features (Guzman and Maalej 2014), and ambiguity (Islam 2014), and on their polarity on their polarity classification, relying on machine-learning techniques trained over vectors of linguistic feature frequencies (Pang et al., 2002; Finin, 2009), although some more ambitious work has been developed to classify reviews into three and five rating classes using a set of linguistic features including intensification, negation, modality and discourse structure (Brooke 2009). To our knowledge, with the exception of initial work by Taboada and Grieves (2004), there are no studies which explore the potential of Appraisal features to classify and quantify the subjective content of these reviews. This paper, therefore, tries to fill a gap in this area by reporting on the recent

Proceedings of the Second Workshop on Computational Modeling of People's Opinions, Personality, and Emotions in Social Media, pages 16–24
New Orleans, Louisiana, June 6, 2018. ©2018 Association for Computational Linguistics

development of a bilingual (English-Spanish) dataset of app store reviews annotated with Appraisal tags. We believe that these tags can help categorize the subjective content of these reviews into more fine-grained and diverse features than those focusing only on polarity, quantify the writer's commitment to the opinion, and specify how focused that opinion is.

2 Appraisal

Appraisal is a linguistic theory of subjectivity developed within Systemic-Functional Linguistics to model language's ability to express and negotiate opinions and attitudes within text (Martin 2000; 2003; Martin & White 2005). Appraisal resources are considered as a system of their own within language, and can be divided into three subsystems: *Attitude, Graduation* and *Engagement,* as shown in Figure 1.

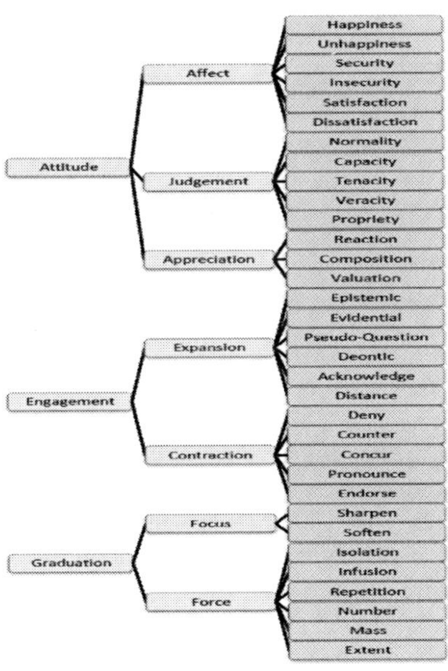

Figure 1: Appraisal subsystems (after Martin and White, 2005)

Attitude is concerned mainly with feelings, such as emotions, judgements and evaluations; it can be further subdivided into *Affect, Judgement* and *Appreciation*, each of which is subdivided into more delicate categories, as shown in Figure 1.
Engagement is concerned with the ways in which the speakers or writers position themselves towards the text and other possible voices, and is further subdivided into *Expansion* and *Contrac-*

tion, with more delicate categories expanding them; *Expansion* presents the author's voice as one in a range of possible viewpoints. In *Contraction* the author restricts or challenges other viewpoints; finally, *Graduation* is concerned with the degrees of intensity of the meanings expressed by *Attitude* and *Engagement* realisations, and includes *Focus* and *Force.*

The work developed so far has been mostly circumscribed to Linguistics and basically focused on English, although some cross-linguistic studies involving both European and non-European languages have emerged during the last decade. This includes contrastive work between English and Spanish journalistic texts (Marín and Perucha 2006; McCabe 2007), consumer reviews (Mora 2011, Carretero and Taboada 2009, 2010a, 2010b, 2011, 2014) and other text types (Taboada, Carretero and Hinnel, 2014; Lavid et al. 2014; Lavid, Carretero and Zamorano 2016).

3 Compiling the corpus

In order to compile the bilingual dataset for annotation purposes, the following steps were carried out:
1. A total of 49687 English reviews and 37304 Spanish reviews published before November 2016 were automatically extracted from Google's Play Store using a crawler designed *ad hoc*, as shown in table 1.

	English	Spanish
Applications	15721	15225
Games	15288	15328
Books	4909	2223
Films	7793	1595
Music	5976	2933
Total	49687	37304

Table 1: English and Spanish reviews extracted

The reviews included the categories of applications, games, films, books and music. For each category, some of the most famous items were selected (Instagram, Angry Birds, Frozen, Fifty Shades of Grey, Adele, etc.).
2) From this initial dataset, we randomly selected a smaller set of 250 reviews for annotation purposes, given the amount of effort needed for fine-grained Appraisal annotation. This smaller set contained equal distribution of reviews in terms of language (English and Spanish), similar length, type of polarity (positive or negative) and app category (applications, games, films, books and mu-

sic). When an item had more reviews than needed for the study, those with a higher length were preferred. Thus, the length of the reviews selected ranges from 4 to 240 words, although most of them are about 30-60 words long.

The dataset of 250 reviews was further divided into two smaller sets as follows:

1. An initial training set of 50 reviews was analysed by two annotators. These annotators shared a common background on Spanish and English linguistic studies, both being PhD students in their last year; however, one of them was familiar with the Appraisal Framework while the other one was not. This training set was used to perform agreement studies to validate the annotation scheme and guidelines of Appraisal in English and Spanish.

2. A larger dataset of 200 reviews was annotated by one of those two initial annotators with the Appraisal tags which had been validated through the agreement studies, using the UAM Corpus Tool (O'Donnell 2008) as shown in Figure 2:

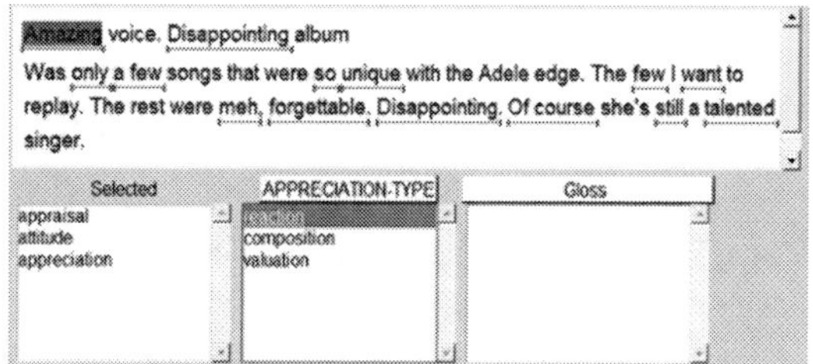

Figure 2: Annotation interface

4 Annotation methodology

We applied the annotation steps suggested by Lavid (2017, 2012) and Hovy and Lavid (2010), as follows:

a) An annotation scheme and guidelines were designed on the basis of the main features proposed in *Appraisal* Theory, along the three axes of *Attitude*, *Engagement* and *Graduation*. This is described in 4.1.

b) Agreement studies were designed to test the empirical validity of the annotation scheme. These were carried out by two independent annotators working separately on a training corpus of fifty mobile application reviews. This is described in 4.2. and 4.3.

c) On the basis of the results of the agreement studies, a larger corpus of two hundred reviews was single-annotated with the validated *Appraisal* tags of the annotation scheme. The results of this annotation is described in 4.4.

d) The distribution of Appraisal tags was examined in the English and the Spanish reviews in order to obtain a characterisation of this genre. This is described in 4.5.

4.1 Annotation scheme and guidelines

On the basis of the Appraisal tags proposed by Martin and White (2005), we designed an initial annotation scheme, consisting of a more general core tagset, and an extended tagset, with some more delicate features. The core tagset was common to English and Spanish and is presented in table 2.

Attitude	Feelings, including emotional reactions, judgements of behaviour and evaluation of qualities of things.
Affect	Emotional reactions and feelings
Judgement	Assessment of behaviour according to normative principles
Appreciation	Evaluation and valuation of things
Engagement	Implication of other possibilities and voices than the speakers'
Expansion	Author's position is one inside a range of possible options or an external source provided for a given opinion
Contraction	Author positions against a contrary position or limits the scope of possibilities
Graduation	Grading phenomena whereby feelings are amplified or softened and categories blurred or sharpened.
Focus	Degree of prototypicality
Force	Degree of intensity or amount

Table 2: Core tagset of annotation schema

4.2 Agreement studies

Three experiments (also called 'agreement studies') were designed to test the reproducibility of the scheme's tags. The first experiment focused on the identification of the spans or markables, the second one addressed the selection of the three main general types of *Appraisal*, and in the third one, coders had to make fine-grained selections from the more delicate subtypes.

The purpose of the first experiment was to investigate which elements were considered as *Appraisal* tags by two coders working independently and to delimit their boundaries. Here coders were instructed to annotate the shortest lexical span expressing *Appraisal*, although one of them was familiar with the theory before the experiment.

Once coders agreed on the spans, the second annotation experiment addressed the labelling of the *Appraisal* markables with one of the three coarser tags and their main subtypes, i.e.: *Attitude* (*Affect, Judgement and Appreciation*), *Engagement* (*Expansion and Contraction*) or *Graduation* (*Force and Focus*).The purpose of this experiment was to investigate whether coders could distinguish among the different coarse tags and their subtypes, before getting deeper into more delicate categories. If significant inconsistencies were found, this step would make it easier to identify any conflictive or confusing aspects of the theory or the guidelines.

In the third annotation experiment, coders were instructed to use more fine-grained tags from the extended tagset to label the selected markable. These include tags such as *Happiness, Unhappiness, Security, Insecurity, Satisfaction* and *Dissatisfaction* in the case of *Affect*; *Normality, Capacity, Tenacity, Veracity* and *Propriety* in the case of *Judgement*; *Reaction, Composition* or *Valuation* in the case of *Appreciation*; *Epistemic, Evidential, Pseudo-Question, Deontic, Acknowledge* and *Distance* in the case of *Expansion; Deny, Counter, Concur, Pronounce* and *Endorse* in the case of *Contraction*; *Sharpen* and *Softer* in the case of *Focus*; and *Isolation, Infusion, Repetition, Number, Mass* and *Extent* in the case of *Force*. The purpose of this experiment was to investigate whether highly delicate categories could be coded consistently by two independent coders, and whether subtle differences in meaning could be distinguished.

4.3 Results of agreement studies

The results of the first experiment yielded a substantially high degree of agreement between coders (Kappa=0.86), although some disagreements also occurred in a small percentage of the cases (4%). These cases occurred when the span was either selected by one of the coders and not by the other, or when the span's length was different. Most of the cases of disagreement occurred in long and complex sentences that do not directly reflect an opinion, but must be contextualised to convey an evaluative meaning, as in (2) below:

(2) *Vale la fama que tiene* [translation: it's worth its popularity] (T43): In this example one coder selected the full phrase while the other one selected only the verb 'vale' [it's worth it].

In the second agreement study the agreement between coders was even higher (Kappa= 0.96). The increase in the k-value was probably due to the fact that the span selection was already decided. Although coders could in most cases distinguish between the three major categories of *Attitude, Engagement* and *Graduation*, the highest mismatches were found when coding *Graduation* followed by *Engagement* and *Attitude*.

Graduation appeared as the most conflictive category, which points to an unclear difference between intensification or additional description and values.

As to disagreements found between different subtypes of categories (i.e.: *Affect, Judgement, Appreciation, Expansion, Contraction, Force* and *Focus*), the category with most conflictive cases was *Attitude: Appreciation*, which was mostly confused with other subtypes of *Attitude*. The second highest disagreements were found within the category of *Graduation*, with more cases confusing *Force* with other subtypes than *Focus*, followed closely by *Engagement*, where *Contraction* was more often confused with other categories than *Expansion*. Figure 3 graphically displays the distribution of these disagreements.

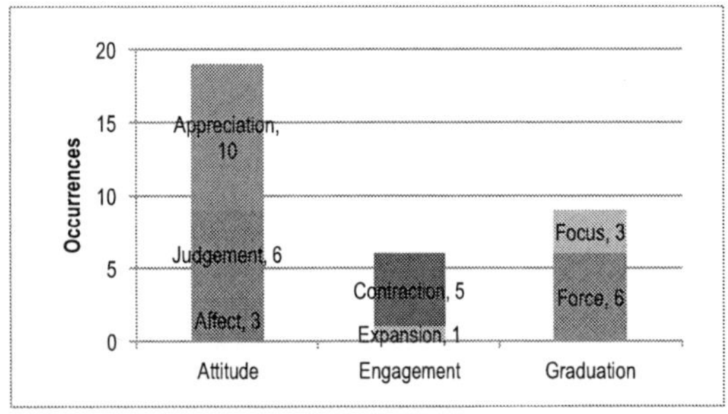

Figure 3: Disagreements among Appraisal subtypes in the bilingual corpus

Finally, Figure 4 shows the distribution of the most controversial combinations, that is, which ones were typically used one instead of the other.

	Attitude Appreciation	Graduation Force	Engagement Contraction
Engagement Expansion			1
Graduation Focus		2	1
Graduation Force	1		3
Attitude Affect	3		
Attitude Judgement	6		

Figure 4: Disagreements in combination of categories

The combinations which caused more disagreement were *Attitude-Appreciation* and *Attitude-Judgement*, since they were often confused by coders. Theoretically, *Judgement* refers to other people's behaviour while *Appreciation* focuses on objects and natural phenomena. However, evaluative elements on moral aspects, typically used for human beings, can be associated with objects in a metaphorical way. Examples which caused disagreement were the use of adjectives such as '*flojísima*' [transl. 'very poor'], '*lenta*' [slow], referring to a novel; '*kid-friendly*' or '*sweet* referring to a film. *Attitude-Appreciation* was also confused with *Attitude-Affect* and vice versa in several cases, probably due to the fact that it is not clear when the focus is on the object causing a feeling or the author having that feeling caused by the object. An example would be the use of '*stunned*'.

The tags of *Graduation-Force* and *Engagement-Contraction* also caused disagreement between coders, as in the case of the item '*really*', which has different meanings that are not always clearly distinguishable.

In the third agreement study, the agreement was only moderate (kappa=0.49). Most disagreements were caused by the difficulty to discriminate among the different subtypes of *Attitude*. The categories which caused more disagreement were *Reaction* and *Valuation*, which were coded differently on several occasions. Thus, for example, in the case of adjectives such as '*pobre*' [poor], or '*lovable*', coders hesitated between considering them as qualities of the object (valuation) to which they were assigned, or a consequence of the user's feelings (reaction).

4.4 Annotation of the larger dataset

Our next step was to annotate a larger dataset with the validated tags of the proposed annotation scheme. This consisted of two hundred texts filtered and selected following the same procedure as the training set: it included comparable English and Spanish texts evenly distributed, as illustrated in Tables 3 and 4 (st. stands for 'stars', regarding the 1-to-5 star rating):

Applications		Games		Books		Films		Music	
20		20		20		20		20	
+	-	+	-	+	-	+	-	+	-
10	10	10	10	10	10	10	10	10	10
5st. 5	1st. 5	5st. 5	1st. 5	5st. 5	1st. 5	5st. 5	1st. 5	5st. 5	1st. 5
4st. 5	2st. 5	4st. 5	2st. 5	4st. 5	2st. 5	4st. 5	2st. 5	4st. 5	2st. 5

Table 3: English dataset

Applications		Games		Books		Films		Music	
20		20		20		20		20	
+	-	+	-	+	-	+	-	+	-
10	10	10	10	10	10	10	10	10	10
5st. 5	1st. 5	5st. 5	1st. 5	5st. 5	1st. 5	5st. 5	1st. 5	5st. 5	1st. 5
4st. 5	2st. 5	4st. 5	2st. 5	4st. 5	2st. 5	4st. 5	2st. 5	4st. 5	2st. 5

Table 4: Spanish dataset

The texts addressed several items inside each of the products in order to enhance diversity in the texts. The reviews addressed at least two items per category, including applications such as *Clean Master, Instagram*, games such as *Angry Birds, Candy Crush*, books such as *All the Light We Cannot See, Fifty Shades of Grey, The Girl on the Train*, films such as *Avatar, Gravity, Frozen, The Wolf of Wall Street*, and music such as AC/DC or Adele.

The annotation tool was the UAM Corpus tool5, a free state-of-the-art annotation platform which supports annotation of multiple texts at multiple linguistic levels (clause, sentence, document, etc.) as well as analysis methods such as instances retrieval and statistical measurements. Also, the first author of this paper single-annotated this larger set, instead of double annotating and adjudicating, following Dligach et al.'s (2010) suggestion, according to which "it is often better to single annotate more data because it is a more cost-effective way to achieve a higher performance".

4.5 Annotation results

At a general level, the most frequently annotated category was *Attitude* (40.89%), followed by *Engagement* (35.64%) and *Graduation* (23.46%). However, when looking at the more specific tags, the most frequent one was *Contraction* (26.93%). This is due to the number of negations (*Deny*) (3a, 3b) and hypothetical situations (*Counter*) (4a, 4b) that are included in both languages. The second most common category was *Appreciation* (24.59%) (5a, 5b), which should be expected since the annotated texts are rich in *Valuation* or expressions conveying a value associated with an object and their aim is to describe those reviewed items. Finally, the tag with the third highest number of occurrences was *Force* (23.14%) (6a, 6b), which includes all those intensifiers and quantifiers that increase or lower the value of other nouns, adjectives or verbs.

(3a) At the beginning, <u>neither</u> is believable (79)
(3b) *A mi <u>no</u> me da <u>ningun</u> problema* (128)
[translation: it doesn't give me any problem]
(4a) <u>However</u>, this is … (74)

(4b) *Pero realmente lo unico que quieren...*(148) [translation: but what they only really want...]
(5a) This is <u>amazing</u> (84)
(5b) *Muy <u>sobrevalorada</u>* (168) [translation: very overrated]
(6a) Shame after <u>so</u> long a wait (90)
(6b) *<u>Muy</u> cara* (200) [translation: very expensive]

The category of *Focus* (0.32%) showed a very low distribution, probably because it is used to soften or sharpen the boundaries of a word, i.e., to express how close it is to the prototypical idea of that item, but users prefer to quantify nouns rather than stress or diminish their core meanings. *Judgement* (6.19%) is used to assign social or moral values to people but here it was used not only to address people but also objects. In any case, this kind of value was not a pivotal one in the items selected. Thirdly, expressions of *Expansion* (8.72%), showing different levels of certainty and allowing for other opinions apart from the authorial one, only appeared in half of the occasions in comparison with *Contraction*. This means that reviewers place the stress on their own voice, limiting the possibilities of other options, instead of presenting their opinion as one of a range of possible choices. Finally, *Affect* is placed in the very middle of the ranking (10.11%). This type of expressions refers to someone's feelings, how the author (or other users) feel with respect to the item reviewed and, in spite of their occurrence in the annotated texts, reviews focus much more on the value or even the effects of the item itself than on users' feelings.

The distribution of these categories in the larger corpus is graphically displayed in Figure 5:

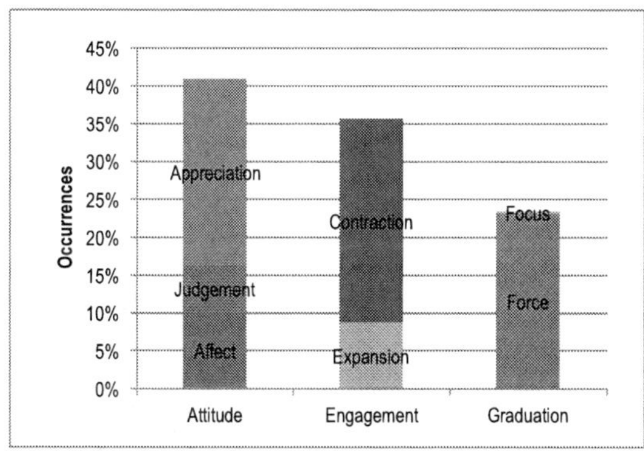

Figure 5: Distribution of Appraisal tags in the larger corpus

As to the language-specific preferences, English shows a slightly higher preference for *Engagement* (36.92%) than Spanish (33.94%), as well as for *Graduation* (24.69% in English vs. 21.82% in Spanish), although these are not statistically significant. However, the most visible difference involves *Attitude*, where it was found that Spanish occurrences go up to 44.24% while only a 38.39% of the English tags are marked as *Attitude*.

When comparing the preferences in the use of specific *Appraisal* tags in the different products (applications, games, books, films, music, etc.), the initial results presented a small difference between two groups: the group of applications and games were characterised by a higher use of *Engagement* resources, while the group of books, films and music showed a more frequent use of *Attitude* categories. *Graduation* did not present a clear tendency with similar results in both groups except for a wider use in games. *Appreciation* was ranked first as an *Attitude* resource in films and books, while *Affect* occurs more frequently in games, as well as in applications and books. *Judgement* is more likely to appear in applications than in any other item reviewed.

Reviews can also be classified according to the number of stars they assign to the item reviewed. This rating goes from 1 to 5 stars, Our corpus was divided in two groups: one group of one hundred negative reviews (with 1 and 2 stars) and another group of one hundred positive reviews (with 4 and 5 stars). While *Attitude* resources were more abundant in positive reviews, negative reviews use *Engagement* expressions more frequently. The use of *Graduation*, on the other hand, is virtually the same in both groups. Also, although the distribution of *Affect* is almost identical in positive and negative reviews (24.07% vs. 25.47%), positive reviews abound in *Appreciation* (64.93% vs. 54.67%), while negative ones make a wider use of *Judgement* (11.00% vs. 19.86%). This is related to the specific use that authors make of *Judgement* expressions, focusing on *Propriety* and, more specifically, negative spans. By contrast, when users are giving a positive evaluation of the item, they use more *Appreciation* resources to describe and justify the positive rating.

5 Summary and Discussion

The results of the annotations in the larger set indicate interesting tendencies in the distribution of *Appraisal* tags in the English and Spanish reviews, although they were not statistically significant. First, mobile applications reviews were shown to be especially rich in *Attitude* tags, followed by *Engagement*, while *Graduation* tags occur much less frequently. This distribution reflects the communicative purpose of these texts, which is to present users' opinions on a given product. Therefore, the majority of the *Appraisal* tags are expressions of *Attitude* which assign a value to the item reviewed, or express someone's feelings related to that item. The need to engage other users in the reviews is also reflected in the quite abundant use of *Engagement* tags in both the English and the Spanish reviews. *Graduation* tags, used to intensify or soften ideas, appear much less frequently in these reviews, indicating that users prefer other *Appraisal* strategies to convey their opinions on a given product.

As to the preferred tags from the extended tagsets, the reviews are rich in *Appreciation* expressions as they focus on the product, including its performance, qualities, effects, etc., while expressions of *Affect* and *Judgement* are less frequently used comparatively. The most frequent subtypes of *Appreciation* tags are *Valuation* and *Reaction*, while *Composition* (how the object is composed) is less frequently used. *Affect* tags are also common, but not as much as *Appreciation*. *Affect* deals with feelings and emotions, expressing the way the author or someone else feels in relation to the product reviewed and are the second-most common subtype of *Attitude* markers in the bilingual corpus. Their role in the reviews is usually supportive with respect to the role of *Appreciation* tags: if the qualities of the object itself are not enough to show why someone's opinion is the way it is, the expression of the users' feelings supports the emotional aspects of their opinion. The most common subtypes of *Affect* used in the larger corpus are *(Un)Happiness* and *(Dis)Satisfaction*. These include messages about how much users like (or dislike) the product or how satisfied and interested they are. Usually, authors tend to include *Happiness* expressions more often than *Unhappiness* elements, although *Satisfaction* and *Dissatisfaction* do not show such a clear distinction. *(In)Security* messages are not recurrent in these texts, so meanings related to fear, surprise, trust and the like are not frequently assigned to these products.

Judgement is the least used category in *Attitude*, probably because it includes meanings used to evaluate people's behaviour and not objects or products. Despite this fact, more occurrences have been found than expected, as when users focused on meanings related to *Capacity* and *Propriety*, classifying a game's bugs as a '*theft*', a character's behaviour as '*reprehensible*' or a singer as '*(un)talented*'.

Engagement, as mentioned before, had the second highest rate after *Attitude*, and it is divided into two main categories: *Expansion*, which presents the author's voice as one in a range of possible voices, and *Contraction*, which delimits and denies other possible voices. *Expansion* was the least frequent choice, while *Contraction* types are highly frequent in the reviews mainly due to *Disclaim* elements (*Counter* and *Deny*), which include common linguistic items such as conjunctions and negative particles.

Finally, *Graduation* was the least used category, with *Force* tags outnumbering *Focus* ones. This is probably because these reviews do not usually modulate the level of prototypicality of the nouns they use to name entities, but they intensify adjectives, verbs and indicate quantities for nouns. Thus, a product is not good but *very* good, a bug did not just happen, but happened *many* times, and they do not just like it, but like it *a lot*.

With respect to the language-specific comparisons, the Spanish reviews use *Attitude* resources much more frequently than the English ones, which prefers *Engagement* and *Graduation* elements. Thus, while the Spanish reviews draw on feelings and qualities, the English ones modulate their voice inside the text through *Engagement* as well as through expressions of *Graduation*. Expressions of *Satisfaction* were more frequently used in the Spanish reviews, while the English ones focused on those expressing *Happiness*. English writers frequently used words like '*love*' and '*like*' for any kind of product while Spanish writers use '*agradecer*' [thank] or '*esperar*' [hope]. Similarly, Spanish writers have a higher interest in describing *Capacity* and *Valuation*, whereas English ones lean more strongly on expressions of *Normality*, *Veracity* and *Reaction*.

As to the distribution of *Engagement* features, English reviews modulate certainty more extensively through *Epistemic* tags and *Pseudo-Questions* and are also more sarcastic by using rhetoric questions in their writings, while Spanish ones are much more direct using *Deontic* resources and basing their opinion on empirical sources. Along the same lines, *Counter* elements are more profuse and varied in English, showing opposition and contrast, while Spanish writers are more direct by simply rejecting any other possibilities by means of *Deny* resources.

With respect to differences among products, the observed distributions allowed the grouping of some products: one formed by applications and games with a higher use of positive *Affect* categories, such as *Happiness, Security* and *Satisfaction*; and a second one formed by books and films, which abound in negative ones such as *Unhappiness* and *Insecurity*. Music shares some characteristics with both groups but it has its own proper qualities.

With respect to the differences between positive and negative reviews, negative reviews abound in expressions of *Judgement* that is not observed in positive texts. As mentioned above, *Judgement* expressions typically address morally incorrect behaviours (*Propriety*), since positive moral actions are taken for granted. Positive *Judgement* realisations usually address *Capacity* meanings, such as talent, an adequate operation or improvements made in a product. The most common *Affect* meanings are *Happiness* and *Satisfaction* in positive reviews and, unsurprisingly, *Dissatisfaction* and *Unhappiness* in the negative ones.

Positive reviews present a higher use of *Epistemic* and *Deontic* resources with authors introducing their opinions by means of spans like *'I think'* and also recommend the product to other users through obligation meanings like *have to*. Negative reviews use *Pseudo-Questions* and *Evidential* markers since they distance from the item by means of sarcastic questions or use verbs like *'seem'* to introduce a negative quality instead of stating it directly. *Counter* realisations were far more common than the other *Disclaim* type, *Deny*, in positive reviews, but they both presented similar percentages in negative reviews. This is due to a higher use of negative elements in negative reviews, as can be expected, instead of a much lower use of *Counter* items.

Finally, *Graduation* differences include a higher use of *Isolation* modifiers in positive reviews, and a more profuse use of *Number* items in negative ones. This means that words like *'so'* or *'very'* are typically attached to positive expressions like *'good'* instead of *'bad'*, while *'many'*, *'some'*, etc. are used when criticising a product.

6   Concluding remarks

The work reported in this paper on the annotation of a bilingual (English-Spanish) dataset of mobile application reviews with *Appraisal* features has shed light on a number of theoretical and applied issues which deserve research attention in the Natural Language Processing (NLP) and the Linguistics communities. From the theoretical perspective, the empirical validation of the annotation scheme will contribute to the refinement and re-formulation of certain *Appraisal* features which have proved problematic in the annotation of the genre of mobile application reviews; and it will hopefully encourage further applied work to other genres and other languages. From the applied NLP perspective, the creation of a bilingual (English-Spanish) dataset containing *Appraisal* features will hopefully be useful for the development of machine learning algorithms for large scale annotation of this genre and other possible ones in the near future.

Future work will be focused on investigating the realisation of *Appraisal* in long phrases and sentences, in order to find common validated features beyond readers' interpretations. Another interesting line of future research is the extension of the empirical validation of more delicate *Appraisal* features for which insufficient evidence was found in the current corpus. It would also be relevant to extend the current range of items reviewed to a wider range of products in order to find possible groupings that share *Appraisal* features, thus confirming or diverging from the tendencies pointed out in this work.

References

Bloom, K., N. Garg and S. Argamon. 2007. Extracting Appraisal Expressions. In *Proceedings of NAACL HLT*. Rochester. 308–315

Bloom, K., S. Stein and S. Argamon. 2007. Appraisal Extraction for News Opinion Analysis at NTCIR-6. In *Proceedings of NTCIR-6 Workshop Meeting*. Tokyo, Japan.

Brooke, Julian. 2009. A Semantic Approach to Automatic Text Sentiment Analysis. M.A. thesis, Simon Fraser University, Burnaby, B.C., Canada.

Carretero, M. and M. Taboada. 2009. Contrastive analyses of Evaluation in text: Key issues raised by the application of Appraisal Theory to corpora of consumer-generated product reviews in English and Spanish. *I CongresoInternacional de Lingüística de Corpus*. Murcia, Spain.

Carretero, M. and M. Taboada. 2010a. Products, consumers and evaluation: a proposal of solutions to problematic issues of Attitude in English and Spanish consumer reviews. *22nd European Systemic Functional Linguistics Conference and Workshop*. University of Primorska, Slovenia.

Carretero, M. and M. Taboada. 2010b. The annotation of Appraisal: How Attitude and epistemic modality overlap. *4th International Conference on*

Modality in English (ModE4). Madrid, Spain.

Carretero, M. and M. Taboada. 2011. Annotating Appraisal: contrastive issues raised in the analysis of consumer reviews in English and Spanish. *38th International Systemic Functional Linguistic Congress*. Lisbon, Portugal.

Dligach, D., R.D. Nielsen and M. Palmer. 2010. To annotate more acccurately or to annotate more. In *Proceedings of the Fourth Linguistic Annotation Workshop.*64{72}, 55, 66, 132, 337, 380, 389.

Hovy, E., and Lavid, J. 2010. Towards a 'Science' of Corpus Annotation: A new Methodological Challenge for Corpus Linguistics. *International Journal of Translation,* 22 (1). 13-36.

Lavid, J. 2012. Corpus analysis and annotation in CONTRANOT: Linguistic and Methodological Challenges. In I. Moskowich and B. Crespo (eds.), *Encoding the past, decoding the future: corpora in the 21st century.* Cambridge: Cambridge Scholars. 205-220.

Lavid, J. 2017. Annotating complex linguistic features in bilingual corpora: The case of MULTINOT. In T. Declerck and S. Kübler (eds.), *Proceedings of the Workshop on Corpora in the Digital Humanities (CDH 2017)*. IN, USA: Bloomington. Available online athttp://ceur-ws.org/Vol-1786.

Lavid J., Carretero, M. and JR. Zamorano (2016): Contrastive Annotation of Epistemicity in the Multinot Project: Preliminary Steps. In Harry Bunt (ed.). *Proceedings of the ISA-12, Twelfth Joint ACL - ISO Workshop on Interoperable Semantic Annotation,* held in conjunction with *Language Resources and Evaluation Conference 2016.* 81-88.

Marín-Arrese, J.I. and B. Núñez Perucha. 2006. Evaluation and Engagement in Journalistic Commentary and News Reportage. *Revista Alicantina de Estudios Ingleses*19. 225-248.

Martin, J. and White, P. 2005. *The language of evaluation: Appraisal in English.* Palgrave, Macmillan.

Mora, N. 2011.*Annotating Expressions of Engagement in Online Book Reviews: A Contrastive (English-Spanish) Corpus Study for Computational Processing.* http://eprints.ucm.es/13754.

O'Donnell, M. 2008. "The UAM CorpusTool: Software for corpus annotation and exploration". Proceedings of the XXVI Congreso de AESLA, Almeria, Spain, 3-5 April 2008.

Pang, B., L. Lee and S. Vaithyanathan. 2002. Thumbs up? Sentiment classification using machine learning techniques. In *Proceedings of the 2002 Conference on Empirical Methods in Natural Language Processing*, Philadelphia, PA, EEUU.

Pang, B. and L. Lee. 2008. Opinion mining and sentiment analysis. *Foundations and Trends in Information Retrieval*, 2(1-2). 1–135.

Taboada, M. and J. Grieve. 2004. Analyzing appraisal automatically. In *Proceedings of AAAI Spring Symposium on Exploring Attitude and Affect in Text (AAAI Technical Report SS-04-07).*). Stanford University, CA, EEUU. 158-16.

Taboada, M. M. Carretero and J. Hinnel. 2014. Loving and hating the movies in English, German and Spanish. *Languages in Contrast*, 14(1). 127-161.

Wiebe, J., T. Wilson, R. Bruce, M. Bell, and M. Martin. 2004. Learning subjective language. *Computational linguistics*, 30(3). 277–308.

Whitelaw, C., Garg, N. and S. Argamon. 2005. Using appraisal taxonomies for sentiment analysis. In *Proceedings of MCLC-05, the 2nd Midwest Computational Linguistic Colloquium*, Colombia, EEUU.

Enabling Deep Learning of Emotion With First-Person Seed Expressions

Hassan Alhuzali, Muhammad Abdul-Mageed
Natural Language Processing Lab
University of British Columbia
muhammad.mageeed@ubc.ca

Lyle Ungar
Computer and Information Science
University of Pennsylvania
ungar@cis.upenn.edu

Abstract

The computational treatment of emotion in natural language text remains relatively limited, and Arabic is no exception. This is partly due to lack of labeled data. In this work, we describe and manually validate a method for the automatic acquisition of emotion labeled data and introduce a newly developed data set for Modern Standard and Dialectal Arabic emotion detection focused at Robert Plutchik's 8 basic emotion types. Using a hybrid supervision method that exploits first person emotion seeds, we show how we can acquire promising results with a deep gated recurrent neural network. Our best model reaches 70% F-score, significantly (i.e., 11%, $p < 0.05$) outperforming a competitive baseline. Applying our method and data on an external dataset of 4 emotions released around the same time we finalized our work, we acquire 7% absolute gain in F-score over a linear SVM classifier trained on gold data, thus validating our approach.

1   Introduction

Emotion is a key aspect of human life, and hence emotion detection systems are poised to have a wide array of applications from health and well-being to user profiling, education, and marketing, among others. Compared to prediction of simple valence (i.e., positive vs. negative sentiment) (Wiebe et al., 2004; Pang and Lee, 2004; Balahur and Steinberger, 2009; Liu, 2012; Rosenthal et al., 2017; Yang and Eisenstein, 2017), natural language processing work on emotion recognition still suffers from the bottleneck of labeled data. This is true for the Arabic language. With the exception of Abdul-Mageed et al. (2016) who develop data for Ekman's (Ekman, 1992) 6 basic emotions {*anger, disgust, fear, joy, sadness, surprise*} and another dataset released very recently as part of SemEval 2018 (Mohammad and Kiritchenko, 2018) that focuses on the 4 emotions {*anger, fear, joy, sadness*}, there are no datasets we know of for the language. In this paper, we seek to partially bridge this gap by creating a larger dataset and expanding to Robert Plutchik's list of 8 primary emotions (Plutchik, 1985, 1994) (which adds *anticipation* and *trust* to Ekman's list). In particular, we describe a newly developed, human-labeled dataset using an approach based on emotion phrase seeds from Modern Standard Arabic (MSA) and Dialectal Arabic (DA). In the process, we also seek to enhance the annotation procedure adopted by (Abdul-Mageed et al., 2016) who ask judges to label emotion existence (i.e., whether there is emotion or not) and emotion intensity (i.e., the degree of emotion arousal when an emotion exists) as a single task (rather then two stages). We believe a single stage set up can cause annotator cognitive overload and empirically show how a more simplified, two-stage annotation process yields higher annotator inter-rater reliability. We then proceed to show the utility of exploiting data acquired with our method to develop emotion detection models, including *supervised*, *distant supervised*, and *hybridly-supervised* (i.e., a mixture of supervised and distant supervised). We also validate our method of data acquisition on an external dataset (i.e., (Mohammad and Kiritchenko, 2018)), further proving its usefulness in capturing emotion signal. Finally, training on machine translation (MT) data, we acquire initial results that may be suggesting emotion does not translate (i.e., it may not be possible to successfully build emotion detection systems using MT).

Overall, we offer the following contributions: (1) We extend a first-person seed phrase approach introduced by (Abdul-Mageed et al., 2016) for emotion data collection from 6 to 8 emotion categories, and improve on the annotation procedure, acquiring higher agreement between the judges, (2) we introduce a new dataset for MSA and DA

Proceedings of the Second Workshop on Computational Modeling of People's Opinions, Personality, and Emotions in Social Media, pages 25–35
New Orleans, Louisiana, June 6, 2018. ©2018 Association for Computational Linguistics

emotion that is over double the size of their data (i.e., $7,268$ vs. $2,984$ tweets), (3) we introduce a hybrid supervision method and apply it to develop promising emotion detection models using a powerful deep gated recurrent neural network (GRU), and (4) we explore the utility of MT in the context of emotion detection, hoping our data-driven findings will lead to work enhancing our understanding of emotion.

The remainder of the paper is organized as follows: Section 2 is a review of related work. Section 3 is an overview of the different datasets acquired and used in our work. Section 4 is a description of both the first-person seed phrase approach to data acquisition and the annotation study we performed. Section 5 is about our methods, and 6 is where we introduce our models and describe negative experiments with MT. We conclude in Section 7.

2 Related Work

There is a small, but growing, body of NLP literature on emotion. A number of papers have focused on creating datasets for emotion detection. The SemEval 2007 Affective Text task (Strapparava and Mihalcea, 2007) focused on emotion annotation and classification where a dataset of $1,250$ news headlines was human labeled with the 6 basic emotions of Ekman (Ekman, 1972) and provided to participants. Similarly, Aman and Szpakowicz (2007) describe an emotion annotation and classification task on blog post data of $4,090$ sentences. The data were collected with identified emotion seeds words. Aman and Szpakowicz (2007) point out that the annotators received no training, but were given samples of annotated sentences to illustrate Ekman's 6 types of emotions. Annotators also labeled the data for *mixed-emotion* and *no-emotion*. In addition, annotators were required to assign emotion intensity tags from the set {*low, medium, high*} to all emotion-carrying sentences (thus excluding sentences tagged with *no-emotion*). Our work differs from these in that we focus on Arabic and the Twitter domain.

A number of works use emotion hashtags (e.g., *#happy, #sad*) as a way of automatically labeling data for emotion (i.e., **distant supervision**) (Mintz et al., 2009). These include Mohammad (2012); Mohammad and Kiritchenko (2015); Wang et al. (2012); Volkova and Bachrach (2016);

Abdul-Mageed and Ungar (2017). For example, Mohammad (2012) collects a corpus of $50,000$ tweets using seed words corresponding to the 6 Ekman emotions and exploits it for building emotion models. More recently, Mohammad and Bravo-Marquez (2017) label a dataset of $7,097$ tweets with emotion intensity tags for the four emotions {*anger, fear, joy, sadness*} using a method they refer to as *best-worst annotation* (Kiritchenko and Mohammad, 2016). They describe the method as producing reliable labels.

In a similar vein, Wang et al. (2012) collect a large emotion corpus (N= 5 million) for 5 of Ekman's 6 basic emotions (skipping *disgust*), but adding *love* and *thankfulness* using a seed set of 131 hashtags representing these emotions. The authors then randomly sample 400 tweets and label them manually with a tag from the set *relevant, irrelevant*. Abdul-Mageed and Ungar (2017) also collect a large dataset of English tweets using 665 hashtags representing 24 different types of emotions. The authors also perform a manual annotation study showing the utility of using hashtags as labels. Other work includes Yan and Turtle (2016) who use crowdsourcing and lab-controlled conditions to label a dataset of $15,553$ tweets that they then exploit to build baseline models. Related to our work is also scholarship on **mood** (Nguyen, 2010; De Choudhury et al., 2012) which also depend on collecting data using seed words. Our work also falls under distant supervision, but is different in that we use seed expressions, rather than hashtags. Our data collection method is most similar to Abdul-Mageed et al. (2016), who also use phrase seeds to acquire tweets for Ekman's 6 basic emotions, but we extend the work to 8 emotions, expand the list of seed expressions used, improve on the manual annotation study, and empirically validate the method on the practical emotion modeling task both on our data and on an external dataset. Our work also has affinity to works on Arabic text classification (Abdul-Mageed et al., 2011; Refaee and Rieser, 2014; Abdul-Mageed et al., 2014; Nabil et al., 2015; Salameh et al., 2015; Abdul-Mageed, 2017, 2018; Alshehri et al., 2018; Abdul-Mageed et al., 2018), but we focus on emotion.

3 Data

Building LAMA: We collect a dataset of Arabic tweets from the Twitter public stream exploiting the Twitter API [1] using a seed set of emotion-carrying expressions following Abdul-Mageed et al. (2016). More specifically, we use a list of seeds for each of the Plutchik 8 primary emotions from the set: {*anger, anticipation, disgust, fear, joy, sadness, surprise, trust*}. As such, we add *anticipation* and *trust* to the 6 categories Abdul-Mageed et al. (2016) work with. In this approach, we collect all tweets where a seed phrase appears in the tweet body text. Note this approach is only conditioned on a given phrase existing in the tweet text as captured by a regular expression. Each phrase is composed of the first person pronoun انا (Eng. "I") + a seed word expressing an emotion, e.g., فرحان (Eng. "happy"). We also follow Abdul-Mageed et al. (2016) in choosing the seed expressions such that they capture data representing Modern Standard Arabic (MSA) as well as Dialectal Arabic (DA). For wider coverage, we expand Abdul-Mageed et al. (2016)'s seeds from 23 to 48 expressions and only include seeds based on complete agreement between two native speakers of the language. From each of the 8 emotion categories, we select $1,000$ tweets with seeds from our list for annotation (total $=8,000$). We ask annotators to manually remove any duplicates in the data, yielding a total of $7,268$ tweets, which we refer to as **LAMA**. To validate this phrase-based approach for emotion data collection, we ask 4 native Arabic speakers to manually label LAMA.

LAMA-DIST: The rest of our dataset acquired with the same seed approach comprises $405,588$ tweets that we automatically clean using a strict pipeline: We remove all re-tweets, use the Python library *pandas* [2] "drop_duplicates" method to compares the tweet texts of all the tweets after normalizing character repetitions [all consecutive characters of > 2 to 2] and user mentions (as detected by a string starting with an "@" sign). We then only keep tweets with a minimal length of 5 words. This procedure leaves us with a total of $182,690$ tweets. We call these **LAMA-DIST**.

DINA: We acquire the **DINA** dataset from Abdul-Mageed et al. (2016) and use it in our experiments as we describe in 6.4.

MT-DIST: We use Google Translate to convert the Twitter English dataset from Abdul-Mageed and Ungar (2017) into Arabic and exploit the data to explore the utility of using MT for emo-

tion detection. The data are collected using hashtags representing the same 8 primary emotions we work with. Similar to e.g., Mohammad (2012); Wang et al. (2012) the tweets only involve emotion hashtags occurring in the end of tweets, that have a minimal length 5 words, and tweets with URLs, retweets, etc. are filtered out. An annotation study was performed by the authors (i.e., (Abdul-Mageed and Ungar, 2017)) to validate use of hashtags in this dataset, with 'substantial' inter-annotator agreement over $> 5,000$ randomly sampled tweets. In total, we use $756,663$ tweets that we translate into Arabic. We refer to this dataset as **MT-DIST**.

SE-18: We use the SemEval 2018 (Mohammad and Kiritchenko, 2018) Arabic data **(SE-18)** developed for the 4 emotion categories {*anger, fear, joy, sadness*}. Since SE-18 is recently released, only the training and development splits are available. The dataset was collected using emotion-related words and comprises a total of $4,037$ tweets. Table 1 provides statistics of the various datasets we exploit in our experiments. We now turn to describing the annotation study we performed on LAMA to validate our first-person phrase seeds approach.

4 Annotation

4.1 Background

The goal of the annotation is to identify tweets carrying the category of emotion expressed by a given phrase from a set of phrase seeds related to each type of emotion. Conceptualized from this perspective, the annotation process is intrinsically a relevance task where a tweet is judged as *relevant* (i.e., carrying the single emotion expressed by the seed phrase) or *irrelevant* (i.e., carrying no emotion at all or > 1 emotion type). Additionally, our goal is to identify the intensity of the emotion in relevant tweets: Given a tweet carrying a single emotion, we direct it to one of three intensity bins. As such, we provide annotators with a tweet where one seed phrase occurs and ask them to approach the task as a two-stage process. In stage one, annotators apply a binary decision using tags from the set {*relevant, irrelevant*}. In stage two, they apply an emotion intensity tag from the set {*low, medium, high*} to all those data points where a *relevant* label was assigned in the first stage. Again, note that we instruct annotators that assigning the

---

Emotion	DINA		LAMA		LAMA-DINA		LAMA-DIST		MT-DIST		SE-18	
	#	%	#	%	#	%	#	%	#	%	#	%
anger	413	0.14	634	0.09	1,047	0.10	3,650	0.02	45,974	0.06	1,027	0.25
anticipation	–	–	934	0.13	934	0.09	24,673	0.14	24,354	0.03	–	–
disgust	449	0.15	621	0.09	1,070	0.10	2,479	0.01	51,452	0.07	–	–
fear	487	0.16	951	0.13	1,438	0.14	28,332	0.16	65,533	0.09	1,028	0.25
joy	476	0.16	888	0.12	1,364	0.13	55,288	0.3	395,251	0.52	952	0.24
sadness	481	0.16	719	0.10	1,200	0.12	27,609	0.15	130,783	0.17	1,030	0.26
surprise	499	0.17	668	0.09	1,167	0.11	15,108	0.08	34,879	0.05	–	–
trust	–	–	865	0.12	865	0.08	25,550	0.14	8,437	0.01	–	–
no-emotion	179	0.06	988	0.14	1,167	0.11	–	–	–	–	–	–
total/percent	2,984	1.00	7,268	1.00	10,252	1.00	182,689	1.00	756,663	1.00	4,037	1.00

Table 1: Data statistics. **DINA**: Twitter gold-labeled data from Abdul-Mageed et al. (2016). **LAMA**: Our newly-developed dataset. **LAMA-DINA**: A merged set of LAMA and DINA. **LAMA-DIST**: Data we automatically acquire with first-person expressions. **MT-DIST**: Twitter emotion data from Abdul-Mageed and Ungar (2017), translated from English into Arabic. **SE-18** SemEval 2018 Arabic data from Mohammad and Kiritchenko (2018).

Class	Kappa *(K-Bin)*	Kappa *(K-Int)*	% 2-jdgs
anger	0.53	0.66	0.57
anticip	1.00	0.85	0.99
disgust	0.49	0.57	0.97
fear	1.00	0.78	0.97
joy	0.93	0.79	0.92
sadness	0.91	0.90	0.86
surprise	0.77	0.64	0.68
trust	1.00	0.80	0.93
average	0.83	0.75	0.86

Table 2: Annotation agreement. **Kappa (K-Bin)**: binary, emotion vs no-emotion; **Kappa (K-Int)**: intensity-based, fine-grained annotation; **% 2-jdgs**: % of emotion captured per category with double-annotated data.

label *relevant* means the tweet carries the single emotion expressed by the seed phrase. To illustrate an annotation scenario, given a tweet like أنا فرحان جداً لأني زرت أمي بالأمس (En "I'm so happy I visited mom yesterday"), where the seed phrase أنا فرحان (Eng. "I'm happy") indicative of the emotion type "joy" occurs, judges are asked whether the tweet carries the respective single "joy" emotion (i.e., *relevant*) or not (i.e., it either carries no emotion or more than one emotion and hence is *irrelevant*). Judges are then tasked to assign one of the intensity labels to that specific tweet if it is labeled *relevant* in stage one. We note that our emotion intensity procedure is similar to Aman and Szpakowicz (2007). To illustrate the *irrelevant* class, even though a tweet like كلما سأله المذيع عن حالته، أجاب: أنا مبسوط. (Eng. "Whenever the reporter asked him how he is doing, he answered 'I'm glad'.") has the same phrase أنا مبسوط (Eng. "I'm glad") as the pre-

vious example, an annotator may decide it does not overall communicate "joy" (i.e., *irrelevant*). Importantly, cast as a two-stage process, our annotation procedure is simpler than Abdul-Mageed et al. (2016)'s single stage set-up where judges are asked to assign one of 4 labels one of which represents *zero* emotion and the rest represent emotion intensity. We believe a two-stage tagging process reduces annotator cognitive overload. As we explain further in Section 4.2, this simplified set-up may be responsible for us acquiring better inter-annotator agreement (Kappa *(K)* = 0.75) than Abdul-Mageed et al. (2016) (Kappa *(K)* = 0.51).

To enable the annotation process and ensure quality, we prepared an annotation guidelines tutorial in the form of a set of presentation slides explaining the overall task, the different emotion categories, the seed expressions chosen to represent each emotion type, and examples of each category. Annotators attended an initial session where the tutorial was shared with them and an expert with native fluency of several Arabic varieties and full knowledge of the task trained them. We had 4 annotators, all of whom are native speakers of Arabic with graduate education. The judges had high proficiency in MSA and reasonable fluency in DA (several dialects). Annotators were advised to consult with one another, consult online sources, and eventually get back to us on cases where a given dialect was not intelligible. Each of the 4 judges labeled data for 2 emotion types. For inter-rater agreement, we chose a sample of 100 labeled tweets from each of the 8 emotions to be double-tagged by the 5*th* judge. We measure inter-annotator agreement using Cohen's (Cohen, 1960) Kappa and also calculate the percentage of per-class agreement. We now turn to describing findings from the annotation study.

4.2 Annotation Study

Do Seed Expressions Capture Emotion? The main goal of the annotation task is to acquire emotion carrying data that we can exploit in computational models. Hence, the most significant question we had is: "To what extent can first-person seed expressions help capture emotion-carrying data?". Considering the labels assigned by the judges, it turns out that, on average, two judges (middle column in Table 2) agree to assign the *relevant* tag (i.e., one or another of the emotion intensity tags) 86% of the time, whereas one judge (last column in Table 2)) assigns it 89% of the time. Table 2 also shows that our seeds are stronger cues for presence of the respective emotion in some cases more than others. For example, in the case of *anticipation*, judges decided that 99% of the data are *relevant* (i.e., carry the *anticipation* emotion), compared to 57% of the data in the case of *anger*. We now describe hand-labeling the data for emotion intensity.

Can We Consistently Label Intensity? To answer the question as to whether, and if so to what extent, we can label emotion intensity, we asked judges to assign one of three intensity tags from the set {*low, medium, high*}. As Table 2 shows, on average, judges agree on these fine-grained labels with a Cohen's Kappa $(K) = 75\%$, thus reflecting 'substantial' agreement (Landis and Koch, 1977). Observably, we acquire higher inter-annotator agreement (Kappa $(K) = 75\%$) than (Abdul-Mageed et al., 2016) (Kappa $(K) = 51\%$). As we mentioned earlier, this may be a result of our simplified, two-stage annotation set up where judges assign *relevant-irrelevant* tags before they assign intensity labels.[3] We now turn to introducing our methods.

5 Methods

Deep Gated Recurrent Neural Networks: For our core modeling, we use *Gated Recurrent Neural Networks (GRNNs)* (Cho et al., 2014; Chung et al., 2015). Like Long Short-Term Memory (LSTM) networks (Hochreiter and Schmidhuber, 1997), GRUs constitute a modern variation of *Recurrent Neural Networks (RNNs)* capable of cap-

turing long-term dependencies while side-walking the problems of vanishing/exploding gradients (Bengio et al., 1994; Pascanu et al., 2013). GRUs are simpler than LSTMs, and tend to run faster usually without sacrificing performance, and so we opt for using them. We run an extensive set of experiments, tuning parameters on our dev data. Once we identified the architecture that worked best on most settings, we fix it across all our experiments. Our GRU architecture is as follows: We use a vocabulary size of $50K$ words, a word embedding vector of 300 dimensions learnt directly from the training data, and an input maximum length of 30 words. We use three hidden GRU layers, each with $1,000$ units[4]. For regularization, we use a dropout (Hinton et al., 2012) of 0.5 after the first hidden layer. We use the Adam (Kingma and Ba, 2014) optimizer, setting our learning rate to 0.001. We use a mini-batch (Cotter et al., 2011) size of 128, and run for 4 epochs. For our loss function, we use categorical cross-entropy.

Baseline classifiers: For comparison, we use an SVM classifier with a linear kernel. Since some of our experiments involve larger datasets than what SVMs can handle within memory bounds, we follow Abdul-Mageed and Ungar (2017) in using 4 additional online classifiers: Multinomial Naive Bayes, Passive Aggressive Classifier, Perceptron, and linear SVMs trained with Stochastic Gradient Descent (SVM-SGD). For these, we use the Python scikit-learn package.[5] With the 5 baseline classifiers, for a fair comparison against the deep network models, we experiment with various lexicalized (i.e., based on N-grams and lexical resources) features where we identify the best settings for the value of N (we experiment with values from the set {*1,2,3*} and combinations of these) and various vocabulary sizes (we experiment with values between $20K$ and $80K$). Here, we typically tune these hyper-parameters on the dev splits of each of the three datasets LAMA, DINA, and LAMA-DINA independently. We identify unigrams+bigrams (1g+2g) with a vocab_size (V) $= 50K$ as our best settings, and so we fix these across all experiments.

Evaluation: Since we run with several classifiers, we limit reported results to the harmonic mean of precision and recall: *F*-score (macro-average). Unless otherwise indicated, we typically

---

[3]While we label intensity in our data, we leave detecting intensity to future work.

[4]Models with as less capacity as 500 units performed only slightly worse in most cases.

[5]http://scikit-learn.org.

use the majority class in the training data of each respective set of experiments as our baseline. We now turn to describing our models under various conditions of supervision.

6 Models

6.1 Supervised Models

Data Splits: We first exploit LAMA and DINA, both of which have gold labels, in a supervised fashion. We split each of these data sets into 80% training (**train**), 10% development (**dev**), and 10% test (**test**) and first learn on each of them independently in a standard way where we train on train, tune performance on dev, and blind-test on test. We also merge the corresponding splits from each dataset (e.g., training set from each to acquire a combined train), forming a unified resource (**LAMA-DINA**) that we then exploit under the same supervised conditions. *We consistently remove all our phrase seeds from the data before we perform any of the experiments, even when we run on external data. This is the case for all the experiments we report in the paper.*

Two-Stage Classification: For all supervised experiments, we have a two-stage classification set-up: (1) *binary* where the models attempt to tease apart the *emotion* from the *no-emotion* categories, and (2) the 8-way *emotion* classification. We now present results with our three data settings.

LAMA: Table 3 shows results of our supervised learning settings in *F*-scores. As the Table shows, for the multiclass task on the 8 emotion categories, the best model on LAMA test is acquired with SVMs. SVMs achieve 63% *F*-score, an absolute gain of 48% over the majority class baseline and 5% higher than GRUs (which performs at 58%). For the binary task (i.e., *emotion, no-emotion*, the highest gains of 93% are with the Perceptron classifier (1% over GRUs), again 6% absolute improvement over the baseline.

DINA: As far as we know, we are the first to develop an Arabic emotion system. As such, there is no previous work to compare to. However, as we mention earlier, we acquire the DINA dataset developed by (Abdul-Mageed et al., 2016) and run experiments on it. As Table 3 shows, both SVMs and GRUs perform best on emotion classification on DINA (both at 54%, which is 36% over the baseline). For binary classification, both the Perceptron and GRUs achieve highest, with 98% (i.e.,

4% above the baseline).

LAMA-DINA: As explained in Section 5, we merge the corresponding splits from LAMA and DINA to form a single resource (LAMA-DINA). For emotion classification, as in Table 3, GRUs performs best (59% *F*-score, 43% over the baseline) on LAMA-DINA. For the binary task, GRUs also achieves better than other classifiers, with 94% *F*-score (4% above the baseline).

Emotion Lexica: Again, for a fairer comparison with our deep learning models, we experiment with adding lexicon-based features to our online classifiers: Fixing N-grams to $1g + 2g$ and $V = 50K$, we use the translated version of the emotion lexicon EmoLex (Mohammad and Turney, 2013) (which has entries for the 8 emotion categories): We add 1 binary feature based on the lexicon to the *emotion vs. no-emotion* stage and 8 binary features (one feature corresponding to each emotion category) to the *emotion* stage. However, we do not find EmoLex features to help, and so we do not use them in further experiments.[6]

Across all the supervised experiments, for both the binary and 8−way emotion classification tasks, our best models are significantly higher than the respective baselines (i.e., at least < p= 0.05).

6.2 Distant Supervision with Seeds

We train exclusively on the LAMA-DIST dataset we acquire with seed expressions (as described in Section 3), directly testing performance on LAMA-DINA test set. Across all classifiers, we use the same hyper-parameters described in Section 5). The current and the next sets of experiments (6.3) are focused on **emotion detection** (the 8 types) and are both reported in Table 4. As Table 4 shows, with more training data, GRUs performs better than all other classifiers (53% *F*-score) and is followed by PAC (42%). GRUs' performance is 23% over the baseline, but 6% less than our best result on the same LAMA-DINA test set reported under full supervised (59%, also acquired with GRUs in Section 6.1). This demonstrates the benefit of our phrase-based approach in absence of gold data. We now turn to investigating the utility of employing distant supervision in a scenario where human-labeled data do exist.

---

[6]We observe a number of issues with the translated version of EmoLex, but leave analysis of these for future work.

TRAIN	Setting	Class	MNB	PAC	PTN	SVM-SGD	SVM	GRU	# test
Lama	emotion	base	0.15	0.15	0.15	0.15	0.15	0.15	–
		avg/total	0.49	0.57	0.48	0.54	**0.63**	0.58	632
	binary	base	0.86	0.86	0.86	0.86	0.86	0.86	–
		emotion	0.92	0.92	**0.93**	0.92	0.92	0.92	632
		no-emotion	0.23	0.29	0.21	0.24	0.33	0.28	94
Dina	emotion	base	0.18	0.18	0.18	0.18	0.18	0.18	–
		avg/total	0.45	0.40	0.46	0.42	**0.54**	**0.54**	278
	binary	base	0.94	0.94	0.94	0.94	0.94	0.94	–
		emotion	0.89	**0.98**	0.97	0.92	0.97	**0.98**	278
		no-emotion	0.30	0.42	0.41	0.25	0.47	0.46	19
Lama-Dina	emotion	base	0.16	0.16	0.16	0.16	0.16	0.16	–
		avg/total	0.43	0.50	0.45	0.47	0.55	**0.59**	910
	binary	base	0.89	0.89	0.89	0.89	0.89	0.89	–
		emotion	0.93	0.93	0.92	0.92	0.93	**0.94**	910
		no-emotion	0.23	0.25	0.38	0.37	0.33	0.30	113

Table 3: **Binary** (i.e., emotion vs. no-emotion) and **emotion** (i.e., a single 8-way classification task) results under supervised conditions. For space, we only report average results across the 8 categories on this set of experiments.

TRAIN	Emotion	MNB	PAC	PTN	SVM-SGD	GRU	#test
Lama-Dist	base	0.30	0.30	0.30	0.30	0.30	—
	avg/total	0.32	**0.42**	0.39	0.41	**0.53**	910
Lama-D2	base-g	0.59	0.59	0.59	0.59	0.59	—
	anger	0.28	0.57	0.53	0.59	0.66	111
	anticip	0.46	0.57	0.54	0.65	0.68	88
	disgust	0.17	0.54	0.50	0.56	0.69	104
	fear	0.60	0.67	0.66	0.69	0.77	145
	joy	0.39	0.48	0.50	0.55	0.68	131
	sadness	0.37	0.49	0.42	0.47	0.63	121
	surprise	0.52	0.59	0.56	0.61	0.72	120
	trust	0.45	0.57	0.60	0.69	0.73	90
	avg/total	0.41	0.56	0.54	**0.60**	**0.70**	910

Table 4: Results of **distant supervision** and **hybrid supervision** on LAMA-DINA test set. **Lama-Dist**: Twitter data we collect with the same phrase-based approach we use in our annotation study. **Lama-D2**: lama-dina+lama-dist. The 59% `base-g` for the LAMA-D2 setting is what we acquire with gold data (LAMA-DINA training data) with GRUs. We only show average performance with our **Lama-Dist** training data, for space.

6.3 Hybrid Supervision with Seeds

In this iteration of experiments, we merge LAMA-DIST with the training split of LAMA-DINA (80% of the LAMA-DINA data) to form a single training set **LAMA-D2**. As Table 4 shows, with LAMA-D2 as train, GRUs model performance reaches its highest F-score of 70%, an absolute gain of 40% over the majority class baseline (`base`) and 11% absolute gain over the best emotion gold model on the same combined LAMA-Dina test set, a second reasonable baseline (`base-g`, acquired with GRUs). *This is the best model we report in this paper, and is **a statistically significant gain over `base` and `base-g` ($< p= 0.01$ and $< p= 0.05$, respectively)**.* These results further demonstrate the advantage of our first-person phrase seed approach for emotion detection. Based on the current and previous set of experiments, we find that this specific distant supervision approach is valuable when used alone but even more so when used to augment existing gold data.

6.4 Validation on External Data

We further validate our data acquistion approach and models on an externa dataset. For this, we use the SemEval 2018 (**SE-18**) (Mohammad and Kiritchenko, 2018) dataset comprised of 4 emotions (described in Table 1) that was recently released. We only use our best-performing classifier, i.e., GRUs with the same settings as described in Section 5, in this set of experiments. We train GRUs with 5 training data splits and acquire results in F-scores as follows: (**a**) SE-18 (36%), (**b**) Lama-Dina (28%), (**c**) Lama-Dist (39%), (**d**) Lama-D2 (41%), and (**e**) Lama-D2+SE-18 (46%). We report only results with conditions (**a**), (**d**), and (**e**) in Table 5. As these results show, using only our automatic data (condition (**c**)), we improve 3% over training with SE-18 (condition (**a**)). When

TRAIN	Emotion	GRU	#dev
SE-18	base	0.26	—
	anger	0.00	149
	fear	0.43	145
	joy	0.64	222
	sadness	0.20	139
	avg/total	**0.36**	655
Lama-D2	anger	0.24	149
	fear	0.39	145
	joy	0.58	222
	sadness	0.35	139
	avg/total	**0.41**	655
Lama-D2+SE-18	anger	0.31	149
	fear	0.41	145
	joy	0.64	222
	sadness	0.41	139
	avg/total	**0.46**	655

Table 5: Experiments on **Sem-Eval 2018 (SE-18)** Arabic data on 4 emotion categories.

we add up our distant supervision and gold data (i.e., with Lama-D2), absolute gain goes up to 5%. Augmenting SE-18 with Lama-D2 gives 46% *F*-score. This is a whole 10% improvement over SE-18 and 20% absolute gain over the 26% majority class baseline. These significant gains on the SE-18 external dataset further demonstrate the utility of our phrase based data acquisition approach, and the advantage of our models.

6.5 Negative Results with MT

In absence of labeled data, MT can be been used for converting labeled data from a source language (often English) into one or more target languages for classification. Although, to the best of our knowledge, there are currently no attempts to exploit MT for emotion detection, there have been successful efforts on the (conceptually relevant) task of sentiment analysis. Examples of sentiment systems employing MT include Hiroshi et al. (2004) (Japanese), Wan (2008) (Chinese), Brooke et al. (2009); Smith et al. (2016) (Spanish), Mihalcea et al. (2007) (Romanian), and Mohammad et al. (2016) (Arabic). Clearly, MT has its limitations. Hence, whether MT will be as useful for emotion as it proved to be for sentiment is in our view an interesting question. As a first attempt to explore answers, we experiment with the MT-DIST data described in Section 3 under two settings: **(a)** We train exclusively on MT-DIST and test on LAMA-DINA, and **(b)** We merge MT-DIST with the training split of LAMA-DINA to form a single training set that we refer to as **MT-D2**. Again, we use the same settings as described in 5 with both the online classifiers and GRUs, and

directly test on LAMA-DINA test set. For space limitations, we do not report the full results from this cycle of experiments with MT here. We do note, however, that we acquire no gains on either of the two settings: With MT-DIST functioning as our training data, the best model we acquire is with GRUs (only at 10% *F*-score, i.e., 5% less than the baseline). Similarly, with MT-D2 as train, GRUs acquires a best result of 20%, a performance 39% less than the 59% we acquire with GRUs using the LAMA-DINA gold data (reported in Table 3). This shows that MT data hurts emotion classification when used for training.

A full understanding of why it is that MT does not help emotion classification is beyond our current work. However, we hypothesize a number of reasons could account for our findings. Intuitively, MT is in general prone to errors and these could be naturally propagating to our models. In addition, the original Twitter dataset which we convert into MT-DIST is acquired via distant supervision, a regime that may have its own biases and noise. From a theoretical perspective, although early psychological research claimed the universality (i.e., cross-cultural nature) of basic emotions, such work is based on facial expression premises, not language, and are not uncontroversial (Barrett, 2017; Mesquita et al., 2017). We suspect there are cross-cultural variations, even in these primary emotions, that current MT technologies cannot capture. Finally, the fact that our test data involves Dialectal Arabic (a range of varieties Google's production MT models do not currently handle) is in all likelihood responsible for a share of the errors.

7 Conclusion

In this paper, we evaluated the feasibility of automatic acquisition of emotion data from the Twitter domain using an approach based on first-person expressions. We validated the method via a careful, manual annotation study. We then developed successful supervised, distant supervised, and hybrid supervised models exploiting the data and validated our methods on an external dataset. We also explored the utility of using MT for emotion detection, providing initial insights that we hope will ultimately lead to enhanced, cross-cultural understandings of emotion. In the future, we plan to extend our models to different emotion categories and possibly other languages.

8   Acknowledgement

This research was enabled in part by support provided by WestGrid (`https://www.westgrid.ca/`) and Compute Canada (`www.computecanada.ca`).

References

Muhammad Abdul-Mageed. 2017. Modeling arabic subjectivity and sentiment in lexical space. *Information Processing & Management* .

Muhammad Abdul-Mageed. 2018. Learning subjective language: Feature engineerd vs. deep models. In *The 3rd Workshop on Open-Source Arabic Corpora and Processing Tools (OSACT 2018), LREC*.

Muhammad Abdul-Mageed, Hassan Alhuzali, and Mohamed Elaraby. 2018. You tweet what you speak: A city-level dataset of arabic dialects. In *LREC*.

Muhammad Abdul-Mageed, Hassan AlHuzli, and Mona Diab DuaaAbu Elhija. 2016. Dina: A multi-dialect dataset for arabic emotion analysis. In *The 2nd Workshop on Arabic Corpora and Processing Tools 2016 Theme: Social Media*. page 29.

Muhammad Abdul-Mageed, Mona Diab, and Mohamed Korayem. 2011. Subjectivity and sentiment analysis of modern standard arabic. In *Proceedings of the 49th Annual Meeting of the Association for Computational Linguistics: Human Language Technologies*. Association for Computational Linguistics, Portland, Oregon, USA, pages 587–591. `http://www.aclweb.org/anthology/P11-2103`.

Muhammad Abdul-Mageed, Mona Diab, and Sandra Kübler. 2014. Samar: Subjectivity and sentiment analysis for arabic social media. *Computer Speech & Language* 28(1):20–37.

Muhammad Abdul-Mageed and Lyle Ungar. 2017. Emonet: Fine-grained emotion detection with gated recurrent neural networks. In *Proceedings of the 55th Annual Meeting of the Association for Computational Linguistics (Volume 1: Long Papers)*. volume 1, pages 718–728.

Ali Alshehri, AlMoetazbillah Nagoudi, Alhuzali Hassan, and Muhammad Abdul-Mageed. 2018. Think before your click: Data and models for adult content in arabic twitter. In *The 2nd Text Analytics for Cybersecurity and Online Safety (TA-COS-2018), LREC*.

Saima Aman and Stan Szpakowicz. 2007. Identifying expressions of emotion in text. In *Text, Speech and Dialogue*. Springer, pages 196–205.

A. Balahur and R. Steinberger. 2009. Rethinking Sentiment Analysis in the News: from Theory to Practice and back. *Proceeding of WOMSA* .

Lisa Feldman Barrett. 2017. *How emotions are made: The secret life of the brain*. Houghton Mifflin Harcourt.

Yoshua Bengio, Patrice Simard, and Paolo Frasconi. 1994. Learning long-term dependencies with gradient descent is difficult. *IEEE transactions on neural networks* 5(2):157–166.

Julian Brooke, Milan Tofiloski, and Maite Taboada. 2009. Cross-linguistic sentiment analysis: From english to spanish. In *RANLP*. pages 50–54.

Kyunghyun Cho, Bart Van Merriënboer, Caglar Gulcehre, Dzmitry Bahdanau, Fethi Bougares, Holger Schwenk, and Yoshua Bengio. 2014. Learning phrase representations using rnn encoder-decoder for statistical machine translation. *arXiv preprint arXiv:1406.1078* .

Junyoung Chung, Caglar Gülçehre, Kyunghyun Cho, and Yoshua Bengio. 2015. Gated feedback recurrent neural networks. In *ICML*. pages 2067–2075.

J. Cohen. 1960. A coefficient of agreement for nominal scales. *Educational and Psychological Measurement* 20:37–46.

Andrew Cotter, Ohad Shamir, Nati Srebro, and Karthik Sridharan. 2011. Better mini-batch algorithms via accelerated gradient methods. In *Advances in neural information processing systems*. pages 1647–1655.

Munmun De Choudhury, Scott Counts, and Michael Gamon. 2012. Not all moods are created equal! exploring human emotional states in social media.

P. Ekman. 1972. Universal and cultural differences in facial expression of emotion. *Nebraska Symposium on Motivation* pages 207–283.

Paul Ekman. 1992. An argument for basic emotions. *Cognition & emotion* 6(3-4):169–200.

Geoffrey E Hinton, Nitish Srivastava, Alex Krizhevsky, Ilya Sutskever, and Ruslan R Salakhutdinov. 2012. Improving neural networks by preventing co-adaptation of feature detectors. *arXiv preprint arXiv:1207.0580* .

Kanayama Hiroshi, Nasukawa Tetsuya, and Watanabe Hideo. 2004. Deeper sentiment analysis using machine translation technology. In *Proceedings of the 20th international conference on Computational Linguistics*. Association for Computational Linguistics, page 494.

Sepp Hochreiter and Jürgen Schmidhuber. 1997. Long short-term memory. *Neural computation* 9(8):1735–1780.

Diederik Kingma and Jimmy Ba. 2014. Adam: A method for stochastic optimization. *arXiv preprint arXiv:1412.6980* .

Svetlana Kiritchenko and Saif M Mohammad. 2016. Capturing reliable fine-grained sentiment associations by crowdsourcing and best-worst scaling. In *HLT-NAACL*. pages 811–817.

J.R. Landis and G.G. Koch. 1977. The measurement of observer agreement for categorical data. *Biometrics* 33(1):159.

Bing Liu. 2012. Sentiment analysis and opinion mining. *Synthesis lectures on human language technologies* 5(1):1–167.

Batja Mesquita, Michael Boiger, and Jozefien De Leersnyder. 2017. Doing emotions: The role of culture in everyday emotions. *European Review of Social Psychology* 28(1):95–133.

Rada Mihalcea, Carmen Banea, and Janyce Wiebe. 2007. Learning multilingual subjective language via cross-lingual projections. In *Annual meeting-association for computational linguistics*. volume 45, page 976.

Mike Mintz, Steven Bills, Rion Snow, and Dan Jurafsky. 2009. Distant supervision for relation extraction without labeled data. In *Proceedings of the Joint Conference of the 47th Annual Meeting of the ACL and the 4th International Joint Conference on Natural Language Processing of the AFNLP: Volume 2-Volume 2*. Association for Computational Linguistics, pages 1003–1011.

S. Bravo-Marquez F. Salameh M. Mohammad and S. Kiritchenko. 2018. Semeval-2018 task 1: Affect in tweets. In *Proceedings of International Workshop on Semantic Evaluation (SemEval-2018)*. Association for Computational Linguistics.

Saif M Mohammad. 2012. #emotional tweets. In *Proceedings of the First Joint Conference on Lexical and Computational Semantics-Volume 1: Proceedings of the main conference and the shared task, and Volume 2: Proceedings of the Sixth International Workshop on Semantic Evaluation*. Association for Computational Linguistics, pages 246–255.

Saif M. Mohammad and Felipe Bravo-Marquez. 2017. Emotion intensities in tweets. In *Proceedings of the sixth joint conference on lexical and computational semantics (*Sem)*. Vancouver, Canada.

Saif M Mohammad and Svetlana Kiritchenko. 2015. Using hashtags to capture fine emotion categories from tweets. *Computational Intelligence* 31(2):301–326.

Saif M Mohammad, Mohammad Salameh, and Svetlana Kiritchenko. 2016. How translation alters sentiment. *J. Artif. Intell. Res.(JAIR)* 55:95–130.

Saif M. Mohammad and Peter D. Turney. 2013. Crowdsourcing a word-emotion association lexicon 29(3):436–465.

Mahmoud Nabil, Mohamed Aly, and Amir F Atiya. 2015. Astd: Arabic sentiment tweets dataset. In *Proceedings of the 2015 Conference on Empirical Methods in Natural Language Processing*. pages 2515–2519.

Thin Nguyen. 2010. Mood patterns and affective lexicon access in weblogs. In *Proceedings of the ACL 2010 Student Research Workshop*. Association for Computational Linguistics, pages 43–48.

B. Pang and L. Lee. 2004. A sentimental education: Sentimental analysis using subjectivity summarization based on minimum cuts. In *Proceedings of the 42nd Annual Meeting of the Association for Computational Linguistics*. pages 271–278.

Razvan Pascanu, Tomas Mikolov, and Yoshua Bengio. 2013. On the difficulty of training recurrent neural networks. *ICML (3)* 28:1310–1318.

Robert Plutchik. 1985. On emotion: The chicken-and-egg problem revisited. *Motivation and Emotion* 9(2):197–200.

Robert Plutchik. 1994. *The psychology and biology of emotion.*. HarperCollins College Publishers.

Eshrag Refaee and Verena Rieser. 2014. An arabic twitter corpus for subjectivity and sentiment analysis. In *LREC*. pages 2268–2273.

Sara Rosenthal, Noura Farra, and Preslav Nakov. 2017. Semeval-2017 task 4: Sentiment analysis in twitter. In *Proceedings of the 11th International Workshop on Semantic Evaluation (SemEval-2017)*. pages 502–518.

Mohammad Salameh, Saif Mohammad, and Svetlana Kiritchenko. 2015. Sentiment after translation: A case-study on arabic social media posts. In *HLT-NAACL*. pages 767–777.

Laura Smith, Salvatore Giorgi, Rishi Solanki, Johannes C. Eichstaedt, Hansen Andrew Schwartz, Muhammad Abdul-Mageed, Anneke Buffone, and Lyle H. Ungar. 2016. Does 'well-being' translate on twitter? In *EMNLP*.

Carlo Strapparava and Rada Mihalcea. 2007. Semeval-2007 task 14: Affective text. In *Proceedings of the 4th International Workshop on Semantic Evaluations*. Association for Computational Linguistics, pages 70–74.

Svitlana Volkova and Yoram Bachrach. 2016. Inferring perceived demographics from user emotional tone and user-environment emotional contrast. In *Proceedings of the 54th Annual Meeting of the Association for Computational Linguistics, ACL*.

Xiaojun Wan. 2008. Using bilingual knowledge and ensemble techniques for unsupervised chinese sentiment analysis. In *EMNLP*. Association for Computational Linguistics, pages 553–561.

Wenbo Wang, Lu Chen, Krishnaprasad Thirunarayan, and Amit P Sheth. 2012. Harnessing twitter" big data" for automatic emotion identification. In *Privacy, Security, Risk and Trust (PASSAT), 2012 International Conference on and 2012 International Confernece on Social Computing (Social-Com)*. IEEE, pages 587–592.

J. M. Wiebe, T. Wilson, R. Bruce, M. Bell, and M. Martin. 2004. Learning subjective language. *Computational Linguistics* 30:227–308.

Jasy Liew Suet Yan and Howard R Turtle. 2016. Exploring fine-grained emotion detection in tweets. In *Proceedings of NAACL-HLT*. pages 73–80.

Yi Yang and Jacob Eisenstein. 2017. Overcoming language variation in sentiment analysis with social attention. *TACL* 5:295–307.

A Dataset of Hindi-English Code-Mixed Social Media Text for Hate Speech Detection

Aditya Bohra[*], Deepanshu Vijay[*], Vinay Singh, Syed S. Akhtar, Manish Shrivastava
International Institute of Information Technology
Hyderabad, Telangana, India
{aditya.bohra, deepanshu.vijay, vinay.singh, syed.akhtar}@research.iiit.ac.in
m.shrivastava@iiit.ac.in

Abstract

Hate speech detection in social media texts is an important Natural language Processing task, which has several crucial applications like sentiment analysis, investigating cyber bullying and examining socio-political controversies. While relevant research has been done independently on code-mixed social media texts and hate speech detection, our work is the first attempt in detecting hate speech in Hindi-English code-mixed social media text. In this paper, we analyze the problem of hate speech detection in code-mixed texts and present a Hindi-English code-mixed dataset consisting of tweets posted online on Twitter. The tweets are annotated with the language at word level and the class they belong to (Hate Speech or Normal Speech). We also propose a supervised classification system for detecting hate speech in the text using various character level, word level, and lexicon based features.

1 Introduction

With recent surge in the amount of user generated social media data, there has been a tremendous scope in automated text analysis in the domain of computational linguistics. Popularity of opinion-rich online resources like review forums and microblogging sites has encouraged users to express and convey their thoughts all across the world in real time. This often results in users posting offensive and abusive content online using hateful speech. These may be directed towards an individual or community to show their dissent. Detecting hate speech is thus important for lawmakers and social media platforms to discourage occurence of any wrongful activities. Previous research related to this task has mainly been focused on monolingual texts (Malmasi and Zampieri, 2017; Schmidt and Wiegand, 2017;

Davidson et al., 2017) due to their large-scale availability. However, in multilingual societies like India, usage of code-mixed languages (among which Hindi-English is most prominent) is quite common for conveying opinions online.

Code-Mixing (CM) is a natural phenomenon of embedding linguistic units such as phrases, words or morphemes of one language into an utterance of another (Myers-Scotton, 1993; Gysels, 1992; Duran, 1994; Muysken, 2000). Following are some instances of Hindi-English code-mixed texts also transliterated in English.

T1 : *"Mujhe apne manager se nafrat hai, I want to kill that guy."*
Translation : "I hate my manager, I want to kill that guy."

T2 : *"Aaj ka day humesha yaad rahega humein because India won the World Cup! :D"*
Translation : "We'll forever remember this day because India won the World Cup! :D "

T3 : *"Jisne bhi Nirbhaya ka rape kiya should be bloody hanged till death."*
Translation : "Whoever raped Nirbhaya, should be bloody hanged till death."

It can be observed that **T1** and **T3** contain hate speech, while **T2** is an instance of normal speech.

To the best of our knowledge, currently there are no online code-mixed resources available for detecting hate speech. We believe that our initial efforts in constructing a Hindi-English code-mixed dataset for hate speech detection will prove to be extremely valuable for linguists working in this domain.

The structure of the paper is as follows. In Section 2, we review related research in the area of

---

* These authors contributed equally to this work.

Proceedings of the Second Workshop on Computational Modeling of People's Opinions, Personality, and Emotions in Social Media, pages 36–41
New Orleans, Louisiana, June 6, 2018. ©2018 Association for Computational Linguistics

code mixing and hate speech detection. In Section 3, we describe the corpus creation and annotation scheme. In Section 4, we present our system architecture which includes the pre-processing steps and classification features. In Section 5, we present the results of experiments conducted using various character-level, word-level and lexicon features. In the last section, we conclude our paper, followed by future work and references.

2 Background and Related Work

(Bali et al., 2014) performed analysis of data from Facebook posts generated by Hindi-English bilingual users. Analysis depicted that significant amount of code-mixing was present in the posts. (Vyas et al., 2014) created a POS tag annotated Hindi-English code-mixed corpus and reported the challenges and problems in the Hindi-English code-mixed text. They also performed experiments on language identification, transliteration, normalization and POS tagging of the dataset. (Sharma et al., 2016) addressed the problem of shallow parsing of Hindi-English code-mixed social media text and developed a system that can identify the language of the words, normalize them to their standard forms, assign their POS tag and segment them into chunks. (Barman et al., 2014) addressed the problem of language identification on Bengali-Hindi-English Facebook comments. They annotated a corpus and achieved an accuracy of 95.76% using statistical models with monolingual dictionaries. (Raghavi et al., 2015) developed a Question Classification system for Hindi-English code-mixed language using word level resources. The shared tasks have been also organized on classifying code-mixed cross-script question and on information retrieval of Hindi-English code-mixed tweets where the task was to retrieve the top k tweets from a corpus for a given query consisting of Hind-English terms where the Hindi terms are written in Roman transliterated form(Banerjee et al., 2016). (Gupta et al., 2014) addressed the problem of Mixed-Script IR (MSIR). They also proposed a solution to handle the mixed-script term matching and spelling variation where the terms across the scripts are modelled jointly in a deep-learning architecture and can be compared in a low-dimensional abstract space. They also did empirical analysis of the proposed method along with the evaluation results in an ad-hoc retrieval setting of mixedscript IR where

the proposed method achieves significantly better results (12% increase in MRR and 29% increase in MAP) compared to other state-of-the-art baselines. (Joshi et al., 2016; Ghosh et al., 2017) performed Sentiment Identification in code-mixed social media text.

(Malmasi and Zampieri, 2017) examined methods to detect hate speech in social media. They presented a supervised classification system which uses character n-grams, word n-grams and word skip grams. They were able to achieve accuracy of 78% on dataset which contains English tweets annotated with three labels, namely, hate speech (HATE), offensive language but no hate speech (OFFENSIVE); and no offensive content (OK). (Del Vigna et al., 2017) addressed the problem of Hate speech detection for Italian language. They built their annotated corpus using comments retrieved from the Facebook public pages of Italian newspapers, politicians, artists, and groups. They conducted two different classification experiments: the first considering three different categories of hate (Strong Hate, Weak Hate and No Hate) and the second considering only two categories, No Hate and Hate, where the last category was obtained by merging the Strong Hate and Weak Hate classes. In the two experiments they were able to achieve the best accuracies of 64.61% and 72.95% respectively.

3 Corpus Creation and Annotation

We constructed the Hindi-English code-mixed corpus using the tweets posted online in last five years. Tweets were scrapped from Twitter using the Twitter Python API[1] which uses the advanced search option of twitter. We have mined the tweets by selecting certain hashtags and keywords from politics. public protests, riots, etc., which have a good propensity for the presence of hate speech. We retrieved 1,12,718 tweets from Twitter in json format, which consists of information such as timestamp, URL, text, user, re-tweets, replies, full name, id and likes. An extensive processing was carried out to remove all the noisy tweets. Furthermore, all those tweets which were written either in pure English or pure Hindi language were removed. As a result of manual filtering, a dataset of 4575 code-mixed tweets was created.

---

[1] https://pypi.python.org/pypi/twitterscraper/0.2.7

```
<tweet>
<id>954297321843433472<\id>
<word lang="eng">Congress</word>
<word lang="hin">ke</word>
<word lang="eng">agents</word>
<word lang="hin">ho</word>
<word lang="hin">ya</word>
<word lang="hin">maha</word>
<word lang="hin">murkh.</word>
<word lang="hin">rape</word>
<word lang="hin">rape</word>
<word lang="hin">hota</word>
<word lang="hin">hai</word>
<word lang="eng">use</word>
<word lang="hin">dalit</word>
<word lang="eng">or</word>
<word lang="hin">non</word>
<word lang="hin">dalit</word>
<word lang="eng">see</word>
<word lang="hin">Jo</word>
<word lang="hin">Kar</word>
<word lang="hin">mat</word>
<word lang="hin">dekho</word>
</tweet>
<class>
Hate Speech
</class>
```

Figure 1: Annotated Instance

3.1 Annotation

Annotation of the corpus was carried out as follows:

Language at Word Level : For each word, a tag was assigned to its source language. Three kinds of tags namely, 'eng', 'hin' and 'other' were assigned to the words by bilingual speakers. 'eng' tag was assigned to words which are present in English vocabulary, such as "School", "Death", etc. 'hin' tag was assigned to words which are present in the Hindi vocabulary such as "nafrat" (Hatred), "marna" (dying). The tag 'other' was given to symbols, emoticons, punctuations, named entities, acronyms, and URLs.

Hate Speech or Normal Speech : An instance of annotation is illustrated in Figure 1. Each tweet is enclosed within <tweet></tweet>tags. First line in every annotation consists of tweet id. Language tags are added before every token of the tweet, enclosed within <word></word>tags. Each tweet is annotated with one of the two tags (Hate Speech or Normal Speech). Hate speech is detected in 1661 tweets. Remaining 2914 code-mixed tweets in the dataset comprise of normal speech. The annotated dataset with the classification system is made available online[2] .

3.2 Inter Annotator Agreement

Annotation of the dataset to detect presence of hate speech was carried out by two human annotators having linguistic background and proficiency in both Hindi and English. A sample annotation set consisting of 50 tweets (25 hate speech and 25 non hate speech) selected randomly from all across the corpus was provided to both the annotators in order to have a reference baseline so as to differentiate between hate speech and non hate speech text. In order to validate the quality of annotation, we calculated the inter-annotator agreement (IAA) for hate speech annotation between the two annotation sets of 4575 code-mixed tweets using Cohen's Kappa coefficient. Kappa score is 0.982 which indicates that the quality of the annotation and presented schema is productive.

4 System Architecture

In this section, we present our machine learning model which is trained and tested on the code-mixed dataset described in the previous sections.

4.1 Pre-processing of the code-mixed tweets

Following are the steps which were performed in order to pre-process the data prior to feature extraction.

1. **Removal of URLs:** All the links and URLs in the tweets are stored and replaced with "URL", as these do not contribute towards any kind of sentiment in the text.

2. **Replacing User Names:** Tweets often contain mentions which are directed towards certain users. We replaced all such mentions with "USER".

3. **Replacing Emoticons :** All the emoticons used in the tweets are replaced with "Emoticon".

4. **Removal of Punctuations:** All the punctuation marks in a tweet are removed. However, before removing them we store the count of

---

[2]https://github.com/deepanshu1995/HateSpeech-Hindi-English-Code-Mixed-Social-Media-Text

each punctuation mark since we use them as one of the features in classification.

4.2 Feature Identification and Extraction :

In our work, we have used the following feature vectors to train our supervised machine learning model.

1. **Character N-Grams (C):** Character N-Grams are language independent and have proven to be very efficient for classifying text. These are also useful in the situation when text suffers from misspelling errors (Cavnar and Trenkle, 1994; Huffman, 1995; Lodhi et al., 2002). Group of characters can help in capturing semantic meaning, especially in the code-mixed language where there is an informal use of words, which vary significantly from the standard Hindi and English words. We use character n-grams as one of the features, where n vary from 1 to 3.

2. **Word N-Grams (W) :** Bag of word features have been widely used to capture emotion in a text (Purver and Battersby, 2012) and in detecting hate speech (Warner and Hirschberg, 2012). Thus we use word n-grams, where n vary from 1 to 3 as a feature to train our classification models.

3. **Punctuations (P):** Punctuation marks can also be useful for hate speech detection. Users often use exclamation marks when they want to express strong feelings. Multiple question marks in the text can denote anger and dissent. Usage of an exclamation mark in conjunction with the question mark indicates annoyed feeling. We count the occurrence of each punctuation mark in a sentence and use them as a feature.

4. **Negation Words (N) :** A list of negation words was taken from Christopher Pott's sentiment tutorial[3]. We count the number of negations in a tweet and use the count as a feature.

5. **Lexicon (L) :** Users often use a particular set of words to express hate. Previous research on various NLP tasks such as Emotion Detection has demonstrated that lexicon

Features	Accuracy
Character N-Grams	71.6
Word N-Grams	70.1
Punctuations	63.6
Lexicon	64.2
Negations	63.6
All features	**71.7**

Table 1: Accuracy of each feature using Support Vector Machines

features provide a significant gain in classification accuracy when combined with corpus-based features, if training and testing sets are drawn from the same domain (Mohammad, 2012). We identified 177 Hindi and English hate words from the dataset and took them as a feature for classification.

5 Results

We performed experiments with two different classifiers namely Support Vector Machines with radial basis function kernel and Random Forest Classifier. Since the size of feature vectors formed are very large, we applied chi-square feature selection algorithm which reduces the size of our feature vector to 1200[4]. For training our system classifier, we have used Scikit-learn (Pedregosa et al., 2011). In all the experiments, we carried out 10-fold cross validation. Table 1 and Table 2 describe the accuracy of each feature along with the accuracy when all features are used, in the case of Support vector machine and Random forest classifier respectively. Support vector machine performs better than Random forest classifier and gives a highest accuracy of 71.7% when all features are used. Character N-Grams proved to be most efficient in SVM, while Word N-Grams resulted in most accuracy in the case of Random Forest Classifier.

6 Conclusion and Future Work

In this paper, we present an annotated corpus of Hindi-English code-mixed text, consisting of tweet ids and the corresponding annotations. We also present the supervised system used for detection of Hate Speech in the code-mixed text. The

---

[3]http://sentiment.christopherpotts.net/lingstruc.html

[4]The size of feature vector was decided after empirical fine tuning

Features	Accuracy
Character N-Grams	66.8
Word N-Grams	**69.9**
Punctuations	63.2
Lexicon	63.8
Negations	63.6
All features	66.7

Table 2: Accuracy of each feature using Random Forest Classifier

corpus consists of 4575 code-mixed tweets annotated with hate speech and normal speech. The words in the tweets are also annotated with source language of the words. The features used in our classification system are character n-grams, word n-grams, punctuations, negation words and hate lexicon. Best accuracy of 71.7% is achieved when all the features are incorporated in the feature vector using SVM as the classification system.

As a part of future work, the corpus can be annotated with part-of-speech tags at word level which may yield better results. Moreover, the annotations and experiments described in this paper can also be carried out for code-mixed texts containing more than two languages from multilingual societies, in future.

References

Kalika Bali, Jatin Sharma, Monojit Choudhury, and Yogarshi Vyas. 2014. " i am borrowing ya mixing?" an analysis of english-hindi code mixing in facebook. In *Proceedings of the First Workshop on Computational Approaches to Code Switching*, pages 116–126.

Somnath Banerjee, Kunal Chakma, Sudip Kumar Naskar, Amitava Das, Paolo Rosso, Sivaji Bandyopadhyay, and Monojit Choudhury. 2016. Overview of the mixed script information retrieval (msir) at fire-2016. *Organization (ORG)*, 67:24.

Utsab Barman, Amitava Das, Joachim Wagner, and Jennifer Foster. 2014. Code mixing: A challenge for language identification in the language of social media. In *Proceedings of the first workshop on computational approaches to code switching*, pages 13–23.

William B Cavnar and John M Trenkle. 1994. N-gram-based text categorization. *Ann arbor mi*, 48113(2):161–175.

Thomas Davidson, Dana Warmsley, Michael Macy, and Ingmar Weber. 2017. Automated hate speech detection and the problem of offensive language. *arXiv preprint arXiv:1703.04009*.

Fabio Del Vigna, Andrea Cimino, Felice Dell'Orletta, Marinella Petrocchi, and Maurizio Tesconi. 2017. Hate me, hate me not: Hate speech detection on facebook. *In Proceedings of the First Italian Conference on Cybersecurity (ITASEC17), Venice, Italy*.

Luisa Duran. 1994. Toward a better understanding of code switching and interlanguage in binguality: Implications for bilingual instruction. *The Journal of Educational Issues of Language Minority Students*, 14(2):69–88.

Souvick Ghosh, Satanu Ghosh, and Dipankar Das. 2017. Sentiment identification in code-mixed social media text. *arXiv preprint arXiv:1707.01184*.

Parth Gupta, Kalika Bali, Rafael E Banchs, Monojit Choudhury, and Paolo Rosso. 2014. Query expansion for mixed-script information retrieval. In *Proceedings of the 37th international ACM SIGIR conference on Research & development in information retrieval*, pages 677–686. ACM.

Marjolein Gysels. 1992. French in urban lubumbashi swahili: Codeswitching, borrowing, or both? *Journal of Multilingual & Multicultural Development*, 13(1-2):41–55.

Stephen Huffman. 1995. Acquaintance: Language-independent document categorization by n-grams. Technical report, DEPARTMENT OF DEFENSE FORT GEORGE G MEADE MD.

Aditya Joshi, Ameya Prabhu, Manish Shrivastava, and Vasudeva Varma. 2016. Towards sub-word level compositions for sentiment analysis of hindi-english code mixed text. In *Proceedings of COLING 2016, the 26th International Conference on Computational Linguistics: Technical Papers*, pages 2482–2491.

Huma Lodhi, Craig Saunders, John Shawe-Taylor, Nello Cristianini, and Chris Watkins. 2002. Text classification using string kernels. *Journal of Machine Learning Research*, 2(Feb):419–444.

Shervin Malmasi and Marcos Zampieri. 2017. Detecting hate speech in social media. *arXiv preprint arXiv:1712.06427*.

Saif Mohammad. 2012. Portable features for classifying emotional text. In *Proceedings of the 2012 Conference of the North American Chapter of the Association for Computational Linguistics: Human Language Technologies*, pages 587–591. Association for Computational Linguistics.

Pieter Muysken. 2000. *Bilingual speech: A typology of code-mixing*, volume 11. Cambridge University Press.

Carol Myers-Scotton. 1993. Dueling languages: Grammatical structure in code-switching. *Oxford University Press*.

Fabian Pedregosa, Gaël Varoquaux, Alexandre Gramfort, Vincent Michel, Bertrand Thirion, Olivier Grisel, Mathieu Blondel, Peter Prettenhofer, Ron Weiss, Vincent Dubourg, et al. 2011. Scikit-learn: Machine learning in python. *Journal of machine learning research*, 12(Oct):2825–2830.

Matthew Purver and Stuart Battersby. 2012. Experimenting with distant supervision for emotion classification. In *Proceedings of the 13th Conference of the European Chapter of the Association for Computational Linguistics*, pages 482–491. Association for Computational Linguistics.

Khyathi Chandu Raghavi, Manoj Kumar Chinnakotla, and Manish Shrivastava. 2015. Answer ka type kya he?: Learning to classify questions in code-mixed language. In *Proceedings of the 24th International Conference on World Wide Web*, pages 853–858. ACM.

Anna Schmidt and Michael Wiegand. 2017. A survey on hate speech detection using natural language processing. In *Proceedings of the Fifth International Workshop on Natural Language Processing for Social Media*, pages 1–10.

Arnav Sharma, Sakshi Gupta, Raveesh Motlani, Piyush Bansal, Manish Srivastava, Radhika Mamidi, and Dipti M Sharma. 2016. Shallow parsing pipeline for hindi-english code-mixed social media text. *arXiv preprint arXiv:1604.03136*.

Yogarshi Vyas, Spandana Gella, Jatin Sharma, Kalika Bali, and Monojit Choudhury. 2014. Pos tagging of english-hindi code-mixed social media content. In *Proceedings of the 2014 Conference on Empirical Methods in Natural Language Processing (EMNLP)*, pages 974–979.

William Warner and Julia Hirschberg. 2012. Detecting hate speech on the world wide web. In *Proceedings of the Second Workshop on Language in Social Media*, pages 19–26. Association for Computational Linguistics.

The Social and the Neural Network:
How to Make Natural Language Processing about People again

Dirk Hovy
Bocconi University
Via Roberto Sarfatti 25
20136 Milan, MI, Italy
mail@dirkhovy.com

Abstract

Over the years, natural language processing has increasingly focused on tasks that can be solved by statistical models, but ignored the social aspects of language. These limitations are in large part due to historically available data and the limitations of the models, but have narrowed our focus and biased the tools demographically. However, with the increased availability of data sets including socio-demographic information and more expressive (neural) models, we have the opportunity to address both issues. I argue that this combination can broaden the focus of NLP to solve a whole new range of tasks, enable us to generate novel linguistic insights, and provide fairer tools for everyone.

1 Introduction

Up until the 1970s, economic theory assumed that people make economic decisions with their own best interest in mind, and based on the full available information. This was a useful assumption, which allowed researchers to model people, firms, and markets as statistical linear models of the form $y = \mathbf{w}^T\mathbf{x}$, to test existing theories and to generate new insights. The seminal work by Tversky and Kahneman (1973), however, showed that this assumption was wrong: they demonstrated experimentally that again and again, people would make economic decisions that were not in their best interest, even with the full available knowledge, but instead relied on biases and heuristics. This did not mean that the linear models were useless they were useful abstractions. It did show, however, that there was more to the subject, and that it was fundamentally about people. Incorpo-

rating people's behavior opened up economics to new insights, and even established a completely new field, behavioral economics.

Up until the 1990s, NLP was largely based on applying heuristics based on linguistic theory. However, in the 1990s, the field underwent a "statistical revolution": It turned out that statistical linear models of the form $y = \mathbf{w}^T\mathbf{x}$ were more robust, accurate, and reliable in extracting linguistic information from text than linguistic heuristics were. This was a useful insight, which enabled us to solve a number of tasks. However, as a consequence, the field focused more and more on tasks that *could* be solved with these models, and moved away from tasks that could not. While this approach enabled a number of breakthroughs, it also increasingly narrowed the focus of the field, in what could be called "streetlamp science": much like the person searching for their keys under the light of the streetlamp (rather than where they lost them), NLP has continued to search for tasks that could be solved by the statistical models we have, rather than the ones that could help us understand the underpinnings of language.

This shift to the streetlamp and away from the social aspects of language has had two practical consequences: it ignored a whole host of applications that are more difficult to model, and it biased our tools. Language is about much more than information: language is used by people to communicate with other people, to establish social order, to convince, entertain, and achieve a whole host of other communicative goals, but also to signal membership in a social group.

The latter is most obvious in teenagers, who become linguistically creative to distinguish themselves from their parents. For most other groups, the process is much less obvious and often subconscious, but all people use language to mark their membership in a variety of demographic groups:

Proceedings of the Second Workshop on Computational Modeling of People's Opinions, Personality, and Emotions in Social Media, pages 42–49
New Orleans, Louisiana, June 6, 2018. ©2018 Association for Computational Linguistics

these groups range from gender to region, social class, ethnicity, and occupation. This property of language has been used in NLP to predict those demographic labels from text in author-attribute prediction tasks (Rosenthal and McKeown, 2011; Nguyen et al., 2011; Alowibdi et al., 2013; Ciot et al., 2013; Liu and Ruths, 2013; Volkova et al., 2014, 2015; Plank and Hovy, 2015; Preoţiuc-Pietro et al., 2015a,b, inter alia).

However, demographics also affect NLP beyond their use as prediction target. Demographic bias in the training data can severely distort the performance of our tools (Jørgensen et al., 2015; Hovy and Søgaard, 2015; Zhao et al., 2017), while accounting for demographic factors can actually improve performance in a variety of tasks (Volkova et al., 2013; Hovy, 2015; Lynn et al., 2017; Yang and Eisenstein, 2017; Benton et al., 2017). In order to move forward as a field, we will have to follow two strands of research: 1) we need to identify the specific demographic factors that do have an influence on NLP models (on bias and performance), and 2) based on this knowledge, we need to develop models that account for demographics to improve performance while preventing bias.

In this position paper, I argue that the recent abundance of demographically rich data sets and complex neural architectures allows us to break out of streetlamp science and to explore those two strands of demographically-based research. This shift will enable a host of new applications that make socio-demographic aspects an integral part of language. I highlight several neural network architectures and procedures that show promise to achieve these goals, and provide some experimental results in applying them.

2 Neural models for sociolinguistic insights

2.1 Representation Learning

Word embeddings have been shown to be effective as input in a variety of NLP tasks, because they are able to capture similarities along a large number of latent dimensions in the data. If language is indeed a signal for socio-demographic factors, it makes sense to assume that these socio-demographic factors are captured as latent dimensions in continuous word representations.

Indeed, Bamman et al. (2014) have shown that neural representations can be used to capture extra-linguistic information about geographic variation, by adding US-state specific representations to general word word embeddings. The resulting vectors capture regional factors, such as the nearest neighbors for landmarks, parks, and sports teams. In the same vein, Hovy (2015) showed that if word embeddings are learned on corpora that have been explicitly based on certain demographic attributes, they capture these underlying factors to influence performance of text-classification tasks sensitive to them.

It is easy to extend this concept to a popular and widely available representation-learning tool, `paragraph2vec` (Le and Mikolov, 2014). `Paragraph2vec`, similar to `word2vec` (Mikolov et al., 2013), learns embeddings through back-propagation of the input (and output) representations in a simple prediction task. Depending on the precise architecture, we either have document labels as inputs and words as output (DBOW), or words and documents as input and words as output (DM).

Instead of separating out different sub-corpora or including modifiers to the general word embeddings, though, we can exploit the unsupervised learning setup of the model, by using socio-demographic attributes (if known) as document labels (rather than unique document identifiers). Crucially, we can provide as many labels as we want for each document (see Table 1 for examples of this).

Through the training process, latent characteristics of the document labels are reflected in the learned word embeddings, while the embeddings of the demographic labels reflect the words most closely associated with them.

TEXT	LABELS
I had a lovely experience with them	F, 60, ID00014
...	
Compared lots of prices and ended up with them. Good value for money	ID16457
...	
Exactly the product I wanted. Good price and speedy delivery.	M, ID243534

Table 1: Example reviews with different amounts of available labels

As a result, we have representations of the word, document, and population-level. The unique document identifiers allow us to represent each training instance as a vector. The socio-demographic labels, on the other hand, are not unique, but shared among potentially many instances.

In the `gensim` implementation of `paragraph2vec`, both word and document-label embeddings are projected into the same high-dimensional space. We can compare them using cosine-similarity and nearest neighbors.

This allows us to qualitatively examine four comparisons:

1. words to words: similar to `word2vec`, this allows us to find words with similar meanings, i.e., words that occur in a similar context. In addition, these words representations are conditioned on the socio-demographic factors, though.

2. words to document labels and

3. document labels to words: this allows us to find the n words best describing a document label, or the n document labels most closely associated to a word

4. document labels to document labels: this allows us to find similarities between socio-demographic factors.

In addition, we can use clustering algorithms on the word and document representations to identify

1. topic-like structures (when clustering on the word representations)

2. extra-linguistic correlations (when clustering on the document representations)

I will illustrate the four different comparisons in a study on the data from Hovy et al. (2015)[1] below, as well as the two clustering solutions. I use English reviews labeled with the age, gender, and location of the author. Note that in the setup described here, we do *not* need to have all the information for all instances! We can use evidence from partial labeling to exploit a larger sample.

Note that the methodology described here is by no means limited to socio-demographic factors, but can be applied to other variables of interest.

The advantage of this method is that it requires no new model, can be used on a wide variety of input sources and problems, and yields interpretable results. We provide an implementation of the entire pipeline suit (representation learning, clustering) as a Python implementation on github: `https://github.com/dirkhovy/PEOPLES`.

2.2 Experimental Results

I preprocess the data to remove stop words and function words, replace numbers with 0s, lowercase all words and lemmatize them. I also concatenate collocations with an underscore to form a single item. This reduces the amount of noise in the data. As labels, I use the seven age decades, as well as the two genders present in the data. Overall, this results in slightly over 2M instances. See Table 1 for examples.

I run the model for 100 iterations, following the settings described in (Lau and Baldwin, 2016), with the embedding dimensions to 300, window size to 15, minimum frequency to 10, negative samples to 5, downsampling to 0.00001.

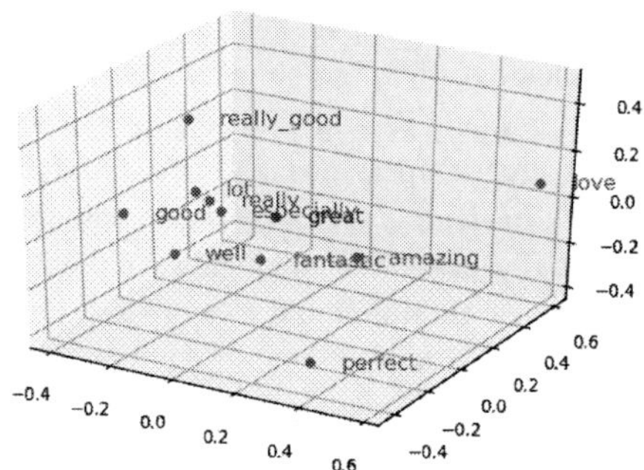

Figure 1: 10 nearest neighbors of *great* in 3-dimensional space.

Comparing words to each other The effect of the modeling process is that semantically similar words get closer in embedding space. The 10 nearest neighbors when querying for the word *great* are *well, fantastic, amazing, really_good, good, really, lot, perfect, especially*, and *love* (see Figure 1 for a graphical depiction). This is not new or surprising, but I will show further results building on this in subsequent sections.

Comparing words to labels We can use each demographic label vector and find the closest words around them. This gives us descriptors of the labels.

10: yesstyle, cd_key, game, cjs_cd_keys, cjs
20: ever, never, today, nothing, anything
30: nothing, actually, complain, today, even
40: sort, company, nothing, fault, -PRON-
50: sort, advise, fault, realise, problem
60: telephone, problem, firm, certainly, sort
70: could_find, certainly, good, problem, certainly_use
F: brilliant, lovely, fab, really_pleased, delighted
M: fault, sort, round, good, first_class

We can also use the well-known vector arithmetics that allow us to subtract and add vectors from each other. Using the example word from the previous paragraph, *great*, but adding and subtracting demographic label representations in the calculation, we can compute

$$great - MALE + FEMALE$$

and

$$great - FEMALE + MALE$$

to see which words women and men, respectively, use with or for *great*.

The first calculation give us *fab*, *fabulous*, *lovely*, *love*, *wonderful*, *really_pleased*, *fantastic*, *brilliant*, *amazing*, and *thrill* for women and *guy*, *decent*, *good*, *top_notch*, *couple*, *new*, *well*, *gear*, *get_good*, and *awesome* for men.

Such knowledge is interesting with respect to sociodemographic studies, but can have practical applications: Reddy and Knight (2016) have shown how gender can be obfuscated online by replacing particularly "male" or "female" words with a neutral or even opposite counterpart. The approach shown here based on vector arithmetics is a possible simple alternative.

Comparing labels to labels Comparing labels to each other is again very similar to the situation we have seen above for words. In the present study, this comparison is less interesting (though we can for example see which age groups are more or less similar to each other, see Figure 2).

However, we will exploit this attribute in the next section (2.3), were we explicitly compare labels to each other.

Clustering Clustering the word representations with k-means gives us a number of centroids in the embedding space, which we

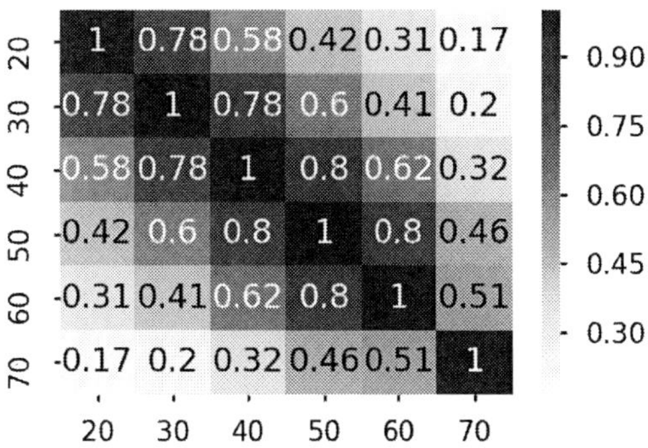

Figure 2: Cosine similarity of vector representations of age groups.

can again characterize by their closest words. For 10 clusters, we see: TROPHIES: trophiesplusmedal, trophy, medal, trophy_store, good_product_good_price_excellent_delivery_time
CUSTOMER SERVICE: confirm_-PRON-_account, wojtek, activate, first_time_order_part_geek, frustrated
MOBILE PHONES: mazuma, send_-PRON-_phone, send_phone, great_service_would_use_recommend_friend, mazuma_mobile
TASTE: taste, flavour, delicious, protein, tasty
CARS: mechanic, bmw, partsgeek, -PRON-_vehicle, -PRON-_car
GLASSES: pair_glass, optician, -PRON-_glass, -PRON-_prescription, glass
SHIPPING: excellent_service_order_arrive_day, first_class_service_would_recommend_-PRON-_friend, guitar, good_service_fast_delivery_excellent_product, reliable_service_prompt
SERVICE: excellent_service_prompt_delivery_good_price, refuse, tell, apparently, akinika
MISC: srv, hendrix, marvin, bankcard, irrational
TRAVEL: hotel, airport, flight, -PRON-_flight, -PRON-_trip

2.3 Including external knowledge

The last section showed how the learned representations are useful for a variety of qualitative analysis. However, their utility can be improved by leveraging existing outside-information that we did not include as document labels in the training process of the model, either because it was un-

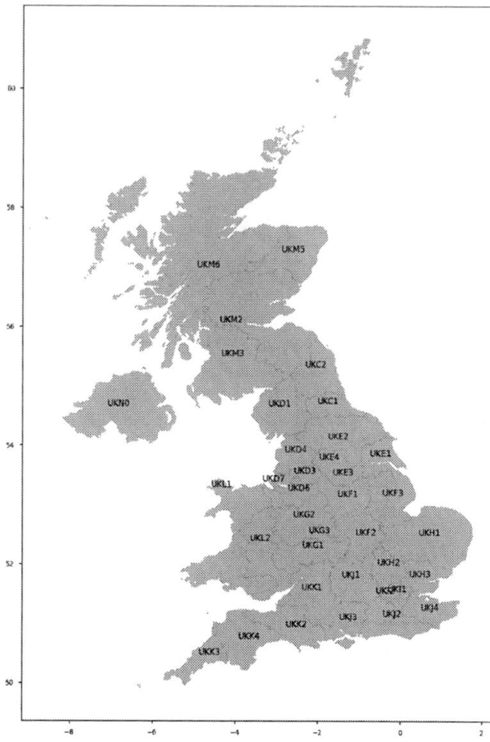

Figure 3: NUTS regions for the UK.

available, could not be incorporated (for example continuous values), or because it serves a different, tasks-specific purpose (whereas the embeddings are general-purpose). Examples of this include knowledge about word or document-label similarities based on some external source.

I provide an intuitive example of these techniques in a setup where we investigate the geographic distribution of terms, and their ability to define larger dialect regions. The input to our model are the geo-tagged tweets and Twitter profile texts (short self-descriptions) from 118K users in the UK, labeled with the statistical geographic region (NUTS2, similar in size to a county) they originated from (see Figure 3). I use the same preprocessing and modeling procedure as before, but in this case only use the regions as document labels.

Due to the nature of online conversations, the most indicative words for each region are typically cities and places in that region (see examples below).[2] An interesting exception to this rule are the

regions in Scotland: here, we see several gaelic words among the top-3 (*wee, aye, nae*).

UKC1: durham, mam, middlesbrough
UKC2: newcastle, sunderland, nufc
UKD1: cumbria, carlisle, workington
UKD3: manchester, mufc, mcfc
UKD4: blackpool, preston, lancashire
UKD6: cheshire, warrington, chester
UKD7: liverpool, everton, lfc
UKE1: hull, hcafc, notohulltigers
UKE2: york, scarborough, harrogate
UKE3: sheffield, reyt, swfc
UKE4: leeds, leed, bradford
UKF1: nottingham, derby, nffc
UKF2: leicester, lcfc, northampton
UKF3: lincoln, lincolnshire, superbull
UKG1: worcester, nuneaton, hereford
UKG2: stoke, coverdrives, nymets
UKG3: birmingham, west_midlands, coventry
UKH1: norwich, suffolk, ipswich
UKH2: hertfordshire, watford, albans
UKH3: essex, colchester, southend
UKI1: london, w/, pic
UKI2: london, loool, lool
UKJ1: oxford, need, find
UKJ2: brighton, sussex, surrey
UKJ3: southampton, portsmouth, hampshire
UKJ4: kent, canterbury, maidstone
UKK1: bristol, bath, cheltenham
UKK2: bournemouth, somerset, dorset
UKK3: cornwall, cornish, truro
UKK4: plymouth, exeter, devon
UKL1: swansea, welsh, wales
UKL2: cardiff, wales, welsh
UKM2: edinburgh, wee, aye
UKM3: glasgow, wee, celtic
UKM5: aberdeen, nae, imorn
UKM6: inverness, caley, rockness
UKN0: belfast, ulster, irish

Clustering with structure We can cluster the document labels with agglomerative clustering. This clustering algorithm starts with each region vector in its own cluster, and recursively merges pairs until we have reached the required number of clusters. The pairs to merge are chosen as to minimize the increase in linkage distance. While a variety of distance measures exist, the most commonly used (and empirically most useful) is Ward

---

[2] Eisenstein et al. (2010) have therefore approached dialects as regionally distributed topics, and Salehi et al. (2017) showed that using such regional terms makes individuals more likely to be correctly geo-located.

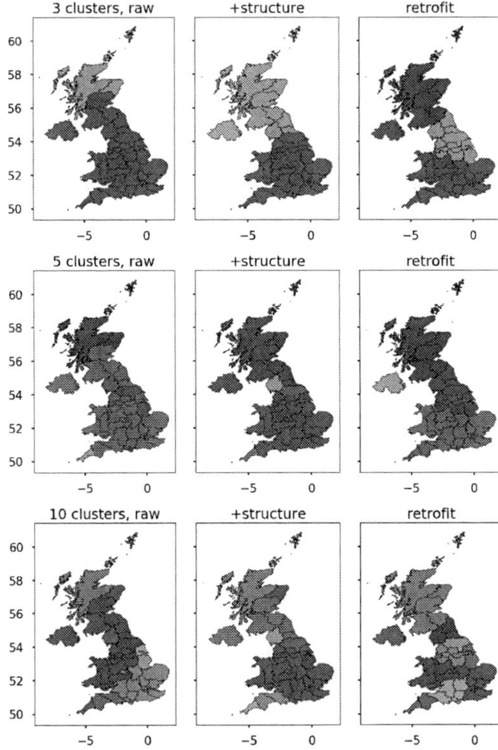

Figure 4: Effect of structure and retrofitting on clustering region embeddings.

linkage, which minimizes the new cluster's variance.

However, while the resulting solutions are stable across runs (as opposed to k-means, which is stochastic), they favor creating small new clusters, before breaking up larger groups. The effect can be seen in the leftmost column of Figure 4: one large area dominates, with some smaller regions scattered about. For 5 and 10 clusters, we also see discontinuities.

The algorithm can be enhanced with structure, by providing a connectivity matrix for the data points (i.e., either a floating point similarity or a binary adjacency), which is used to select cluster pairs during the merging process. This structure allows us to infuse the representations with additional knowledge.

Using a binary adjacency matrix over neighboring regions adds additional geographic information to the clustering process, which before was only based on linguistic similarity. We see larger dialect areas emerge, and no more discontinuous dialect areas (center column in Figure 4).

Note that we are not restricted to binary adjacency: if we were comparing points rather than regions (say, individual cities), we could instead use a similarity matrix with the inverse distance between cities (closer cities are therefore merged before more distant cities). This structure lets us express continuous values, which are impossible to include in the learning setup of `doc2vec`.

Retrofitting   Faruqui et al. (2015) introduced the concept of retrofitting vectors to external dictionaries. This allows us to adjust the positions of the vectors according to categorical outside information.

Here, we convert the adjacency matrix used before into an external dictionary that lists for each region its directly neighboring regions. Retrofitting the region representations under this dictionary forces the representations of adjacent regions to become more similar in vector space. Retrofitting therefore allows us to bring external, geographic knowledge to bear that could not be encoded in the representation learning process.

Clustering the retrofit region embeddings (rightmost column in Figure 4) results in continuous, large dialect areas.[3]

Similarly, we could derive a dictionary that lists for each word all other words observed in the same regions. This second dictionary could be used to adjust the word embeddings along the same lines as the region representations.

3   Debiasing and other applications

The previous sections have outlined how representation learning allows us to encode socio-demographic attributes in word and document representations. I have shown a number of qualitative studies that allow us to explore the effect of demographics on language. This is useful in discovering demographic traits,

However, it has been shown that knowledge of socio-demographic variables can improve a variety of NLP classification tasks, either by using them as input features (Volkova et al., 2013), or by conditioning embeddings on various demographic factors (Hovy, 2015). This theme was extended on by (Lynn et al., 2017), who show that user-demographics can be incorporated in a variety of ways, including from predicted labels. Benton

---

[3]Using structure when clustering these retrofit vectors has no effect, since the information is already encoded in the vectors, so the adjacency matrix adds no additional information.

et al. (2017) show how multitask-learning allows us to include demographic information in prediction tasks by making one of the auxiliary tasks a user-attribute prediction task. Especially in cases where the main task is strongly correlated with the prediction target, MTL can be a promising neural architecture to improve performance. Yang and Eisenstein (2017) have shown another way in which external knowledge about social structures can be incorporated into neural architectures (via attention), to improve prediction accuracy.

At the same time, demographic factors do create a demographic bias in the training data that influences NLP tools like POS taggers (Jørgensen et al., 2015; Hovy and Søgaard, 2015), leading to possible exclusion of under-represented demographic groups (Hovy and Spruit, 2016). Current methods, however, still fail to explicitly account for such biases, and can in fact even increase the demographic bias (Zhao et al., 2017). While it is possible to counter-act this bias, it requires our specific attention. Adversarial learning techniques could present a way to address this problem directly in a neural architecture, similarly to its use in domain-adaptation. This is an area that deserves special attention, if we want to use NLP for social good, and counteract the prevailing problem of biased machine learning.

4   Conclusion

In this position paper, I have argued that language is fundamentally about people, but that we have de-emphasized this aspect in NLP. However, with the increased availability of demographically-rich data sets and neural network methods, I argue that we can re-incorporate socio-demographic factors into our models. This will both improve performance, reduce bias, and open up new applications, especially in dialogue, chat, and interactive systems. I show the basic usefulness of representation learning for qualitative socio-demographic studies, and demonstrate several ways that allow us to include further outside knowledge into the representations. In the future, we need to better understand the exact influence of various demographic factors on our models, and develop ways to deal with them. Adversarial learning, multitask learning, attention, and representation learning currently look like promising instruments to achieve these goals.

References

Jalal S Alowibdi, Ugo A Buy, and Philip Yu. 2013. Empirical evaluation of profile characteristics for gender classification on twitter. In *Machine Learning and Applications (ICMLA), 2013 12th International Conference on*. IEEE, volume 1, pages 365–369.

David Bamman, Chris Dyer, and Noah A Smith. 2014. Distributed representations of geographically situated language. In *Proceedings of the 52nd Annual Meeting of the Association for Computational Linguistics (Volume 2: Short Papers)*. volume 2, pages 828–834.

Adrian Benton, Margaret Mitchell, and Dirk Hovy. 2017. Multitask learning for mental health conditions with limited social media data. In *Proceedings of the 15th Conference of the European Chapter of the Association for Computational Linguistics: Volume 1, Long Papers*. volume 1, pages 152–162.

Morgane Ciot, Morgan Sonderegger, and Derek Ruths. 2013. Gender Inference of Twitter Users in Non-English Contexts. In *Proceedings of the 2013 Conference on Empirical Methods in Natural Language Processing, Seattle, Wash.* pages 18–21.

Jacob Eisenstein, Brendan O'Connor, Noah A Smith, and Eric P Xing. 2010. A latent variable model for geographic lexical variation. In *Proceedings of the 2010 Conference on Empirical Methods in Natural Language Processing*. Association for Computational Linguistics, pages 1277–1287.

Manaal Faruqui, Jesse Dodge, Sujay Kumar Jauhar, Chris Dyer, Eduard Hovy, and Noah A Smith. 2015. Retrofitting word vectors to semantic lexicons. In *Proceedings of the 2015 Conference of the North American Chapter of the Association for Computational Linguistics: Human Language Technologies*. pages 1606–1615.

Dirk Hovy. 2015. Demographic factors improve classification performance. In *Proceedings of the 53rd Annual Meeting of the Association for Computational Linguistics and the 7th International Joint Conference on Natural Language Processing (Volume 1: Long Papers)*. volume 1, pages 752–762.

Dirk Hovy, Anders Johannsen, and Anders Søgaard. 2015. User review-sites as a source for large-scale sociolinguistic studies. In *Proceedings of WWW*.

Dirk Hovy and Anders Søgaard. 2015. Tagging performance correlates with author age. In *Proceedings of the 53rd Annual Meeting of the Association for Computational Linguistics*.

Dirk Hovy and Shannon L Spruit. 2016. The social impact of natural language processing. In *Proceedings of the 54th Annual Meeting of the Association for Computational Linguistics*. volume 2, pages 591–598.

Anna Jørgensen, Dirk Hovy, and Anders Søgaard. 2015. Challenges of studying and processing dialects in social media. In *Workshop on Noisy User-generated Text (W-NUT)*.

Jey Han Lau and Timothy Baldwin. 2016. An empirical evaluation of doc2vec with practical insights into document embedding generation. page 78.

Quoc Le and Tomas Mikolov. 2014. Distributed representations of sentences and documents. In *Proceedings of the 31st International Conference on Machine Learning (ICML-14)*. pages 1188–1196.

Wendy Liu and Derek Ruths. 2013. What's in a name? using first names as features for gender inference in twitter. In *Analyzing Microtext: 2013 AAAI Spring Symposium*.

Veronica Lynn, Youngseo Son, Vivek Kulkarni, Niranjan Balasubramanian, and H Andrew Schwartz. 2017. Human centered nlp with user-factor adaptation. In *Proceedings of the 2017 Conference on Empirical Methods in Natural Language Processing*. pages 1146–1155.

Tomas Mikolov, Ilya Sutskever, Kai Chen, Greg S Corrado, and Jeff Dean. 2013. Distributed representations of words and phrases and their compositionality. In *Advances in neural information processing systems*. pages 3111–3119.

Dong Nguyen, Noah A Smith, and Carolyn P Rosé. 2011. Author age prediction from text using linear regression. In *Proceedings of the 5th ACL-HLT Workshop on Language Technology for Cultural Heritage, Social Sciences, and Humanities*. Association for Computational Linguistics, pages 115–123.

Barbara Plank and Dirk Hovy. 2015. Personality traits on twitterorhow to get 1,500 personality tests in a week. In *Proceedings of the 6th Workshop on Computational Approaches to Subjectivity, Sentiment and Social Media Analysis*. pages 92–98.

Daniel Preoţiuc-Pietro, Vasileios Lampos, and Nikolaos Aletras. 2015a. An analysis of the user occupational class through twitter content. In *ACL*.

Daniel Preoţiuc-Pietro, Svitlana Volkova, Vasileios Lampos, Yoram Bachrach, and Nikolaos Aletras. 2015b. Studying user income through language, behaviour and affect in social media. *PloS one* 10(9):e0138717.

Sravana Reddy and Kevin Knight. 2016. Obfuscating gender in social media writing. In *Proceedings of the First Workshop on NLP and Computational Social Science*. pages 17–26.

Sara Rosenthal and Kathleen McKeown. 2011. Age prediction in blogs: A study of style, content, and online behavior in pre-and post-social media generations. In *Proceedings of the 49th Annual Meeting of the Association for Computational Linguistics: Human Language Technologies-Volume 1*. Association for Computational Linguistics, pages 763–772.

Bahar Salehi, Dirk Hovy, Eduard Hovy, and Anders Søgaard. 2017. Huntsville, hospitals, and hockey teams: Names can reveal your location. In *Proceedings of the 3rd Workshop on Noisy User-generated Text*. pages 116–121.

Amos Tversky and Daniel Kahneman. 1973. Availability: A heuristic for judging frequency and probability. *Cognitive psychology* 5(2):207–232.

Svitlana Volkova, Yoram Bachrach, Michael Armstrong, and Vijay Sharma. 2015. Inferring latent user properties from texts published in social media (demo). In *Proceedings of the Twenty-Ninth Conference on Artificial Intelligence (AAAI)*. Austin, TX.

Svitlana Volkova, Glen Coppersmith, and Benjamin Van Durme. 2014. Inferring user political preferences from streaming communications. In *Proceedings of the 52nd annual meeting of the ACL*. pages 186–196.

Svitlana Volkova, Theresa Wilson, and David Yarowsky. 2013. Exploring demographic language variations to improve multilingual sentiment analysis in social media. In *Proceedings of EMNLP*. pages 1815–1827.

Yi Yang and Jacob Eisenstein. 2017. Overcoming language variation in sentiment analysis with social attention. *Transactions of the Association for Computational Linguistics* 8:295–307.

Jieyu Zhao, Tianlu Wang, Mark Yatskar, Vicente Ordonez, and Kai-Wei Chang. 2017. Men also like shopping: Reducing gender bias amplification using corpus-level constraints. In *Proceedings of the 2017 Conference on Empirical Methods in Natural Language Processing*. pages 2979–2989.

Observational Comparison of Geo-tagged and Randomly-drawn Tweets

Tom Lippincott and **Annabelle Carrell**
Johns Hopkins University
tom@cs.jhu.edu, belle.carrell@gmail.com

Abstract

Twitter is a ubiquitous source of micro-blog social media data, providing the academic, industrial, and public sectors real-time access to actionable information. A particularly attractive property of some tweets is *geo-tagging*, where a user account has opted-in to attaching their current location to each message. Unfortunately (from a researcher's perspective) only a fraction of Twitter accounts agree to this, and these accounts are likely to have systematic diffences with the general population. This work is an exploratory study of these differences across the full range of Twitter content, and complements previous studies that focus on the English-language subset. Additionally, we compare methods for querying users by self-identified properties, finding that the constrained semantics of the "description" field provides cleaner, higher-volume results than more complex regular expressions.

1 Motivation

Twitter users can opt-in to include their current geographic location with their tweets. This fine-grained information has been used for a number of down-stream tasks, including bot and spam account detection ((Guo and Chen, 2014)), demographic analysis ((Malik et al., 2015), (Pavalanathan and Eisenstein, 2015)), and enhancing situational awareness for disaster or public health crises ((Amirkhanyan and Meinel, 2016)).

As many of these studies note, there are a number of reasons to be suspicious of geo-tagged tweets as a direct source of realistic communications between people. Popular media has raised public awareness of the dangers in sharing one's location, while for a non-human user (e.g. a business, pseudonymous personality, government entity) this may be exactly the information intended for dissemination. More specific factors like country, culture, and technology further complicate the relationship between geo-tagged accounts and the general user base.(Sunghwan Mac Kim and Paris, 2016; Karbasian et al., 2018)

2 Previous studies

A number of prior work has investigated how Twitter users, and subsets thereof, relate to more general populations. (Malik et al., 2015) collate two months of geo-tagged tweets originating in the United States with county-level demographic data, and determine that geo-tagged users differ from the population in familiar ways (higher proportions of urban, younger, higher-income users) and a few less-intuitive ways (higher proportions of Hispanic/Latino and Black users). (Sloan et al., 2015), (Sloan, 2017) combined UK government and targeted surveys, human validation, and information from user descriptions to compare Twitter and general population distributions over age and occupation, reporting significant differences between both the data sets and the quality of classifiers. (Pavalanathan and Eisenstein, 2015) compared aggregate properties of tweets whose location was determined from geo-tagging with those determined from the free-form user "location" field. They focused on the 10 large urban centers in the US, and found significant variation in age and gender demographics. They note that such differences, which are correlated with linguistic properties and classification difficulty for automatic geo-tagging, and the higher activity of geo-tagged users, can produce inflated accuracies as an evaluation set. These studies focused on English-language data, and regions in either the United States or United Kingdom: this study expands attention to previously-unstudied languages and geographies.

Proceedings of the Second Workshop on Computational Modeling of People's Opinions, Personality, and Emotions in Social Media, pages 50–55
New Orleans, Louisiana, June 6, 2018. ©2018 Association for Computational Linguistics

3 Methods

We used Twitter's streaming API to collect a *geo-tagged* (GT) data set of all geo-tagged content from the final week of November 2017, and a *non-geo-tagged* (NGT) data set of the 1% uniform random sample from the same time period, *minus* geo-tagged content. We then indexed the tweet and user JSON objects in ElasticSearch(Gormley and Tong, 2015) to facilitate comparisons between the two data sets. After examining several high-level properties, we chose *language*, *hash tag*, *user mention* and *time zone* as the most well-populated categorical fields to focus on.[1]

Following the work of (Beller et al., 2014) we extracted user self-identification in tweets based on the case-insensitive regular expression "I('m|am) an? (\S+)", limiting our results to the same 33 roles considered in that study. We also target the same set of roles by simply querying for users whose "description" field contains the role. The authors examined 20 randomly-chosen hits for each combination of role and methodology to determine precision, shown in Figure 1. We consider pattern matches on "retweets" to be false positives. Interestingly, despite its relative simplicity, the description queries are almost universally more precise, while also pulling back orders of magnitude more results. We therefore use it as our source for this demographic information, and perform the same comparisons for role-distributions as for other categorical fields. Note that our focus on precision is partly due to our focus on building high-quality training data sets, and partly due to the difficulty of measuring recall, particularly for low-frequency roles. We leave this for future work.

To compare distributions over discrete outcomes (e.g. GT versus NGT language use, role occurrence, etc) we calculate the Jensen-Shannon divergence (JSD)(Grosse et al., 2002), a symmetric variant of the Kullbeck-Liebler divergence.

Finally, we compared the same discrete features conditioned on *language*, with the hypothesis that possible causes like spam and commercial content may be particularly focused on particular communities for which language is a reasonable proxy. To explore whether different axes of GT-NGT varia-

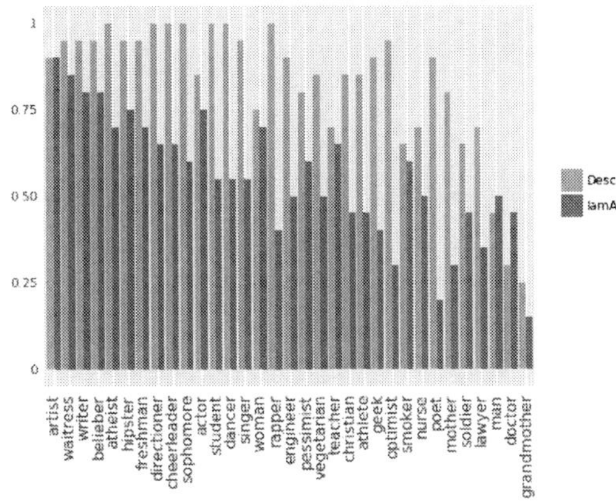

Figure 1: Precision of roles extracted via the "IamA" pattern versus the "description" field

tion (e.g. hashtags, roles) behave across different language communities, we calculate the Spearman rank correlation coefficient(Hollander et al., 2013) over the JSD values.

4 Results

4.1 Macro-level comparisons

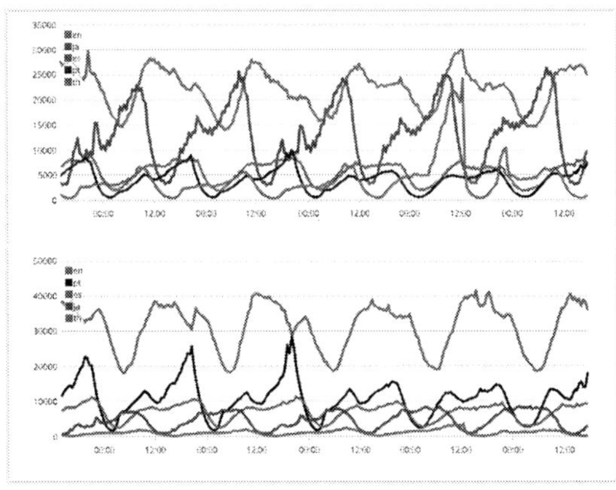

Figure 2: Comparison of GT and NGT tweet volume for several languages over one week

Figure 2 compares GT and NGT tweet volume over time in several high-frequency languages. The expected diurnal pattern from Twitter's overall language distribution is accentuated by the GT skew towards English and Portuguese, with large populations in the Americas. The sharp spike in NGT for Thai is due to a high-profile contestant in the Miss Universe competition.

The number of tweets collected in the GT and NGT data sets is of similar scale (28.5m and 23m,

---

[1] Twitter's terms of service prevent distribution of the underlying data, but we make the fine-grained counts available as pickled query results from ElasticSearch at `www.cs.jhu.edu/~tom/naacl18_PEOPLE_ES_query.pkl.gz`

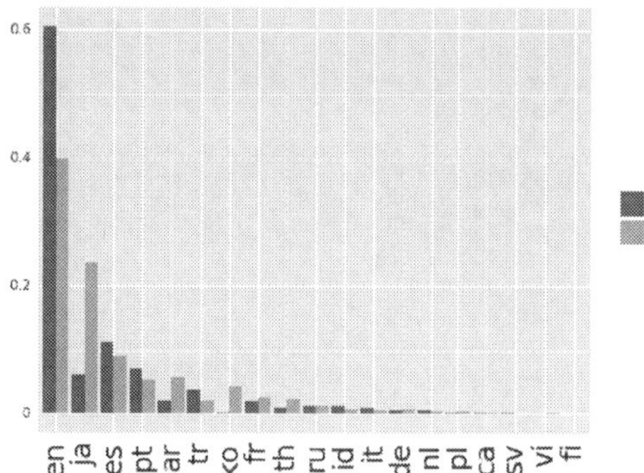

Figure 3: User languages

respectively) but GT users tweet at over triple the rate (8.4 and 2.5 average per user, respectively).[2] Additionally, GT accounts tend to be about twice the age of NGT accounts (Dec. 2012 and Feb. 2015 average creation dates, respectively), and 1% of GT users are verified, compared to NGT at 0.5%.[3] Table 1 shows aggregate information related to how users in each data set participate in Twitter's community structure on average.

Data	Friends	Followers	Favorites
GT	670	2096	4912
NGT	601	1569	4408

Table 1: Average counts of user behavior

Note that, in all of these dimensions, the GT users appear to be more active and engaged with Twitter's structure. How this behavior is attributable to self-selectiveness of individuals, the nature of institutional and spam accounts, or other causes is an open question.

Figure 3 compares user distributions over languages. Among the most common languages, Japanese, Arabic, Thai, and particularly Korean-language accounts have low proportions of geo-tagging, while Spanish, Portuguese, and particularly English and Turkish have high proportions.

The time zone comparison reflects similar trends, and also allows zeroing in on some specific locales, like Irkutsk, Baghdad, and Paris. It

would be useful to determine the various ways in which the *time zone* field can be set, perhaps in tandem with source information (device, app), to better understand this data.

4.2 Hash tags and user mentions

Figures 4 and 5 compare counts of the most-frequent hash tags and user mentions, respectively. Hash tags are dominated by discussion of the Miss Universe competition, particularly from Thailand. Discounting such one-off events, the majority of tags are English-language and related to potential employment, with general values like *job*, *CareerArc*, *hiring*, and industries like *Hospitality*, *HealthCare*, *CustomerService*. These are almost universally geo-tagged, supporting the hypothesis that institutional accounts are a likely source for much of the geo-tagged content. Not visible in the figure, tags relating to various crypto-currencies tend to *not* be geo-tagged, perhaps reflecting cultural and technological aspects of that demographic.

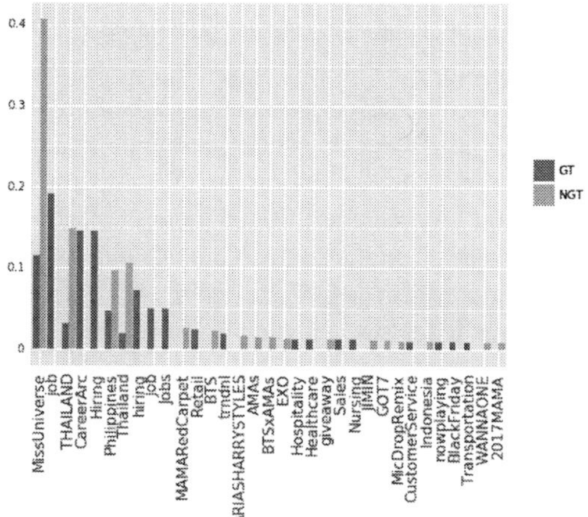

Figure 4: Comparison of most-frequently-used hashtags

Geo-tagged users most frequently mention accounts that are institutional (publicly-traded companies, news organizations, sports franchises) with the notable outliers of accounts associated with Donald Trump, while NGT users are more likely to mention pop stars.[4] Most institutional accounts are only mentioned by GT users, likely self-referentially (e.g. *StarbucksTR*, *NissanUSA*)

---

[2] We thank a reviewer for pointing out a methodological problem with the original comparison: however, we performed the same comparison of between the full account histories of GT and NGT users from a large window in the 1% sample, and found the same proportion.

[3] Twitter recognizes accounts that are "maintained by users in music, acting, fashion, government, politics, religion, journalism, media, sports, business, and other key interest areas"

[4] This is likely biased by services that transfer messages from other social media service in e.g. Asia, which appear to not include geotagging

and more for broadcasting information than active engagement. *FoxNews* is an outlier in this respect, as NGT users often address it directly.

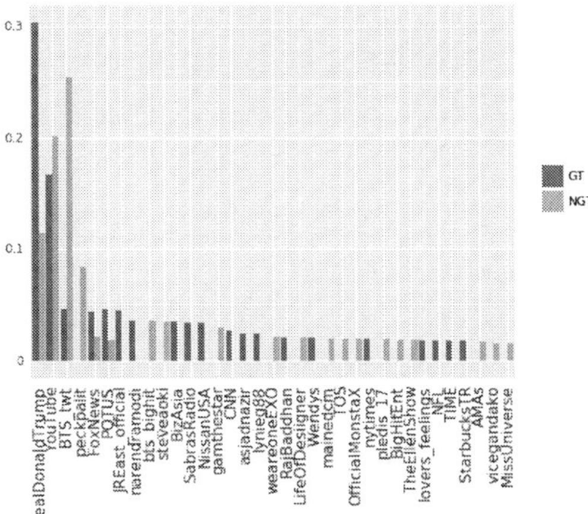

Figure 5: Comparison of most-frequently-mentioned user accounts

4.3 Self-identification

Figure 6 compares relative frequency of each role in the GT and NGT data sets, which have a high Spearman correlation of 0.944. Roles focusing on religion (*Christian*, *atheist*) and musical fandom (*Belieber*, *Directioner*) have a strong preference against geo-tagging, while roles involving performance (*singer*, *actor*, *athlete*, *cheerleader*) seem more inclined to publicize location.

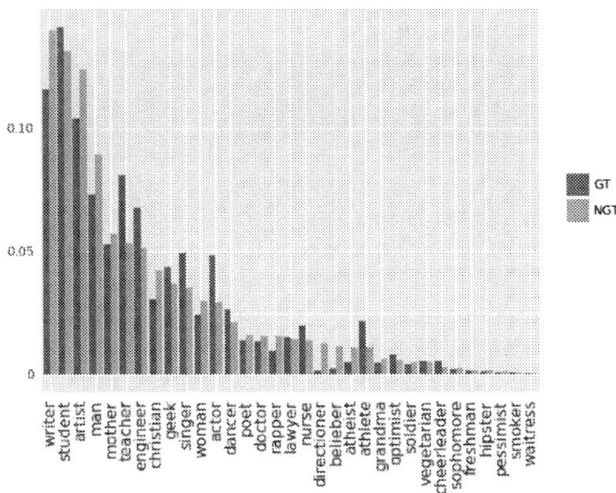

Figure 6: Comparison of role frequencies between the data sets, extracted from user descriptions

4.4 Variation by language

Figure 7 plots JSD divergence between GT and NGT distributions over several discrete spaces.

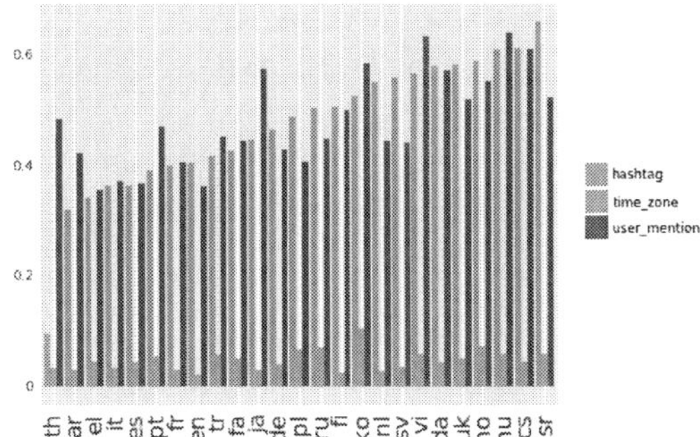

Figure 7: Jensen-Shannon Divergence calculated between GT and NGT hashtag, user mention, and time zone distributions, per language

The Spearman correlations between the variations are shown in Table 2. The values all indicate a positive association, but at a much lower level than the English role distributions. User mention and hash tag variations are more correlated with each other than either with time zone, which may be due to their intentional use compared to the passive setting of time zone by user devices (again, a better understanding of how time zones are set would help with interpreting this). [5] An interesting question for future work is whether the variations correlate with factors outside the scope of Twitter, such as government-driven propaganda, internet infrastructure, or cultural norms.

	hashtag	time_zone
user_mention	0.733	0.608
hashtag		0.638

Table 2: Pairwise Spearman correlation between JSD based on different distributions

5 Conclusion

We expanded previous work on differences between geo-tagged and non-geo-tagged English-language tweets to the full set of observed languages. In pursuit of aggregate user statistics, we determined that keyword search over user descriptions provides higher precision and recall than regular expressions applied to messages. We plan to exploit this further as supervised input to discrim-

---

[5]Note that the low divergences of the time zone distributions are likely because there is a strong correlation between the aggregate distributions of languages and time zones, while specific content (a political campaign, high-profile event, etc) can be very localized, and/or draw global interest.

inative models for extracting unconstrained self-identification in future work, and experiments on extending the method beyond English. Other interesting extensions include exploring correlations between the regional and language-specific variation and known cultural and political axes, and additional indexing of structure/content to compare other modes of variation. Finally, this study did not directly examine *content* fields (tweet texts and user descriptions) beyond the special case of role-extraction to generate additional categorical fields for English. Future work could extend it to variation over simple lexical features, which are easily extracted without language-specific processing.

References

Aragats Amirkhanyan and Cristoph Meinel. 2016. Analysis of the Value of Public Geotagged Data from Twitter from the Perspective of Providing Situational Awareness. *Social Media: The Good, the Bad, and the Ugly* .

Charley Beller, Rebecca Knowles, Craig Harman, Shane Bergsma, Margaret Mitchell, and Benjamin Van Durme. 2014. I'm a Belieber: Social Roles via Self-identification and Conceptual Attributes. In *The Annual Meeting of the Association for Computational Linguistics (ACL)*. `http://www.aclweb.org/anthology/P14-2030`.

Clinton Gormley and Zachary Tong. 2015. *Elasticsearch: The Definitive Guide*. O'Reilly Media, Inc., 1st edition.

Ivo Grosse, Pedro Bernaola-Galván, Pedro Carpena, Ramón Román-Roldán, Jose Oliver, and H. Eugene Stanley. 2002. Analysis of symbolic sequences using the Jensen-Shannon divergence. *Physical Review E* 65(4).

Diansheng Guo and Chao Chen. 2014. Detecting Non-personal and Spam Users on Geo-tagged Twitter Network. *Transactions in GIS* 18(3):370–384. `https://doi.org/10.1111/tgis.12101`.

M. Hollander, D.A. Wolfe, and E. Chicken. 2013. *Nonparametric Statistical Methods*. Wiley Series in Probability and Statistics. Wiley. `https://books.google.com/books?id=-V7jAQAAQBAJ`.

Habib Karbasian, Hemant Purohit, Rajat Handa, Aqdas Malik, and Aditya Johri. 2018. Real-Time Inference of User Types to Assist with more Inclusive and Diverse Social Media Activism Campaigns. *Association for the Advancement of Artificial Intelligence* .

Momin M. Malik, Hemank Lamba, Constantine Nakos, and Jurgen Pfeffer. 2015. Population Bias in Geotagged Tweets. *Standards and Practices in Large-Scale Social Media Research: Papers from the 2015 ICWSM Workshop* .

Umashanthi Pavalanathan and Jacob Eisenstein. 2015. Confounds and Consequences in Geotagged Twitter Data. *CoRR* abs/1506.02275. `http://arxiv.org/abs/1506.02275`.

Luke Sloan. 2017. Who Tweets in the United Kingdom? Profiling the Twitter Population Using the British Social Attitudes Survey 2015. *Social Media + Society* .

Luke Sloan, Jeffrey Morgan, Pete Burnap, and Matthew Williams. 2015. Who Tweets? Deriving the Demographic Characteristics of Age, Occupation and Social Class from Twitter User Meta-Data. *PLOS ONE* 10(3):1–20. `https://doi.org/10.1371/journal.pone.0115545`.

Stephen Wan Sunghwan Mac Kim and Cecile Paris.
2016. Detecting Social Roles in Twitter. *Proceedings of The Fourth International Workshop on Natural Language Processing for Social Media* .

Johns Hopkins or johnny-hopkins:
Classifying Individuals versus Organizations on Twitter

Zach Wood-Doughty, Praateek Mahajan, Mark Dredze
Center for Language and Speech Processing
Johns Hopkins University, Baltimore, MD 21218
`zach@cs.jhu.edu, praateek@cs.jhu.edu, mdredze@cs.jhu.edu`

Abstract

Twitter accounts include a range of different types of users. While many individuals use Twitter, organizations also have Twitter accounts. Identifying opinions and trends from Twitter requires the accurate differentiation of these two groups. Previous work (McCorriston et al., 2015) presented a method for determining if an account was an individual or organization based on account profile and a collection of tweets. We present a method that relies solely on the account profile, allowing for the classification of individuals versus organizations based on a single tweet. Our method obtains accuracies comparable to methods that rely on much more information by leveraging two improvements: a character-based convolutional neural network, and an automatically-derived corpus an order of magnitude larger than the previously available dataset. We make both the dataset and the resulting tool available[1].

1 Introduction

Twitter has been a boon to researchers who study trends in opinions and behaviors at scale (Velasco et al., 2014). Numerous applications from political science (O'Connor et al., 2010), linguistics (Bamman et al., 2014), health (Paul and Dredze, 2017) and the computational social sciences (Schwartz et al., 2013) have utilized Twitter and other social media platforms as datasets.

Phone surveys and other traditional analyses in these fields often involve collecting demographic information for the individuals in a study (Kempf and Remington, 2007). This has led social media analyses to also include such demographic contextualization (Chen et al., 2015).

However, Twitter and other social media platforms generally do not provide demographic characteristics of users. As such, multiple systems have been developed to automatically infer demographic characteristics of users. Various systems have been shown to perform well at classifying gender (Ciot et al., 2013; Burger et al., 2011), ethnicity (Culotta et al., 2015; Pennacchiotti and Popescu, 2011), and geographic location (Jurgens et al., 2015; Dredze et al., 2013). These classifiers leverage user data to predict these missing demographic attributes; some methods use the tweets written by the user (Al Zamal et al., 2012), while others track who the user follows (Culotta et al., 2015; Jurgens, 2013).

These tools make a central assumption: the account for which demographic inference is performed belongs to an individual. Yet Twitter accounts do not just belong to individuals; the platform is widely used by organizations to represent their interests on the platform, and it may not make sense to infer the gender of an organization. McCorriston et al. (2015) estimated that 9.4% of users on Twitter are brands or organizations. While we address the issue of bots and other types of Twitter accounts in §2.3, we make the simplifying assumption that all accounts on Twitter are either individuals or organizations, and rely on bot detection systems to first filter other types of accounts. When using Twitter data for studies, researchers should not conflate individuals on Twitter with the organizations and brands who use the platform. An analysis of opinions on vaccinations should not treat the official @CDC account as a particularly prolific individual, and a study of grassroots political preferences should not use tweets from a major political party as representative of a specific individual's beliefs.

Despite the differences between individual and

---

[1] `http://bitbucket.org/mdredze/demographer`

Proceedings of the Second Workshop on Computational Modeling of People's Opinions, Personality, and Emotions in Social Media, pages 56–61
New Orleans, Louisiana, June 6, 2018. ©2018 Association for Computational Linguistics

organizational accounts, most Twitter analyses do not make any such distinction. This is the easiest option and may be a reasonable simplification in some analyses, but conflating the two groups may introduce biases. The only previous readily-available tool for this task is from McCorriston et al. (2015). The authors built a dataset of 19k users annotated as individuals or organizations by crowdsourced annotation. Using a classifier built on metadata features as well as a sample of tweets from the account, they achieved good accuracy at differentiating these account types and released a Python tool. Unfortunately, the solution of McCorriston et al. (2015) poses several problems. First, the tool requires 200 tweets per account to achieve the reported accuracy. Many datasets collected from Twitter have few tweets per user, and downloading sufficient additional data for each account may be expensive. Second, while their annotated corpus has high quality labels, it is relatively small. Since only the user labels are released with the annotations, others who wish to train new models on this corpus will suffer over time as accounts are deleted or made private, removing them from consideration. This can be an issue as the models become stale, as behaviors of individuals and organizations on Twitter continue to shift over time (Laroche et al., 2013; Liu et al., 2014; Zhu and Chen, 2015). A larger corpus would maintain its utility for longer, and ideally, the necessary data collection should be as close to automated as possible.

We address these two issues for the task of identifying individuals versus organizations. First, we propose a primarily-automatic way of constructing a large corpus of annotated individuals and users. Our dataset is almost an order of magnitude larger than that provided by McCorriston et al. (2015). While our data collection uses weak supervision and contains errors, we can achieve comparable accuracy to a method trained on the dataset produced with high-quality annotations by McCorriston et al. (2015). Researchers can use this corpus, or reconstruct a fresh corpus in the future following our approach. Second, we propose a method for classifying individuals versus organizations based on a character-based convolutional neural network (CNN) that examines only a single tweet from a user account, with a focus on the user profile.

This simplifies the process of dividing a dataset into individuals and organizations by obviating the need for additional data downloads. By combining our larger corpus and improved model, we obtain results that are comparable to McCorriston et al. (2015).

2 Data

Our goal was the construction of a large set of Twitter accounts annotated as individual or organization. Rather than rely on manual labeling of accounts, we seek an automated method based on weak supervision (Li et al., 2014) for the discovery and labeling of these accounts. We describe our process in this section, and evaluate the efficacy of our resulting dataset by evaluating models trained on this corpus.

2.1 Twitter Lists

Twitter users can create "lists," collections of Twitter accounts organized by topic. Examples of lists include "social-justice organizations" or "volleyball teammates." Lists are useful ways for crowdsourcing the identified and organization of Twitter accounts.

We identified Twitter lists that predominantly contained either organizations or individuals. We used a search engine to find user-generated lists which included key terms such as "businesses" or "companies" to identify lists of organization accounts. For each list that we verified as likely containing organizations, we downloaded the Twitter accounts that were members of the list and labeled them organizations. We repeated this process for individuals by searching for terms such as "friends" or "family."

Using this approach to gather about 250 lists, we collected 19k accounts labeled as individuals and 28k accounts labeled as organizations. After data collection was complete, we randomly sampled 100 organizations and 100 individuals for verification, and found 98% were labeled correctly[2].

2.2 LinkedIn

We identified individuals on Twitter through the presence of a link to a LinkedIn profile page in the users' Twitter profile. We examined the `user.url` field for links with the domain

---

[2] According to two authors' subjective assessments, with Cohen's κ=0.88.

`linkedin.com` or `lnkd.in`. We examined all tweets collected from Twitter's 1% feed in 2017, about 3 billion tweets. We then extracted the set of unique authors of these tweets, yielding a corpus of 161k users we believe to be individuals. After finishing data collection, we randomly sampled 100 of these accounts and found that all were correctly labeled.

In total, these two methods produced a list of 180k individuals and 28k organizations.

2.3 Limitations

Our work makes the simplifying assumption that all accounts are either individuals or organizations, and ignores other possible types of Twitter accounts. We assume that accounts are first processed by bot detection systems to identify them as either "human and non-human" users (Dickerson et al., 2014), where the non-human users can be subdivided into "spambots, paybots, or influence bots" (Subrahmanian et al., 2016). In this work, we treat these bot categories as orthogonal – that is, a spambot or influence bot may *impersonate* an individual or an organization, but our tool only considers this latter designation. This simplifying assumption may be reasonable given the data we consider. In the dataset constructed by McCorriston et al. (2015), human annotators were only allowed to code a random selection of Twitter users as either individuals or organizations, and yet 90.7% of the accounts had a unanimous labeling across three annotators, with an inter-annotator Cohen's κ=0.95. Twitter bots who cannot be labeled as individuals or organizations may exist, but we expect they are rare. Further research should consider the correlation between our tool's predictions and the predictions made by systems such as BotOrNot (Davis et al., 2016) or SentiBot (Dickerson et al., 2014). Future work could improve our tool by incorporating features used by these bot classifiers, though many such features cannot be computed when using only one tweet per user.

In the lists and LinkedIn data we collected, we found that these methods identified accounts that agreed with the inferred label with high probability. However, some labels may be blatantly wrong and others may be ambiguous in the eyes of human annotators. Twitter lists are generated and named by users, and may have misleading titles or contain erroneous accounts.

Similarly, some organizational accounts may link their Twitter profile to a `linkedin.com` page, which would cause us to incorrectly label their account in our dataset.

A second drawback of our training data is that it is not drawn from a representative sample of the Twitter user population. Accounts which are added into other users' lists are likely more popular than a randomly-selected account, and individuals who link their Twitter account to a LinkedIn page likely present a more professional appearance in their profile or tweets. This may bias our classifier to misjudge less popular organizational users or the accounts of individuals who do not use Twitter professionally.

We evaluate the impact of our data limitations by using this corpus as a training set for classifications on a high-quality test set. We leave the considerations of Twitter bots for future work.

3 Methods

We present three models for the task of classifying users as either organizations or individuals: a baseline method and two new methods that require only a single tweet per user.

3.1 Humanizr

McCorriston et al. (2015) proposed a method (named Humanizr) for classifying individuals and organizations based on features extracted from the profile and tweet history of Twitter users. This method requires the downloading of multiple tweets for each account for classification. The extracted features are then used by an SVM to learn a binary classifier. We used their released code to train their models on a March 2018 download of their dataset, for which we successfully retrieved 86% of the users.

3.2 N-gram Model

Knowles et al. (2016) developed a model for gender classification of Twitter users based on a linear model trained on character n-gram features from users' names. They found that their model outperformed several available baselines for gender prediction. Furthermore, since the model considered the username, it required only a single tweet from a user to make a prediction. We extend their n-gram feature selection by incorporating new name-based features which we expect to be indicative of the organization

	Balanced	Full
Majority	50.0	89.5
Humanizr	**89.6**	**94.8**
N-gram	85.2	93.8
CNN	84.5	93.4

(a) Results from training on the data released by McCorriston et al. (2015).

	Balanced	Full
Majority	50.0	89.5
Humanizr	-	-
N-gram	84.0	94.1
CNN	**85.8**	**94.6**

(b) Results from training on our collected data. Humanizr was not evaluated due to data constraints.

Figure 1: Experimental results. In both experiments, the test sets are 20% of the data released by McCorriston et al. (2015).

versus individual task, such as the occurrence of capitalization and numeric characters. We combine these name-based features with the profile-based features described below.

3.3 Convolutional Neural Network

We use a character-based CNN to learn a representation of a Twitter user's name. After some initial experiments, we used a simple stack of two convolutional layers of 256 filters of width 3. The name representation learned by the CNN is concatenated with the profile-features described below, and this combined vector is passed through two fully-connected layers to produce a distribution over the labels.

3.4 Profile-based features

Both our n-gram and CNN models incorporate features extracted from the user fields contained in the metadata of a single tweet object. Some of these features – the ratio of followers to friends, verification status, and the number of tweets – were used in previous work (McCorriston et al., 2015). We also introduce new features, such as the presence of personal pronouns (e.g. "my" vs. "our") and the use of repetitive punctuation (e.g. "!!") in users' descriptions. A complete list of our profile features is included in the released code. For all continuous features (e.g. follower to friends ratio), we normalize them to take values between -1 and 1 using a piecewise linear function constructed from their deciles.

3.5 Parameter Estimation

For both the n-gram and CNN models, we used the held-out development set for hyper-parameter tuning. For the n-gram model, we considered hinge or perceptron loss functions, and L1 or L2 regularization, using the implementations from sklearn (Pedregosa et al., 2011). For the CNN, experimentation led us to use a SGD optimizer with learning rate 0.5, a character

embedding of 256, and dropout rate of 0.2, using implementations in Tensorflow (Abadi et al., 2016). We train for up to 200 epochs, using the dev set for early stopping.

4 Evaluation

We ran two experiments, each focused on one major question. First, how well do our proposed models perform on this task, when using only a single tweet per user, compared to the Humanizr method? Second, how useful is the dataset we created for training models to discriminate between organizations and individuals?

To answer the first, we apply our two methods to the dataset collected by McCorriston et al. (2015) and compare against their method. We take data for the 17k users we could scrape and split them into train, dev, and test sets. We do this for two experimental settings: a 'balanced' setting in which we subsample individuals so that each split has an equal number of individuals and organizations, and a 'full' setting in which we use the ratio of individuals to organizations (approximately 8:1) that occurs in the scraped data. Empirically, we found that a training set ratio of 7:1 individuals to organizations improved dev performance in the class-imbalanced, 'full' experimental setting.

To answer the second question, we use the dataset we collected as training data, but use the McCorriston et al. (2015) data for dev and test sets. This examines whether the features learned from Twitter users in our noisy and cheap dataset are useful for classifying users in a high-quality and expensive dataset. In this experiment, we did not evaluate the Humanizr method due to the cost associated with downloading 200 tweets per user for 180k users. We again considered both balanced and full experimental settings.

For each experimental setting, we use 20% of the McCorriston et al. (2015) data for the dev and test sets, either class-balanced or not. To highlight the difference between the balanced and full settings, we include the proportion of the majority label as a baseline classification accuracy.

4.1 Results

Table 1 (a) shows the results for the first experiment. While the Humanizr method slightly outperforms both our n-gram and CNN models, it requires significantly more data per user. The Humanizr method's test accuracy on our splits was slightly lower than the five-fold cross validation accuracy reported in McCorriston et al. (2015). This may be because we were unable to download 14% of the users in the original dataset or because we did not retune their hyper-parameters to the tweet data from 2018.

Table 1 (b) shows the result for the second experiment, evaluating our models trained on our collected dataset. The CNN improves considerably, almost matching the performance of Humanizr. In fact, in the full setting, the difference between the two is not statistically significant[3]. This provides strong evidence that our dataset, while cheaply collected with noisy labels, is valuable for classifying organizations and individuals on a random sample of Twitter.

While the n-gram model slightly outperformed the CNN in the first experiment, the trend was reversed in the second. This may be because the smaller dataset in the first experiment was sufficient for our hand-engineered n-gram features, but not large enough for the CNN models to learn robust character-level features from data alone.

Together, these two experiments demonstrate that a method which requires just a single tweet per user can be trained on cheaply-gathered data to classify organizations on Twitter, and perform comparably to a tool trained on high-quality data with hundreds of tweets per user. Our method makes it possible to classify organizations in an analysis of billions of tweets without having to download significant additional data per user. Our method also makes possible analyses in a streaming setting in which their decisions must be made in real-time without additional data collection.

Future work should see whether our tool's predictions are correlated with the predictions of bot-detection systems, and whether our model could be used to predict bot or other non-human account types. We could also incorporate the content features from Humanizr with our name and profile features we introduce. Another avenue for future work is to consider whether we can control for any biases in our weakly-supervised dataset to produce better predictions on the ground-truth data. As it is often easier to collect a large amount of noisy data than a small amount of gold-standard data, such an approach could be widely applicable to studies of Twitter users' emotions and personalities.

We release the account-type labels and the Twitter userids for our training dataset, as well as our code for our feature extraction and experiments. We also provide a pre-trained model for classification of Twitter accounts. The code, data, and models are available as an extension to the Demographer tool at `http://bitbucket.org/mdredze/demographer`.

5 Acknowledgements

This work was supported in part by the National Institute of General Medical Sciences under grant number 5R01GM114771.

References

Martin Abadi, Ashish Agarwal, Paul Barham, Eugene Brevdo, Zhifeng Chen, Craig Citro, Greg S Corrado, Andy Davis, Jeffrey Dean, Matthieu Devin, et al. 2016. Tensorflow: Large-scale machine learning on heterogeneous distributed systems. *arXiv preprint arXiv:1603.04467*.

Faiyaz Al Zamal, Wendy Liu, and Derek Ruths. 2012. Homophily and latent attribute inference: Inferring latent attributes of twitter users from neighbors. *ICWSM*, 270.

David Bamman, Jacob Eisenstein, and Tyler Schnoebelen. 2014. Gender identity and lexical variation in social media. *Journal of Sociolinguistics*, 18(2):135–160.

John D Burger, John Henderson, George Kim, and Guido Zarrella. 2011. Discriminating gender on twitter. In *EMNLP*, pages 1301–1309. ACL.

Xin Chen, Yu Wang, Eugene Agichtein, and Fusheng Wang. 2015. A comparative study of demographic attribute inference in twitter. *ICWSM*, 15:590–593.

Morgane Ciot, Morgan Sonderegger, and Derek Ruths. 2013. Gender inference of twitter users in non-english contexts. In *EMNLP*, pages 1136–1145.

---

[3] p=0.36 when using a two-proportion t-test. For the balanced setting, Humanizr's 89.6% is significantly better than the best CNN's 85.8%, with p=0.014 using the same test.

Aron Culotta, Nirmal Ravi Kumar, and Jennifer Cutler. 2015. Predicting the demographics of twitter users from website traffic data. In *AAAI*, pages 72–78.

Clayton Allen Davis, Onur Varol, Emilio Ferrara, Alessandro Flammini, and Filippo Menczer. 2016. Botornot: A system to evaluate social bots. In *WWW*, pages 273–274. International World Wide Web Conferences Steering Committee.

John P Dickerson, Vadim Kagan, and VS Subrahmanian. 2014. Using sentiment to detect bots on twitter: Are humans more opinionated than bots? In *ASONAM*, pages 620–627. IEEE.

Mark Dredze, Michael J Paul, Shane Bergsma, and Hieu Tran. 2013. Carmen: A twitter geolocation system with applications to public health. In *AAAI Workshop on Expanding the Boundaries of Health Informatics Using AI (HIAI)*.

David Jurgens. 2013. That's what friends are for: Inferring location in online social media platforms based on social relationships. *ICWSM*, 13:273–282.

David Jurgens, Tyler Finethy, James McCorriston, Yi Tian Xu, and Derek Ruths. 2015. Geolocation prediction in twitter using social networks: A critical analysis and review of current practice. In *ICWSM*, pages 188–197.

Angela M Kempf and Patrick L Remington. 2007. New challenges for telephone survey research in the twenty-first century. *Annu. Rev. Public Health*, 28:113–126.

Rebecca Knowles, Josh Carroll, and Mark Dredze. 2016. Demographer: Extremely simple name demographics. *NLP+ CSS 2016*, page 108.

Michel Laroche, Mohammad Reza Habibi, and Marie-Odile Richard. 2013. To be or not to be in social media: How brand loyalty is affected by social media? *International Journal of Information Management*, 33(1):76 – 82.

Jiwei Li, Alan Ritter, and Eduard Hovy. 2014. Weakly supervised user profile extraction from twitter. In *ACL*, volume 1, pages 165–174.

Yabing Liu, Chloe Kliman-Silver, and Alan Mislove. 2014. The tweets they are a-changin: Evolution of twitter users and behavior. In *ICWSM*, volume 30, pages 5–314.

James McCorriston, David Jurgens, and Derek Ruths. 2015. Organizations are users too: Characterizing and detecting the presence of organizations on twitter. In *ICWSM*, pages 650–653.

Brendan O'Connor, Ramnath Balasubramanyan, Bryan R Routledge, and Noah A Smith. 2010. From tweets to polls: Linking text sentiment to public opinion time series. *ICWSM*, 11(122-129):1–2.

Michael J Paul and Mark Dredze. 2017. Social monitoring for public health. *Synthesis Lectures on Information Concepts, Retrieval, and Services*, 9(5):1–183.

Fabian Pedregosa, Gaël Varoquaux, Alexandre Gramfort, Vincent Michel, Bertrand Thirion, Olivier Grisel, Mathieu Blondel, Peter Prettenhofer, Ron Weiss, Vincent Dubourg, et al. 2011. Scikit-learn: Machine learning in python. *Journal of machine learning research*, 12(Oct):2825–2830.

Marco Pennacchiotti and Ana-Maria Popescu. 2011. A machine learning approach to twitter user classification. *Icwsm*, 11(1):281–288.

H Andrew Schwartz, Johannes C Eichstaedt, Margaret L Kern, Lukasz Dziurzynski, Stephanie M Ramones, Megha Agrawal, Achal Shah, Michal Kosinski, David Stillwell, Martin EP Seligman, and Lyle H Ungar. 2013. Personality, gender, and age in the language of social media: The open-vocabulary approach. *PloS one*, 8(9):e73791.

V. S. Subrahmanian, Amos Azaria, Skylar Durst, Vadim Kagan, Aram Galstyan, Kristina Lerman, Linhong Zhu, Emilio Ferrara, Alessandro Flammini, Filippo Menczer, Rand Waltzman, Andrew Stevens, Alexander Dekhtyar, Shuyang Gao, Tad Hogg, Farshad Kooti, Yan Liu, Onur Varol, Prashant Shiralkar, V. G. Vinod Vydiswaran, Qiaozhu Mei, and Tim Huang. 2016. The DARPA twitter bot challenge. *CoRR*, abs/1601.05140.

Edward Velasco, Tumacha Agheneza, Kerstin Denecke, Gan Kirchner, and Tim Eckmanns. 2014. Social media and internet-based data in global systems for public health surveillance: A systematic review. *The Milbank Quarterly*, 92(1):7–33.

Yu-Qian Zhu and Houn-Gee Chen. 2015. Social media and human need satisfaction: Implications for social media marketing. *Business horizons*, 58(3):335–345.

The Potential of the Computational Linguistic Analysis
of Social Media for Population Studies

Letizia Mencarini

Bocconi University, Dondena Centre for Research on Social Dynamics and Public Policy
via Roentgen 1, 20136 Milan, I.
letizia.mencarini@unibocconi.it

Abstract

The paper provides an outline of the scope
for synergy between computational linguistic analysis and population studies. It
first reviews where population studies
stand in terms of using social media data.
Demographers are entering the realm of
big data in force. But, this paper argues,
population studies have much to gain from
computational linguistic analysis, especially in terms of explaining the drivers behind population processes. The paper gives
two examples of how the method can be
applied, and concludes with a fundamental
caveat. Yes, computational linguistic analysis provides a possible key for integrating
micro theory into any demographic analysis of social media data. But results may
be of little value in as much as knowledge
about fundamental sample characteristics
are unknown.

1 The incomplete data revolution in demography

Demography is the study of population. Tradi-
tionally, demography is concerned with measuring and estimating population change by births,
deaths and migration. Demography is rooted in
quantitative methods, with data at its heart. As the
field moved through different epochs of data
availability, in demography data have always
been "big" (Billari and Zagheni, 2017). Starting
with the exercise of mapping macro-level trends
through population level parameters, based largely on census and administrative records, the field
became more theory driven as individual data became available. It is fair to say that with the ex-
plosion in available survey data, a revolution in

demographic studies took place. Rather than
simply describing demographic patterns, today
demographers are equally concerned in understanding both the drivers and the consequences of
demographic processes. In doing so, demographers have assembled an enormously rich set of
data for explaining not only population processes,
but also the motivational and behavioral drivers
behind these processes. However, data generated
by surveys may have peaked. As survey and polling agencies struggle with increasing costs and
declining survey response rates, statistic produc-
ers are increasingly looking towards big data.
Still, given their quantitative pedigree, demographers are perhaps better placed than most other
social scientists to take on the challenge of the
new big data revolution.

Demographers are, in fact, already using big
data to describe demographic processes, including
data derived from social media. But there are challenges. Big data is messy and unstructured, and this
is a considerable challenge for a scientific field
acutely concerned with representativeness and un-
biased estimation. Social media provides a promising avenue, however, as demographers are interested not only in describing population processes, but
also in the motivations that individuals have for
their behavior, which, ultimately, generates observed population processes. For demographers in
search of the determinants and consequences of
demographic behavior, the linguistic analysis of social media texts can offer a precious and rich new
source. Caution – as this paper highlights – is necessary, since its non-representativeness and partiali-
ty makes it problematic in social-science terms.

The rapid emergence of big data from social
media outpaced social scientists' capacity for using and analyzing them. That having been said,

Proceedings of the Second Workshop on Computational Modeling of People's Opinions, Personality, and Emotions in Social Media, pages 62–68
New Orleans, Louisiana, June 6, 2018. ©2018 Association for Computational Linguistics

demographers have made a start in exploiting social media data. For example, Reis and Brownstein (2010) show that the volume of Internet searches for abortion is inversely proportional to local abortion rates and directly proportional to local restrictions on abortion. Billari et al. (2013) show that Google searches for fertility-related queries, like 'pregnancy' or 'birth', can be used to predict fertility intentions and consequently fertility rates, several months ahead of them being made public through other data sources. Ojala et al. (2017) use Google Correlate to detect evidence for different socio-economic contexts related to fertility (e.g., teen fertility, fertility in high income households, etc.). Email data have been used to track migrants (Zagheni and Weber, 2012); Facebook data to monitor migrant stocks (Zagheni et al., 2017); patterns of short- and long-term migration (Zagheni et al., 2014); and family change have been derived from Twitter data (Billari et al., 2017). These applications are important, and have demonstrated that the combination of survey and internet data improve predictive power and the accuracy of the described demographic phenomena. Billari and Zagheni (2017) triumphally affirm that the Data Revolution is already here for the study of population processes. However, these studies are all ultimately about describing demographic processes. So far, progress in exploiting content analysis of texts and corpora has been limited, and existing studies have not yet tackled how social media data can explain the behavioral motivations that drive observed population processes. On this point, there is massive potential for synergy between demography and computational linguistics. Certain strands of the social sciences have started looking in this direction, as there are several examples in political science and political economy.

2 Why people's opinions matter

In order to exploit social media data to explain the determinants of population processes, one has, perforce, to delve into the behavioral theories commonly invoked in demographic studies. For population studies, there is no single theory. Instead, being an interdisciplinary science, demographers borrow from a host of theoretical concepts from across the social sciences. One example is the Second Demographic Transition theory (Van de Kaa, 1987; Lesthaeghe, 2010), which has been a point of reference in family demography in re-

cent decades. The theory stems from Inglehart's work (1971). He argued that with the onset of modernization, individuals now cared more about self-realization and less about traditional family life, which consequently fostered new demographic behaviors, such as out-of-wedlock childbearing, cohabitation replacing marriage and fertility decline. In other words, values, attitudes and opinions, play a critical role. Another example concerns the theoretical concept of gender equality and equity. As women increasingly attain the same levels of higher education as men their attitudes change. Other than having children, they also want fulfilling work careers (Esping-Andersen and Billari, 2015; Aassve et al., 2015). The sense of gender equity (Mencarini, 2014) changes as women reach men's level in terms of education, but traditional attitudes may prevail within households. If so, there is a mismatch between gender equity and actual equality, which, McDonald (2000) argues, creates a gender conflict, which eventually leads to lower fertility. Yet, another important theoretical concept originates in economics. Economic models are used to explain changes in divorce, migration drivers, and fertility and so forth. Starting with individual preferences, behavior come out through a process of decision making, where individuals' (presumed) rational evaluations are made in order to maximize their wellbeing. As one moves from survey data to a social media *corpus*, these theoretical concepts offer both challenges and opportunities. On the one hand, new methods, not always familiar to demographers, must be implemented. On the other, there is opportunity in the fact that social science theories can show us what one should be looking for in an otherwise complex and sometimes overwhelming amount of data.

3 Social media linguistic analysis as a middle ground between qualitative and quantitative analysis

One important reason behind the slow progress in the field, is, perhaps, that demographers are more confident with the analysis of numbers than with text: i.e. with quantitative rather than qualitative analysis. Or, perhaps, there is still uncertainty and suspicion about the extent to which social media data can be used to properly infer theoretical concepts for demography. Developments are being made elsewhere in the social sciences. However, the most prominent examples are based on digitized historical texts. The approach taken is similar to what is being done with social media data, in the sense that one exploits distributional semantic techniques. This is a 'usage-based' theory of meaning built upon similarities of linguistic distributions in a corpus (Lenci 2008), and it allows for the extraction of (near-) synonyms in a context-dependent way, for each document and period under consideration. As we discuss below, the key lies in defining, and coding, the concepts that are to be captured (Kenter et al., 2015, Betti and van den Berg, 2016; Fokkens et al., 2016).

The challenge lies in how theoretical concepts commonly used in demographic analysis (such as the ones mentioned earlier) can be integrated into computational linguistic analysis. Social media has created an extraordinary quantity of potential research material that would have unimaginable even just a few years ago. This material, especially those texts where individuals express opinions through conversation and other ways of communications, where they reveal subjective perceptions, expression of feelings and reasons for their actions, are of tremendous value. Those spontaneous texts are very similar in their nature to certain kinds of qualitative data collection. Texts are the central form of data in qualitative research, in the form of interview transcripts, observations, field notes and primary documents (Mills, 2017). Compared to classical qualitative text analysis, social media texts are much more disordered, but they have two important positive features: they are spontaneous and they are enormous in quantity. These are important issues. The sheer quantity of social media data effectively deals with one of the most frequent criticisms of classic qualitative studies, i.e. the small number of observations. Moreover, classical qualitative studies, do not lend themselves easily to tracking how concepts change over time.

The fact that social media texts are the product of conversations between individuals, groups, and organizations, instead of responses to questions created by researchers (who usually have only *post-hoc* intuitions about the relevant factors in making meaning) is relevant, and gives hints of how perceptions, values, etc., evolve in real time. The quantity of material can, instead, create challenges for social scientists. Often linguistic analysis looks for positive or negative expressions of sentiment. This, though, in itself is not enough.

The challenge lies in *how* text data can be investigated for research questions which require closer analysis and nuanced interpretation. But neither traditional qualitative approaches requiring the manual screening and classification of all the material, nor quantitative statistical analysis, can be applied. In this sense, social media data texts provide a middle ground between qualitative studies and more standard quantitative approaches. Some studies have recently and successfully used a mixture of manual coding and machine learning techniques (as discussed next).

4 The analytical approach: the importance of coding

When the concepts of interest are theory driven, they are often complex, multifaceted, and not always directly measurable. Therefore, considerably more effort is needed in annotating texts so as to get meaningful classification results. This, note, is also the case for demographic analysis and for family research.

One method is to combine a conventional classification method in qualitative social science (i.e. manual coding), with algorithmic classification using supervised machine learning. After having collected social media texts over a given period and in a given geographical area, the first step is to get at the texts that contain relevant topics for the research question. This kind of research cannot rely simply on hashtags or other similar holistic tools that allow for the identification of texts and posts. Usually one encounters situations where the potentially relevant data are broad in scope. Consequently, it becomes difficult to identify the presence of information related to the topics one is interested in. The filtering should be based on theoretical guided keywords (using hashtags when available), or by users: i.e. in some cases we are interested in individuals but not companies, institutions or newspapers. Duplicates (e.g. re-tweets) can be deleted. As a result of the filtering, a *corpus* of potentially relevant texts is obtained. The idea is to first manually examine the texts, according to a pre-defined and theoretically-based semantic scheme, thus creating an annotated *corpus* (e.g. of tweet messages). Then an annotation model should be created and operationalized as a clear guide for manual annotators. The approach needs then to be tailored to the specific research question, which may require tweaks. As noted in

Karamshuk et al. (2017), if, for instance, crowdsourcing is used to increase the set of manual labels, slightly different approaches or different decision trees may need to be developed to enable adequate levels of agreement amongst crowd workers. The coding scheme that can be interpreted and applied by crowd workers to create reliable high quality labels is central in this process and clear guidance should be provided for crowd workers. Karamshuk et al. (2017) used a decision tree to help to create greater consistency in labelling. As a result of this fundamental step, what is known as a *gold standard corpus* of annotated texts (with sentiment but also with topics labels) is created. This will constitute the base for the algorithmic classification of the rest of the texts using machine learning, thereby mimicking the human researcher in coding the texts. It is, naturally, important to see how the machine algorithm is able to generate labels in agreement with the crowd labels, i.e. with what levels of accuracy. An acceptable percentage of accuracy from a linguistic point of view, may not be satisfactory to social scientists.

Examples of this analytical approach include Karamshuk et al. (2017) and Mencarini et al. (2017 and 2018), two works from quite different fields with different research questions. Karamshuk et al. (2017) use a case study approach, applying semi-automated coding, for public social media empathy in the context of high-profile deaths by suicide. Five cases were chosen which had a high rate of public response on Twitter, with the aim of exploring what types of response were more or less common in the public Twitter space, and what factors might affect these responses. The analysis suggests that the combination of qualitative analysis with machine learning can offer both a big picture view of public events and a close analysis of particular turning points or key moments in discussions of such events, yielding new insights that were not easily achievable with traditional qualitative social science methods. The paper develops semi-automated coding, where the authors first manually bootstrap a coding scheme from a micro-scale sample of data, then use a crowdsourcing platform to achieve a meso-scale model, and finally apply machine learning to build a macro-scale model.

In Mencarini et al. (2017) the aim is to investigate how computational linguistic techniques can be used to explore opinions and semantic orientations related to fertility and parenthood. There was a two-step approach: first, we developed a Twitter Italian corpus annotated applying a novel multi-layered semantic annotation scheme for marking information not only about sentiment polarity, but also about the specific semantic areas/sub-topics which are the target of sentiment in the fertility-SWB domain. As a reference dataset, we collected all the tweets posted in Italian language in 2014 from the TWITA collection[1]. Then we applied a multi-step thematic filtering, which included a keyword-based filtering stage through the inflection of a list of hashtags and keywords resulting from a combination of a manual content analysis on 2,500 tweets sampled at completely random (taken as a starting point) and a linguistic analysis on synonyms (see Sulis et al. 2017 and Mencarini et al. 2018 for the more details on the development of the corpus). A random sample of about 6,000 tweets has been manually annotated by using the CrowdFlower platform. The annotator's task was, first, to mark if the post is *in-* or *off-topic*[2] (or unintelligible), and then to mark for *in-topic* posts, on the one hand, the polarity and presence of irony, on the other hand, the sub-topics. An analysis of the manually annotated tweets to highlight relationships between the use of affective language and sub-topics of interest has been carried out. This step sheds lights on the social media content of messages related to fertility domains. The end product of this phase is a *gold standard corpus*, TW-SWELLFER, available to the community, which is essentially a body of trustworthy texts used for training and for meaningful evaluation in the next stage. The second phase consisted of a supervised machine learning experiment carried out on the overall dataset and based on the annotated tweets from the previous stage. Employing well-known algorithms from NLP, messages concerning children, parenthood or fertility (*in-topic*) from others (*off-topic*) were distinguished. Also sentiment *polarity,* with a standard annotation (as provided for the Senti-polc shared task in Basile et al. 2014) was de-

---

[1] http://valeriobasile.github.io/twita/about.html

[2] Topics related to fertility and parenthood. are somehow spread in the dataset and it is not an easy task to filter messages which contain relevant information on such subjects. Then, we decided to apply this manual check to identify and remove noise.

tected. This step was devoted to infer to what extent social media users report negative or positive affects on topics relevant to the fertility domain. The prevalence of positive tweets was then correlated with relevant regional characteristics regarding fertility. Data was derived from tweets in Italian and, since there is currently no up-to-date survey data on individual subjective well-being that can be connected to childbearing and parenthood for Italy, this material is, thus, potentially of real value for socio-demographic research.

5 Features and caveats in the study of demographic behavior

The growing deluge of digitally-generated texts and the development of computational algorithms to analyze them, create an unprecedented opportunity for the study of socio-demographic behavior. First, social media texts allow for the harvesting of opinions which are expressed spontaneously, not responding to a specific question and often as a reaction to some emotional driven observation. Second, social media coverage in time and space offers a continuity that surveys cannot provide. These two features are very important and offer a unique opportunity for learning about social media users and, therefore, for providing new perspectives on socio-demographic behavior.

Still, a fundamental question is who the users are. Which population do they represent? As data is generated from social media platforms, one is necessarily relying on a biased, or non-representative base of users. Despite using data with millions of data points, we are focusing on small biased subsets of the population, which otherwise, should be sampled through parameters such as gender, race, geography, age, income and education. For instance, there are studies suggesting that Twitter users in the Netherlands are young and female with specific personality traits (Nguyen et al., 2013; Plank and Hovy, 2015; Verhoeven et al., 2016). Individuals from such groups, will necessarily provide different kinds of information. In other words, despite the massive quantities of social media data available, we risk ignoring parts of the population, relevant to policy makers and social scientists. There are now efforts being made to overcome this issue. Studies attempt to calibrate non-representative digital data against reliable official statistics, thereby evaluating and modeling possible biases, or, when offi-

cial statistics are not available, relative trends are compared (Zagheni and Weber, 2015). Some have suggested retrieving information on the socio-demographic traits of Twitter users with the crowd-sourcing platform CrowdFlower and the image-recognition software Face++ (Yildiz et al., 2017) or by manually inspecting data that they have published elsewhere, e.g. on LinkedIn profiles. When age is not given, it could be estimated by taking into account, if present, the information included, say, in the LinkedIn education section, such as the starting date of a degree. Gender could be inferred from profile photos and names, by following a methodology similar to that in Rangel et al. (2014). In particular, the idea of extracting information about the age and gender of users by automatically analyzing their pictures, relying on advanced face-recognition techniques, might allow a novel methodological framework for a demographic-oriented analysis of social media and an assessment of theoretical ideas. Another fundamental piece of information for demographic studies, refers to the geographical location where social media users live or operate. Geocoded texts are available of course, but again, not universally so (e.g., in Mencarini et al. 2017 only one out of four messages were geo-tagged), and establishing residence is difficult since a large number of social media texts are generated on portable devices. Nevertheless, these stable or semi-stable socio-demographic traits of users are fundamental in making sense of social media data for demographic purposes, not least because they are instrumental in judging the representativeness of the social media sample applied.

6 The end of theory is not here, yet

The message of this paper is twofold. First, computational linguistic analysis offers great potential in advancing social science and demographic analysis. To do so successfully, however, one must develop an annotation procedure to incorporate the key theoretical concepts from the social sciences. On this point, social sciences and demography have the potential to provide huge advances in computational linguistics analysis. Second, there is no way (yet), to ignore the issue of representativeness. For social media data to make sense for demographic analysis, or more generally, for the social sciences, one needs to know something about the sample used for one's analysis. Perhaps one day we will reach the point where the quantity of big data is so huge, so all encompassing, and so comprehensive, that it will capture and answer all possible social questions. In the defense of the classical approach, however, one can always argue that such data will produce biases; and that there will be digital divides, both in the way information and technology is produced (Graham, 2012). Despite the enormity of digital data and the development of statistical tools designed to crunch data, social scientists will, at least for the foreseeable future, set the research questions and agendas, search for causation, and contribute useful theories for demographic analysis. As such, we are still some distance away from the supremacy of unsupervised machine learning, where the power of correlation supersedes causation, and where an epistemological revolution will effectively end social theory simply by letting data speak for themselves (Anderson, 2008; Chandler, 2015). At least for research into socio-demographic behavior, sociologists and demographers, with computer scientist colleagues, will still, for some time yet, be in the business of torturing the data until they talk.

References

Arnstein Aassve, Letizia Mencarini, and Maria Sironi. 2015. Institutional change, happiness and fertility. *European Sociological Review*, 31(6), 749-765. https://doi.org/10.1093/esr/jcv073

Anderson Chris. 2008. The end of theory: the data deluge makes the scientific method obsolete. *Wired*, 23 June.

Ben Y. Reis and John S. Brownstein. 2010. Measuring the impact of health policies using Internet search patterns: the case of abortion. *BMC public health*, 10(1): 514. https://doi.org/10.1186/1471-2458-10-514

Arianna Betti, and Hein van den Berg. 2016. Towards a Computational History of Ideas. In *Proceedings of the Third Conference on Digital Humanities in Luxembourg with a Special Focus on Reading Historical Sources in the Digital Age. CEUR Workshop Proceedings.* CEUR-WS.Org, edited by Lars Wieneke, Catherine Jones, Marten Düring, Florentina Armaselu, and René Leboutte. Vol. 1681. Aachen.

Francesco C. Billari, Nicolò Cavalli, Eric Qian, and Ingmar Weber. 2017. Footprints of Family Change: A Study Based on Twitter, Paper presented Annual Meeting of the Population Association of America, Chicago, IL, April 27-29 2017.

Francesco C. Billari, Francesco D'Amuri, and Juri Marcucci. 2013. Forecasting births using google. Paper presented at Annual Meeting of the Population Association of America, New Orleans, LA, April 11-13 2013.

Francesco C. Billari, and Emilio Zagheni. 2017. Big Data and Population Processes: A Revolution?. SocArXiv. July 1, published also in: Alessandra Petrucci, Rosanna Verde (edited by), SIS 2017. Statistics and Data Science: new challenges, new generations. 28-30 June 2017 Florence (Italy). *Proceedings of the Conference of the Italian Statistical Society*, Firenze University Press, 2017, pages 167–178. https://doi:10.17605/OSF.IO/F9VZP

David Chandler. 2015. A world without causation: big data and the coming of age of posthumanism. *Millennium: Journal of International Studies,* 43(3): 833–851. https://doi.org/10.1177/0305829815576817

Gosta Esping Andersen, and Francesco C. Billari. 2015. Retheorizing Family Demographics. *Population and Development Review,* 41(1), 1-31. https://doi.org/10.1111/j.1728-4457.2015.00024.x

Antske Fokkens, Serge ter Braake, Isa Maks, and D. Ceolin. 2016. On the Semantics of Concept Drift: Towards Formal Definitions of Semantic Change, paper presented at "Drift-a-LOD", Detection, Representation and Management of Concept Drift in linked Open Data, Workshop EKAW, Bologna, Italy, 20th November, 2016.

Mark Graham. 2012. Big data and the end of theory?, *The Guardian*, 9 March 2012.

Ronald Inglehart. 1971. The Silent Revolution in Europe: Intergenerational Change in Postindustrial Societies. *American Political Science Review*, 65: 991–1017. https://doi.org/10.2307/1953494

Dmytro Karamshuk, Frances Shaw, Julie Brownlie, and Sastry Nishanth, 2017. Bridging big data and qualitative methods in the social sciences: A case study of Twitter responses to high profile deaths by suicide, *Online Social Networks and Media*, 1: 33-43. https://doi.org/10.1016/j.osnem.2017.01.002

Tom Kenter, Melvin Wevers, Pim Huijnen, and Maarten de Rijke. 2015. Ad Hoc Monitoring of Vocabulary Shifts over Time. *CIKM '15 Proceedings of the 24th ACM International on Conference on Information and Knowledge Management*, Pages 1191 – 1200.

Alessandro Lenci. 2008. Distributional Semantics in Linguistic and Cognitive Research. *Italian Journal of Linguistics*, 20: 1–31.

Ronald Lesthaeghe. 2010. The unfolding story of the second demographic transition. Population and

Development Review, 36(2): 211-251. https://doi.org/10.1111/j.1728-4457.2010.00328.x

Peter McDonald (2000). Gender equity, social institutions and the future of fertility. *Journal of population Research*, 17(1), 1-16. https://doi.org/10.1007/BF03029445

Letizia Mencarini. 2014. Gender equity, In: Michalos AC (Ed*.). Encyclopedia of Quality of Life and Well-Being Research*. Springer, Dordrecht, Netherlands: Springer, Pages 2437-2438.

Letizia Mencarini, Viviana Patti, Mirko Lai, and Emilio Sulis, Happy parents' tweets. 2017. In: Alessandra Petrucci, Rosanna Verde (edited by), *SIS 2017. Statistics and Data Science: new challenges*, new generations. 28-30 June 2017 Florence (Italy). Proceedings of the Conference of the Italian Statistical Society, Firenze University Press, 2017, 693-700. https://doi:10.17605/OSF.IO/F9VZP

Letizia Mencarini, Delia Irazú Hernández-Farías, Mirko Lai, Viviana Patti, Emilio Sulis, Daniele Vignoli. 2018. *Italian happy parents in Twitter*, Dondena WP 117, Bocconi University.

Kathy A. Mills. 2017. What are the threats and potentials of big data for qualitative research?, *Qualitative Research*, First Published November 30. https://doi.org/10.1177/1468794117743465

Dong Nguyen, Rilana Gravel, Dolf Trieschnigg, and Theo Meder. 2013. "How Old Do You Think I Am?": A Study of Language and Age in Twitter. *Proceedings of the Seventh International AAAI Conference on Weblogs and Social Media.*

Jussi Ojala, Emilio Zagheni, Francesco C Billari, and Ingmar Weber. 2017. Fertility and its meaning: Evidence from search behavior. *Proceedings of the International Conference on Web and Social Media* (ICWSM) 2017.

Barbara Plank and Dirk Hovy. 2015. Personality traits on twitter—or—how to get 1,500 personality tests in a week. In Proceedings of the 6th Workshop on Computational Approaches to Subjectivity, Sentiment and Social Media Analysis, pages 92–98.

Francisco Rangel Pardo, Paolo Rosso, Irina Chugur,Martin Potthast, Martin Trenkmann, Benno Stein, Ben Verhoeven, Walter Daelemans. 2014. Overview of the 2nd author profiling task at PAN 2014, in: L. Cappellato, N. Ferro, M. Halvey, W. Kraaij (eds.), CLEF 2014 Labs and Workshops, *Notebook Papers*, 1180, CEUR-WS.org, pages 898-927.

Emilio Sulis, Cristina Bosco, Viviana Patti, Mirko Lai, Delia Irazú Hernández Farías, Letizia Mencarini, Michele Mozzachiodi, Daniele Vignoli. 2016. Subjective Well-Being and Social Media. A Semantically Annotated Twitter Corpus on Fertility

and Parenthood. *Proceedings of Third Italian Conference on Computational Linguistics (CLiC-it 2016)*, Napoli, Italy, December 5-7, 2016. CEUR Workshop Proceedings volume 1749, CEUR-WS.org.

Dirk J. Van de Kaa. 1987. Europe's second demographic transition. *Population Bullettin,* 42(1):1–59.

Ben Verhoeven, Walter Daelemans, and Barbara Plank. 2016. TWISTY: a Multilingual Twitter Stylometry Corpus for Gender and Personality Profiling. *Proceedings of the 10th International Conference on Language Resources and Evaluation* (LREC 2016).

Dilek Yildiz, Jo Munson, Agnese Vitali, Ramine Tinati, and Jennifer A. Holland. 2017. Using Twitter data for demographic research. Demographic Research, 37 (46). https://doi.org/10.4054/DemRes. 2017.37.46

Emilio Zagheni, and Ingmar Weber. 2012. You are where you E-mail: Using E-mail Data to Estimate International Migration Rates. *Proceedings of the 4th Annual ACM Web Science, Evanston, IL*, pages 348-351.

Emilio Zagheni, Kiran Garimella, and Ingmar Weber. 2014. Inferring international and internal migration patterns from twitter data. In *Proceedings of the23rd International Conference on World Wide Web*. ACM, pages 439-444.

Emilio Zagheni, Ingmar Weber. 2015. Demographic research with non-representative internet data. *International Journal of Manpower*. 36(1): 13-25. https://doi.org/10.1108/IJM-12-2014-0261

Emilio Zagheni, Ingmar Weber, Krishna Gummadi. 2017. Estimate stock of migrants using Facebook's advertising platform, *Population and Development Review*, on-line first. https://doi.org/10.1111/padr.12102

Understanding the Effect of Gender and Stance on Opinion Expression in Debates on "Abortion"

Esin Durmus
Cornell University
ed459@cornell.edu

Claire Cardie
Cornell University
cardie@cs.cornell.edu

Abstract

In this paper, we focus on understanding linguistic differences across groups with different self-identified gender and stance in expressing their opinions about ABORTION. We provide a new dataset consisting of users' gender, stance on ABORTION, as well as the debates in ABORTION drawn from *debate.org*. We use the gender and stance information to identify significant linguistic differences across individuals with different gender and stance. We show the importance of considering the stance information along with the gender, since we observe significant linguistic differences across individuals with different stance even within the same gender group.

1 Introduction

Understanding the differences in writing style and content across different demographic groups has been an important research focus (Argamon et al., 2003; Chong and Druckman, 2007). For example, Schler et al. (2006) has studied how the writing style and the content of blogs varies with the age and the gender of the blogger. We hypothesize that to study the actual linguistic differences across different gender groups' opinion expression on a topic, it is necessary to control for the differences that could potentially be correlated with the individuals' stances on the topic rather than their gender.

In this paper, we analyze linguistic factors that are significantly different across individuals with different gender and stance. We limit out discussions to the topic of ABORTION in order to control for the differences in language that are correlated with the topic. We include the text of debates where a FEMALE and a MALE with opposing stances on ABORTION discusses some aspect of this topic. We observe significant differences in language usage across FEMALE and MALE. Moreover, we see significant differences even within a gender when the individuals' stances on the topic is different. This suggests that the stance information should be taken into account while studying the impact of differences in demographics on language use. The main contributions of our study are three-fold:

- To the best of our knowledge, this is the first work which computationally studies the effect of gender in opinion expression accounting for the individuals' stance.

- We provide a dataset of debates on ABORTION and user information of the debaters participated in these debates.

- We investigate which linguistic features are important for discriminating between groups with different gender and stance in expressing opinions about ABORTION.

2 Related Work

There has been a tremendous amount of work on understanding differences in writing styles between gender groups. Argamon et al. (2003) has found that females use many more pronouns whereas males use noun specifiers more frequently in British National Corpus covering a range of genres. Litvinova et al. (2017) has looked at the differences in the frequencies of some parts of speech (POS) between different genders in Russian written texts. Morphological features have shown to be important to discriminate between genders in many European languages (Mikros, 2013; Bortolato, 2016). Schofield and Mehr (2016) has studied significant linguistic and structural features of dialogue to differentiate genders in conversation and analyzed how these

Proceedings of the Second Workshop on Computational Modeling of People's Opinions, Personality, and Emotions in Social Media, pages 69–75
New Orleans, Louisiana, June 6, 2018. ©2018 Association for Computational Linguistics

effects relate to existing literature on gender in film.

Mohammad and Yang (2011) has shown that there are marked differences across genders in how they use emotion words in work-place email. They found that women use many words from the joy-sadness axis, whereas men prefer terms from the fear-trust axis. Thelwall et al. (2010) has looked at the comments on MySpace and found that females are more likely to give and receive more positive comments than are males, but there is no difference for negative comments.

Although previous work investigates discriminative features to distinguish between different gender groups, the effect of the stance on the linguistic differences across these groups has not been very well studied. It has been shown that people with different stance talk about a particular topic in a different way (Chong and Druckman, 2007; Diermeier et al., 2012; McCaffrey and Keys, 2000). Given that the linguistic differences may also be correlated with the stance on a topic, to better understand the actual effect of gender vs stance, we propose a controlled setting where we can account for differences in stance on the topic. This allows us to study the effect of gender and the stance simultaneously.

3   Data Description

For this work, we present a dataset of 1639 debates on ABORTION from October of 2007 until November of 2017 drawn from *debate.org*[1]. The dataset includes information for 1545 users that participated in debates on ABORTION. 265 of these users have identified their gender as FEMALE and 648 of them have identified their gender as MALE. Some examples for the debate titles on ABORTION are as follows: "ABORTION IS A CHOICE, NOT A RIGHT.", "ABORTION IS GENERALLY IMMORAL.","ABORTION IS MURDER AND SHOULD BE ILLEGAL.". From 1639 debates on ABORTION, we limit our study to the debates in which one debater identifies their gender as FEMALE and the other one identifies their gender as MALE. We preferred to include only the debates where a debater interacts with someone having opposing gender since it controls for the linguistic differences that can be correlated with interacting with people from the same vs.

different gender group.

Opinions on Abortion. Each user profile on *debate.org* includes the user's opinions on the most controversial debate topics[2]. As ABORTION is one of these controversial topics, each user shares their stance on ABORTION[3]: either PRO (in favor), CON (against), N/O (no opinion), N/S (not saying) or UND (undecided). To study how the stance along with the gender of the debaters affect the language, from the debates including debaters with opposing genders, we keep the debates where each debater identifies their stance on ABORTION either as PRO or CON and two debaters' self-identified stance on ABORTION is opposing (e.g. if DEBATER 1's stance on ABORTION is PRO then DEBATER 2's stance is CON).
This controlled setting allows us to study the differences in linguistic features across people with different self-identified gender and stance when they are interacting with someone from the opposing gender and stance.
In the following sections, we will use the following abbreviations: (PRO-FEMALE) for the debaters who self-identified their gender as FEMALE and their stance on ABORTION as PRO, (CON-FEMALE) for the debaters who self-identified their gender as FEMALE and their stance on ABORTION as CON. Similarly, for MALE, we use the abbreviations PRO-MALE and CON-MALE.

4   Divergence of language across different groups

To understand how people with different genders (FEMALE and MALE) and stance (PRO and CON) talk about ABORTION, first, we applied the method proposed by Monroe et al. (2009). This method estimates the divergence between the two groups' language by modeling word-usage as multinomial distributions smoothed with a uniform Dirichlet prior. The divergence between these two distributions is measured by log-odds ratio. Table 1 shows the most discriminating words for each side of every combinations of FEMALE/MALE genders and PRO/CON sides[4].
We observe that people who are PRO vs CON use different terminologies to refer to the same concept. For example, PRO- uses the word "fe-

---

[2]http://www.debate.org/big-issues/
[3]The website asks the users if ABORTION should be legal or not.
[4]We performed stemming and lemmatization on the text.

PRO-FEMALE	fetus, right, woman, sex, body, care, medical, emotion, really, alive.
CON-FEMALE	baby, kill, cause, murder say, moral, wrong, abortion, human, womb.
PRO-MALE	will, women, birth, pain, force, pregnancy, good, bad, society, reason.
CON-MALE	human, unborn, kill, innocent, life, baby, development, crime, wrong, alive.
PRO-FEMALE	sex, people, woman, adopt, care, choice, pregnancy, emotion, really, child, legal.
PRO-MALE	moral, source, argument, will, human, conclusion, show, given, claim, logic.
CON-FEMALE	baby, I'm, woman, don't, health, want, mother, birth, think.
CON-MALE	human, argument, fetus, right, unborn, crime, case, moral, definition, claim.

Table 1: The most discriminating words for FEMALE/MALE genders and PRO/CON sides (e.g. first two rows shows the words which are important to discriminate between the word-usage distribution of PRO-FEMALE and CON-FEMALE. The most discriminating words for PRO-FEMALE includes "fetus", "right", and "woman" while the most discriminating words for CON-FEMALE includes "baby", "kill", and "babies".).

tus" while CON- emphasizes words like "baby" and "unborn". This distinction is mainly because PRO- differentiates between a "fetus" and "baby" as they claim that a "fetus" is not alive and does not have rights unlike a "baby". However, CON- mainly argues that life starts at conception. This suggests that the differences in terminology can be indicative of the differences in stance. Also, the discriminative words suggests that different gender groups have different motivations and justifications for their stance. We see that the words used by PRO-MALE focuses more on to the ethical, moral aspects of abortion, and how society perceives ABORTION, providing examples from other sources. However, PRO-FEMALE emphasizes more on women's rights and choices. Moreover, while CON-MALE emphasizing more on the morality and human rights to justify their arguments, CON-FEMALE emphasizes more on women, women's health and provides more personal information and experiences. This initial analysis suggests that there may be significant differences in language usage of different groups and the aspects these groups focus on. In the next section, we conduct a more fine-grained analysis for certain linguistic features to explore which linguistic features are important to discriminate between these groups.

5 Analysis

In this section, we analyze the important features to discriminate the opinions from people with different genders and stance. We describe the linguistic features for which we observe a significant difference for at least one the four groups.

For our analysis in this section, we combined all the text utterances of PRO-FEMALE, CON-FEMALE, PRO-MALE, and CON-MALE from the debates. Then, we split combined text for each group to sentences. Our final dataset includes 2716 sentences for PRO-FEMALE, 2215 sentences for CON-FEMALE, 3010 sentences for PRO-MALE and 2444 for CON-MALE. All our analysis in this section is done at the sentence-level.

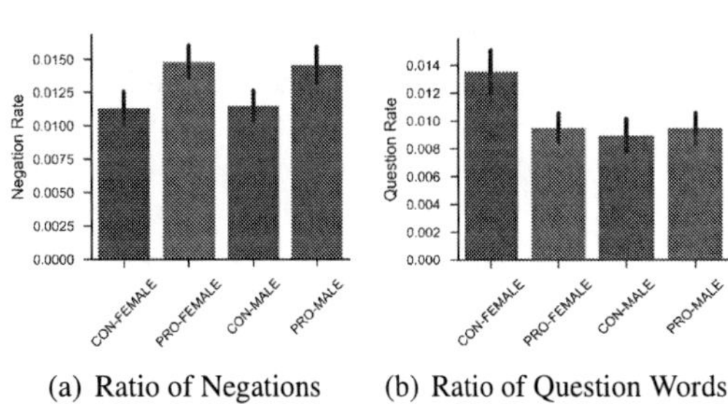

(a) Ratio of Negations   (b) Ratio of Question Words

Figure 1: Ratio of negations and questions to number of tokens. PRO-MALE and PRO-FEMALE uses significantly more negation marks than CON-MALE and CON-FEMALE. CON-FEMALE uses significantly more question words than any other group.

Sentence length. Previous work has found that when mean sentence length is calculated, women come out as the wordier gender in writing (Weitz, 1976; Mulac and Lundell, 1994). However, in our experiments, we find that number of tokens of the text of CON-MALE is significantly higher than PRO-MALE and CON-FEMALE ($p < 0.05$)[5]. Similarly, number of characters of the text of CON-MALE is significantly higher than

---

[5]All reported p values are computed with Welch's t-test.

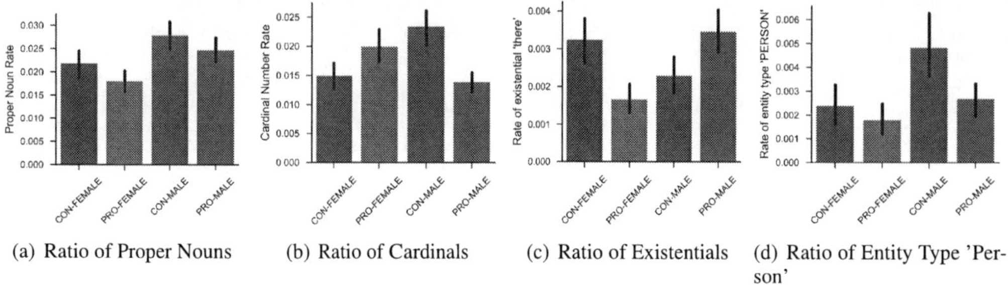

(a) Ratio of Proper Nouns   (b) Ratio of Cardinals   (c) Ratio of Existentials   (d) Ratio of Entity Type 'Person'

Figure 2: Ratio of Proper Nouns, Cardinals, Existential "there" and PERSON named entity.

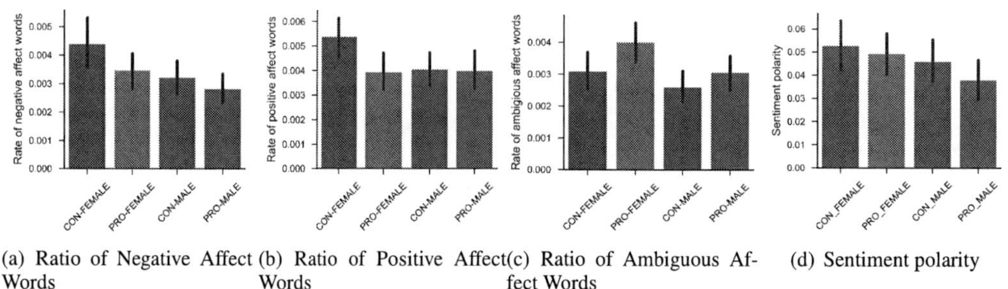

(a) Ratio of Negative Affect Words   (b) Ratio of Positive Affect Words   (c) Ratio of Ambiguous Affect Words   (d) Sentiment polarity

Figure 3: Ratio of negative, positive and ambiguous affect words, and sentiment polarity.

PRO-MALE ($p < 0.05$). We do not observe any significant differences in sentence length between other groups.

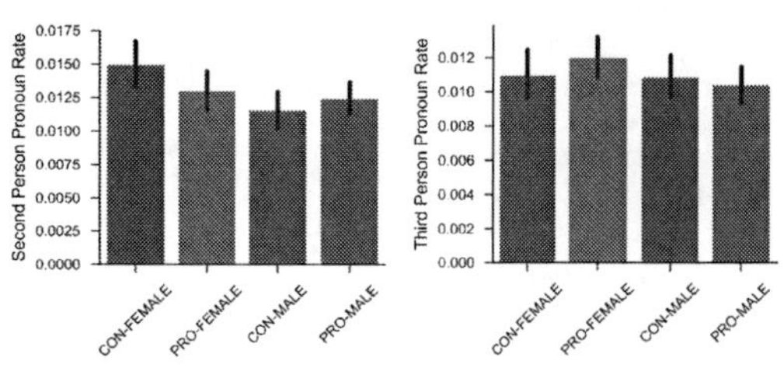

(a) Ratio of Second Person Pronouns   (b) Ratio of Third Person Pronouns

Figure 4: Ratio of number of personal pronouns to number of tokens.

Personal pronouns. Gleser et al. (1959) and Mulac et al. (1986) have shown that women frequently are the higher users of the personal pronouns when the entire category of personal pronouns is considered. Despite this finding, we do not observe any significant differences across different groups when we look at the total number of personal pronouns. We also do not observe any significant difference across these groups in first-

person pronoun usage. Figure 4 shows the ratio of number of second-person pronouns and third-person pronouns to number of tokens for each group. We find that PRO-FEMALE uses significantly more[6] third person pronouns than PRO-MALE. Moreover, CON-FEMALE uses significantly ($p < 0.05$) more second person pronouns than any other group.

Negation. Mulac et al. (2000) has shown that male uses more negation words than female in a setting where 36 female and 50 male managers giving professional criticism in a role play. In our experiments, we did not observe significant differences across individuals with different genders; however, we observed significant differences across individuals with different stance. Figure 1(a) shows the ratio of negation marks to number of tokens. PRO-MALE and PRO-FEMALE uses significantly ($p < 0.001$) more negation marks than both CON-MALE and CON-FEMALE.

Question words. We look at the ratio of total number of question words[7] to number of tokens. As we see in Figure 1(b), CON-FEMALE uses

---

[6]Our comparisons are made after we normalize the feature values with number of tokens in the sentences.

[7]includes "why","when","how","what","who","whose", "whom","where", "whose","whether".

significantly more question words than any other group ($p < 0.0001$). We observe that the question words are used not only to ask questions but also to form adjective clauses. These clauses are used to provide more specific information.

POS tag types. In Figure 2, we see the ratio of Proper Nouns 2(a), Cardinals 2(b), and Existential "there" 2(c) to number of tokens for each group. We observe that CON-MALE uses significantly more ($p < 0.001$) Proper Nouns than both PRO-FEMALE and CON-FEMALE. Moreover, PRO-MALE uses significantly more ($p < 0.001$) Proper Nouns than PRO-FEMALE. We find that users use Proper Nouns generally to cite relevant sources.

CON-MALE uses significantly more Cardinals than any other group[8]. PRO-FEMALE uses significantly more Cardinals than CON-FEMALE and PRO-MALE ($p < 0.05$). We observe that Cardinals are used to refer to a source or something happened in the past (e.g. to provide a date). We also find that CON-FEMALE and PRO-MALE uses significantly more existential "there" than any other group ($p < 0.001$) and CON-MALE uses significantly more existential "there" than PRO-FEMALE ($p < 0.05$).

Named Entity Mentions. For each entity type such as PERSON, LOCATION, ORGANIZATION, we look at the ratio of words belonging to these classes to number of tokens. As 2(d) shows, CON-MALE has significantly more mentions for entity type PERSON than any other group. We observe that CON-MALE uses PERSON entity type while citing other people's ideas.

Affect and Sentiment. We used Wordnet-Affect (Valitutti, 2004) to find affective concepts correlated with affective words and compare the affective concepts across these different groups. We look at the words associated with negative, positive and ambiguous emotions. Figure 3 shows the ratio of negative 3(a), positive 3(b) and ambiguous 3(d) affect words to number of tokens for each group. We find that CON-FEMALE uses significantly more ($p < 0.05$) negative and positive affect words than any other group and PRO-FEMALE uses significantly more ambiguous affect words any other group ($p < 0.05$). We also look at the overall sentiment of the sentences and we see that both CON-FEMALE and PRO-FEMALE have significantly more positive sentiment than PRO-MALE ($p < 0.05$). Although we observe that

female uses more affect and sentiment words in some cases as also found by Danner et al. (2001), the usage of affect and sentiment words changes depending on the stance.

Our analysis in this section shows that there are significant differences in linguistic features between different genders and the individuals with different stance within the same gender group. For example, we see that the linguistic differences in use of negation is more correlated with stance than the gender. This finding highlights the importance of accounting for the stance information to understand actual linguistic differences between different genders.

6 Task : Predicting the gender and the stance.

In the previous section, we demonstrate some linguistic differences between groups with different gender and stance. This analysis highlights the importance of considering the stance while analyzing the differences in opinion expression for different gender groups. In this section, we look at whether the linguistic features we analyze in the previous section are predictive of the group of the person who utters a given piece of text. From the debates we described, we extracted all the turns and label whether they come from PRO-FEMALE, CON-FEMALE, PRO-MALE or CON-MALE. Our dataset for this task includes 451 turns[9]. The task is given a turn, predicting which one of these four groups the person who utters this turn belongs to.

6.1 Methodology

We treat this task as a multi-class (4-class) classification task and we used Logistic Regression[10]. We evaluate prediction accuracy, precision and recall using 5-fold cross validation approach. We pick the model parameters for each split with 3-fold cross validation on the training set. We perform ablation tests for the linguistic features analyzed in the previous section.

---

[8] $p < 0.0001$ for CON-FEMALE and PRO-MALE, $p < 0.05$ for PRO-FEMALE.

[9] 105 of them are coming from CON-MALE, 120 of them are coming from CON-FEMALE, 127 are coming from PRO-MALE, and 99 of them are coming from PRO-FEMALE.

[10] with one-vs.-rest strategy. We optimized the regularizer ($\ell 1$ or $\ell 2$) and the regularization parameter C (between 10^{-5} and 10^5).

Features	Accuracy	Precision	Recall
Majority	26.61	6.65	25.00
Length	27.48	19.82	26.65
Tf-idf	43.46	43.86	42.82
Negation	29.25	14.84	27.06
Named entity: PERSON	31.04	23.30	28.78
Questions	32.37	18.00	29.77
Ambiguous affect words	29.92	21.08	27.93
Tf-idf+Questions+Ambiguous affect words	**44.34**	**44.01**	**43.34**

Table 2: Results for the ablation tests. The best model includes *Tf-idf*, *Questions* and *Ambiguous affect words* features.

6.1.1 Baselines

Majority. Picking the majority group from the training data, as the predicted group.

Length. Using number of tokens in the utterance as a feature.

6.2 Result and Analysis

Table 2 includes the macro-average scores for the baselines and results for the ablation tests for the linguistic features performing better than the baselines. We see that *Tf-idf* features perform significantly better than baseline. We see that important *Tf-idf* features corresponds to the discriminative words described in Section 4. These features include "kill", "murder", "right", "life", "woman", "baby", "mother" etc. This suggest that *Tf-idf* features are helpful to capture the differences in terminology and the motivation behind an individual's reasoning. We see that some of the linguistic features such as *Negation, Named Entity:* PERSON, *Questions* and *Ambiguous affect words* that we find to be discriminative in Section 5 have significantly more predictive power than majority and length baselines. The best predictive model includes *Tf-idf* features, questions, and *Ambiguous affect words*.

7 Conclusion

In this paper we show that accounting for the stance is important in order to effectively study the difference in linguistic features between different genders. We used both stance and gender information of the users and we analyzed differences in language across these different groups. We find that some linguistic features are more correlated with the stance of the individuals while others are more correlated with the gender. As a future direction, we would like to explore methods for rep-

resenting user information, that captures various aspects of a user such as education level, political ideology, and religious beliefs, in order study linguistic difference across different groups of people in a more controlled manner.

8 Acknowledgements

This work was supported in part by NSF grant SES-1741441 and DARPA DEFT Grant FA8750-13-2-0015. The views and conclusions contained herein are those of the authors and should not be interpreted as necessarily representing the official policies or endorsements, either expressed or implied, of NSF, DARPA or the U.S. Government. We thank Faisal Ladhak, Ana Smith, Amr Sharaf and the anonymous reviewers for their helpful feedback and suggestions. We also thank the Cornell NLP group for their insightful comments.

References

Shlomo Argamon, Moshe Koppel, Jonathan M. Fine, and Anat Rachel Shimoni. 2003. Gender, genre, and writing style in formal written texts.

Claudia Bortolato. 2016. Intertextual distance of function words as a tool to detect an author's gender: A corpus-based study on contemporary italian literature. *Glottometrics*, 34:28–43.

Dennis Chong and James N. Druckman. 2007. Framing theory. *Annual Review of Political Science*, 10(1):103–126.

Deborah D Danner, David A Snowdon, and Wallace V Friesen. 2001. Positive emotions in early life and longevity: Findings from the nun study. *Journal of Personality and Social Psychology*, 80(5):804–813.

Daniel Diermeier, Jean-Franois Godbout, Bei Yu, and Stefan Kaufmann. 2012. Language and ideology in congress. *British Journal of Political Science*, 42(1):3155.

Goldine C. Gleser, Louis A. Gottschalk, and Watkins John. 1959. The relationship of sex and intelligence to choice of words: A normative study of verbal behavior. *Journal of Clinical Psychology*, 15(2):182–191.

Tatiana Litvinova, Pavel Seredin, Olga Litvinova, and Olga Zagorovskaya. 2017. Differences in type-token ratio and part-of-speech frequencies in male and female russian written texts. In *Proceedings of the Workshop on Stylistic Variation*, pages 69–73. Association for Computational Linguistics.

Dawn McCaffrey and Jennifer Keys. 2000. Competitive framing processes in the abortion debate: Polarization-vilification, frame saving, and frame debunking. *The Sociological Quarterly*, 41(1):41–61.

GK Mikros. 2013. Systematic stylometric differences in men and women authors: a corpus-based study. *Issues in quantitative linguistics 3. Dedicated to Karl-Heinz Best on the occasion of his 70th birthday*, pages 206–223.

Saif M Mohammad and Tony Wenda Yang. 2011. Tracking sentiment in mail: How genders differ on emotional axes. In *Proceedings of the 2nd workshop on computational approaches to subjectivity and sentiment analysis*, pages 70–79. Association for Computational Linguistics.

Burt L. Monroe, Michael Colaresi, and Kevin M. Quinn. 2009. Fightin words: Lexical feature selection and evaluation for identifying the content of political conflict.

Anthony Mulac and Torborg Louisa Lundell. 1994. Effects of gender-linked language differences in adults' written discourse: Multivariate tests of language effects. *Language & Communication*, 14(3):299–309.

Anthony Mulac, Torborg Louisa Lundell, and James J. Bradac. 1986. Male/female language differences and attributional consequences in a public speaking situation: Toward an explanation of the genderlinked language effect. *Communication Monographs*, 53(2):115–129.

Anthony Mulac, David R Seibold, and Jennifer Lee Farris. 2000. Female and male managers and professionals criticism giving: Differences in language use and effects. *Journal of Language and Social Psychology*, 19(4):389–415.

Jonathan Schler, Moshe Koppel, Shlomo Argamon, and James Pennebaker. 2006. Effects of age and gender on blogging. In *Computational Approaches to Analyzing Weblogs - Papers from the AAAI Spring Symposium, Technical Report*, volume SS-06-03, pages 191–197.

Alexandra Schofield and Leo Mehr. 2016. Gender-distinguishing features in film dialogue. In *Proceedings of the Fifth Workshop on Computational Linguistics for Literature*, pages 32–39. Association for Computational Linguistics.

Mike Thelwall, David Wilkinson, and Sukhvinder Uppal. 2010. Data mining emotion in social network communication: Gender differences in myspace. *Journal of the American Society for Information Science and Technology*, 61(1):190–199.

Ro Valitutti. 2004. Wordnet-affect: an affective extension of wordnet. In *In Proceedings of the 4th International Conference on Language Resources and Evaluation*, pages 1083–1086.

Shirley Weitz. 1976. Sex differences in nonverbal communication. *Sex Roles*, 2(2):175–184.

Frustrated, Polite or Formal: Quantifying Feelings and Tone in Emails

Niyati Chhaya[✉1], Kushal Chawla[1], Tanya Goyal[2], Projjal Chanda[3], and Jaya Singh[4]

[1]Big Data Experience Lab, Adobe Research, India
[2]University of Texas, Austin, USA
[3]Indian Institute of Technology, Kharagpur, India
[4]Indian Institute of Technology, Guwahati, India
[1]*nchhaya,kchawla@adobe.com*
[2]*tanyagoyal@utexas.edu*
[3,4]*projjalchanda1996,jayasinghiitg@gmail.com*

Abstract

Email conversations are the primary mode of communication in enterprises. The email content expresses an individual's needs, requirements and intentions. Affective information in the email text can be used to get an insight into the sender's mood or emotion. We present a novel approach to model human frustration in text. We identify linguistic features that influence human perception of frustration and model it as a supervised learning task. The paper provides a detailed comparison across traditional regression and word distribution-based models. We report a mean-squared error (MSE) of 0.018 against human-annotated frustration for the best performing model. The approach establishes the importance of affect features in frustration prediction for email data. We further evaluate the efficacy of the proposed feature set and model in predicting other *tone* or *affects* in text, namely formality and politeness; results demonstrate a comparable performance against the state-of-the-art baselines.

1 Introduction

Emails are the primary mode of communication in professional environments. Both formal and informal communication is prevalent through emails. In customer care organizations, email and instant messaging are used for conversations. The content in these communications includes information, conversations, requirements, actions and opinions. Every individual and organization has a style of language, topic of choice as well as patterns in which they communicate. Their personality and at times position (authority, social relationships) drive the choice of words and the tone of their content. Similarly, different recipients react differently to different kinds of content. For example, a professional is more likely to respond to a formal request than a casual request from his subordinate at the workplace. A customer care agent can easily calm down an agitated individual if he is polite. *Tone* in text is defined as this expression of affects or feelings in content. We present a study to measure this *Tone* in text content, specifically in email conversations.

Quantifying text sentiment based on lexical and syntactic features is well studied. Further, measuring ease of read (Kate et al., 2010) as well as coherency of text content has been explored. Sentiment and emotion analysis have been explored for specific affect dimensions (e.g. polarity and Ekman's six Emotion categories). Interpersonal communication illustrates fine–grained affect categories, beyond emotions and sentiments. Frustration is one such dominant affect that is expressed in human interactions (Burgoon and Hale, 1984). We present a study of Frustration.

Expressions, tone of the voice (audio), actions, and physical reactions are easy cues to detect the presence of frustration. In the case of text content, identifying the correct sentence formations, use of words, and lexical content structure for affect detection, specifically frustration, is a hard problem (Calvo and D'Mello, 2010; Munezero et al., 2014). We show how using affect lexica to quantify frustration in text content improves the performance as against using just lexical and syntactic features. Our experiments highlight the importance of using word–level affect features for the prediction task. We show that affect features also contribute to the prediction of formality and politeness, which are *tone* dimensions that have been explored earlier. We compare and contrast a traditional regression model with models based on

Proceedings of the Second Workshop on Computational Modeling of People's Opinions, Personality, and Emotions in Social Media, pages 76–86
New Orleans, Louisiana, June 6, 2018. ©2018 Association for Computational Linguistics

word embeddings. The traditional feature–based models outperform the rest for this dataset and the task.

This paper investigates frustration in online written communication. The contributions are:

- We present a state–of–the–art statistical model for frustration prediction, evaluate it against human judgments, and present an in–depth feature analysis: highlighting the importance of affect features. We also evaluate our model for formality and politeness detection and report comparable accuracy as against the state–of–the–art prior work.

- We present an analysis that studies the relationship of Frustration with Formality and Politeness in text data and report negative correlation across these dimensions. High frustration is observed in content with low formality and low politeness.

- We provide an analysis of what humans tag as frustration in written text across 6 different topics.

2 Related Work

Research around understanding text features and quantifying them has been explored. Methods to measure various lexical, syntactic, and semantic text analysis features have been studied on various datasets and mentioned earlier across different emotion and sentiment dimensions (Das and Kalita, 2017). We are concerned with the specific dimensions of frustration, formality, and politeness in text and hence will not present a detailed review for all other work.

To the best of our knowledge, this is the first work that attempts at a computational model for frustration in text. However, dimensions such as formality and politeness have been explored earlier. The closest work in frustration detection is related to interactions and conversations with intelligent chatbots (Wang et al., 2004; D'Mello et al., 2008). These approaches measure human frustration in either online tutoring systems on chat systems or online game interactions. The features used for affect detection include speech, video, and lexical or syntactic features such as use of emoticons. Ciechanowski et al. (2018) provide an overview of approaches of the current models and algorithms in this space using electromyography as well as other psycho-physiological data and a detailed set of questionnaires focused on assessing interactions and willingness to collaborate with a bot, which is one of the most recent work in the paradigm. The above systems, however, do not try to model and quantify these tone dimensions in long texts such as email or blogs.

Tutoring systems and e-learning systems need to evaluate the quality of the responses as well as the student experience. McQuiggan et al. (2007) model student frustration in their work. Student frustration and boredom along with confusion and concentration is studied by researchers who evaluate the efficiency of online tutoring systems and educational computer games (Conati and Maclaren, 2009; Sabourin et al., 2011). These approaches are based on probabilistic modeling and bayesian reasoning use sensors from multiple physiological and audio–video signals. Our work focuses on modeling similar tone from text. Vizar et al. (2009) study frustration in the process of modeling stress using keystrokes and language information. Their work uses speech data and not written text, which is the focus of this paper. While prior art in frustration and similar tone dimensions exists, it has been modeled only based on multi–modal and multi–sensor data as against the text–based content that we present in this paper.

Two complementary affects along with frustration, are formality and politeness in text. Formality has been defined in different works in varied ways (Brooke et al., 2010; Lahiri, 2015). Pavlick et. al. (2016) assume a user–based definition of formality, we use a similar approach to define frustration in this work. The authors focus on semantic (ngram), lexical and syntactic features to present an empirical study of quantifying formality in various types of text content. Their work ignores the affect–related features. We use their model as a baseline in the experiments for formality prediction. Our approach out performs their model for the email dataset. We study politeness to understand the relationship between politeness and frustration. The state–of–the–art in politeness detection predicts politeness in online requests (Danescu-Niculescu-Mizil et al., 2013). We use that approach as a baseline. Most of the published work in this space of text tone dimensions looks at either social media data or chat related datasets. This paper focuses on an email dataset.

Linguistic analysis of email data has gained popularity since the release of the ENRON dataset (Cohen, 2009). This dataset provides the text, user information as well as the network information. In this work, we use a subset of this publicly available dataset. Enron has been a very popular dataset for social network analysis (Chapanond et al., 2005; Diesner et al., 2005; Shetty and Adibi, 2005; Oselio et al., 2014; Ahmed and Rossi, 2015) and sentiment and authority analysis (Diesner and Evans, 2015; Liu and Lee, 2015; Miller and Charles, 2016; Mohammad and Yang, 2011). Peterson et al. (2011) present an approach to model formality on the ENRON corpus and Kaur et al. (2014) compare emotions across formal and informal emails. Jabbari et al. (2006) analyze business and personal emails as different classes of data. Approaches that study the social relationships in the ENRON dataset (Prabhakaran et al., 2012; Zhou et al., 2010; Miller and Rye, 2012; Cotterill, 2013) refer to formality and politeness as indicative features for such tasks. This vast usage of the ENRON dataset supports our choice of the corpus for modeling frustration in interpersonal text communication.

Human Perceptions and Definitions

Tone or affects such as frustration and formality are highly subjective. As seen in section 2 there are various definitions for these measures. We need to specify our own definitions for frustration before we try to automate the prediction. This work does not attempt to introduce a novel or an accurate measure of frustration (or formality and politeness), but we assume that these are defined by human perception and each individual may differ in their understanding of the metrics. This approach of using untrained human judgments has been used in prior studies of pragmatics in text data (Pavlick and Tetreault, 2016; Danescu-Niculescu-Mizil et al., 2013) and is a suggested way of gathering gold-standard annotations (Sigley, 1997). We define frustration as the frustration expressed in text for our study. The aim is to answer whether there is any coherence across individual's perception of frustration (3.1.1). If so, what linguistic features, specifically affect features, contribute towards this collective notion? Based on this, we present an automated approach for frustration prediction in text (Section 4).

3 Data and Annotation

Table 1: Dataset Description

Property	Value
Total number of emails (Main Experiment)	960
Total number of emails (Pilot Experiment)	90
Min. sentences per email	1
Max. sentences per email	17
Average email size (no. of sentences)	4.22
Average number of words per email	77.5

Table 2: Annotations on Varying Email sizes

Dimension	Email size (# sentences)	# emails	mean	std. dev.
Frustration	$0 - 2$	258	-0.06	0.11
(-2,-1,0)	$3 - 5$	452	-0.07	0.13
	$6 - 17$	250	-0.08	0.11
Formality	$0 - 2$	258	0.11	0.55
(-2,-1,0,1,2)	$3 - 5$	452	0.37	0.54
	$6 - 17$	250	0.65	0.46
Politeness	$0 - 2$	258	0.35	0.33
(-2,-1,0,1,2)	$3 - 5$	452	0.51	0.34
	$6 - 17$	250	0.64	0.29

We study the human perception of frustration expressed in text across different topics and message (text) lengths. Prior research on dimensions such as formality and politeness present a similar analysis of how they vary across types of text and genres. Due to the lack of annotated data for frustration, we conducted a crowd sourcing experiment using Amazon's Mechanical Turk. We work off a subset of about 5000 emails from the ENRON email dataset (Cohen, 2009). This contains emails exchanged between over 100 employees and spans across various topics. The analysis presented in this section is based on a subset of about 1050 emails that were tagged across one pilot and one full scale experiment. Table 1 provides an overview of the data statistics of the annotated data.

We follow the annotation protocol of the Likert Scale (Allen and Seaman, 2007) for three affect dimensions: Frustration, Formality, and Politeness. Each email is considered as a single data point and only the text in the email body is provided for tagging. Frustration is tagged on a 3 point scale with neutral being equated to 'not frustrated'; 'frustrated' and 'very frustrated' are marked with -1 and -2 respectively. Formality and politeness follow a 5 point scale from -2 to $+2$ where both extremes mark the higher degree of presence and absence of the respective dimension. We use a mean of 10 annotators score for each input email.[1]

---

[1]Dataset can be accessed at https://goo.gl/WFkDnS

3.1 Analysis

The data has been tagged by 69 individuals, where the average time spent per email is 28.2 seconds. The average number of emails annotated by an individual are approximately 139.

3.1.1 Inter-annotator Agreement

To measure whether the individuals intuition of the affect dimensions is consistent with other annotators' judgment, we use interclass correlation[2] to quantify the ordinal ratings. This measure accounts for the fact that we may have a different group of annotators for each data point. Agreements reported for 3 class and 5 class annotations are 0.506 ± 0.05, 0.73 ± 0.02, and 0.64 ± 0.03 for frustration, formality, and politeness respectively. These numbers are comparable to any other psycholinguistic task. Example emails with their corresponding annotations are provided in Table 3.

3.1.2 Email size and Tone dimensions

Table 2 shows the variance in frustration, formality and politeness in comparison to the email size. We observe that while formality and politeness vary with content size, frustration does not have a significant variance.

3.1.3 Comparison with Readability

We observe that the Readability of the content does not impact the tagged frustration values as against the case with formality and politeness. Figure 1 shows how frustration varies across different readability scores. Prediction experiments (see Table 5) support this observation.

3.1.4 Affective Content

One purpose of this study is to understand the words that are associated with emotions and whether affect plays a role in understanding frustration in this data. Figure 2 shows this analysis. The graphs show the variance in frustration with respect to three psycholinguistic features. As seen in the figure, PERMA relationship(POS) has a very different behavior with the positive and the negative frustration class. This analysis helps in confirming the hypothesis on relationship between frustration in text and psycholinguistic features.

4 Modeling Frustration

We analyze whether an algorithm can distinguish between existence and non-existence of the expression of frustration in text and which linguistic features are important for this task.

4.1 Setup

The data described in section 3 is used for training, using the mean of the annotators' scores as the gold-standard label. We model the problem as a regression task. The task is to predict frustration in given text. We also report results for formality and politeness prediction and compare against baselines for both these dimensions. The model is implemented using the Scikit[3] package in Python.

4.2 Features

Table 4 provides a summary of the features considered. Ngrams and other semantic features are ignored as they introduce domain-specific biases. Word-embeddings are treated separately and considered as raw features to train a supervised model. 55 features are divided into 4 sub-groups: Lexical, Syntactic, Derived(e.g. readability) and Affect-based features. The lexical and syntactic features are defined based on standard definitions. These include features such as 'averageNumberofWords per sentence' and 'number of capitalizations'. The derived features focus on features that can help quantify the readability of text. Hedges, Contractions, and Readability scores are included in this set of features. The fourth group of features are the Affect–related features. These features are lexica–based and quantify the amount of affective content present in the input text. We use Stanford Corenlp[4] and TextBlob[5] for our linguistic processing and feature extraction. All features used by Pavlick et. al. (2016) for formality detection and by Danescu et al. (2013) for politeness detection have been included in our analysis for a comparison against baselines. To the best of our knowledge, this is not only the first of its kind work for quantifying frustration in text using linguistic features but also the first attempt at explicitly using affect features for such an affect detection task.

---

[2]We report the average raters absolute agreement (ICC1k) using the psych package in R.

[3]http://scikit-learn.org/
[4]https://stanfordnlp.github.io/CoreNLP/
[5]https://textblob.readthedocs.io/en/dev/

Table 3: Example emails with high and low inter-annotator agreements.

Affect Dimension	Example	Annotations
Frustration: Low Agreement	See highlighted portion. We should throw this back at Davis next time he points the finger.	(-1, -1, 0, 0, -2, -2, 0, 0, -2, 0)
Frustration: High Agreement	Please see announcement below. Pilar, Linda, India and Deb, please forward to all of your people. Thanks in advance, adr	(0, 0, 0, 0, 0, 0, 0, 0, 0, 0)
Formality: Low Agreement	I talked with the same reporters yesterday (with Palmer and Shapro). Any other information that you can supply Gary would be appreciated. Steve, did Gary A. get your original as the CAISO turns email? GAC	(0, 0, -1, 1, 1, 1, 0, -1, -2, -1)
Politeness: High Agreement	John, This looks fine from a legal perspective. Everything in it is either already in the public domain or otherwise non-proprietary. Kind regards, Dan	(1, 1, 1, 1, 1, 1, 1, 1, 2, 1)

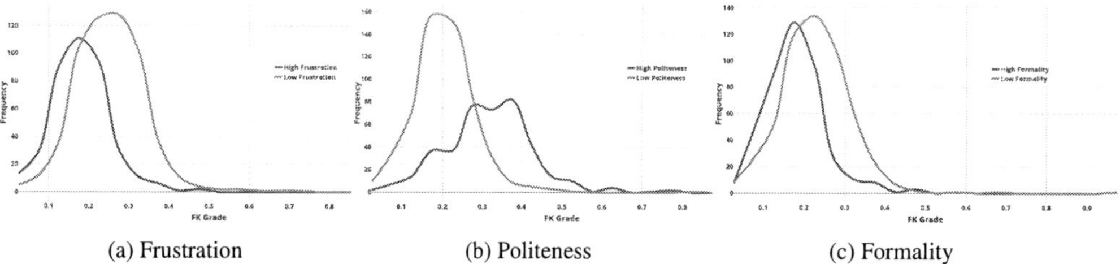

(a) Frustration (b) Politeness (c) Formality

Figure 1: Comparing Readability Index (Flesh–Kincaid readability score-FKGrade- with *Tone* Dimensions: Graphs show the distribution of readability score for the positive and negative class for each of the dimensions. The two classes correspond to the presence or absence of the respective tone.

Lexical and Syntactic Features: The lexical features capture various counts associated with the content. Prior art in formality and politeness prediction extensively relies on such features for their analysis and hence we hypothesize that the lexical properties will contribute to our task. Syntactic features include NER–based features, Number of blank lines, and text density. Text density is defined as follows:

$$\rho = \frac{\#(sentences)}{1 + \#(lines)}$$

where ρ is the text density, $\#(sentences)$ denotes number of sentences in the text content and $\#(lines)$ number of lines including blank lines in the text message.

Derived: Readability Features: The derived features capture information such as readability of text, existence of hedges, subjectivity, contractions, and sign–offs. Subjectivity, contractions, and hedges are based on the TextBlob implementation.

Readability is measured based on Flesh–Kincaid readability score which is given by the following equation:

$$FKGrade = 0.39\frac{words}{sentences} + 11.8\frac{syllables}{words} + 15.59$$

This score is a measure of ease of reading of given piece of text. We use the textstat package[6] in Python for the implementation.

Affect Features: The affect features used in our analysis include:

1. **Valence-Arousal-Dominance (PAD) Model** (Mehrabian, 1980): This three dimensional model quantifies the valence which is the happy-unhappy scale, arousal: the excited–calm scale, and dominance, which indicates the forcefulness of the expressed affect. We use the Warriner's lexicon (Warriner et al., 2013) for the feature extraction.

2. **Ekman's Emotions (Ekman, 1992)**: Ekman's model provides the 6 basic human emotions: anger, disgust, admiration, surprise, anticipation, and sadness. We use the

---

[6]https://pypi.python.org/pypi/textstat/0.1.6

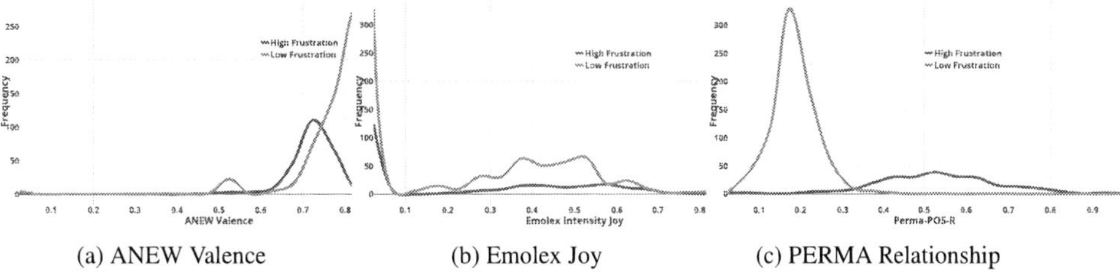

(a) ANEW Valence   (b) Emolex Joy   (c) PERMA Relationship

Figure 2: Frustration and Affect: Graphs show how specific affect dimension (based on lexica) varies for the positive and negative class of Frustration. PERMA relationship (POS) has a sharp peaked distribution for one class where as a flat distribution for the other. ANEW-Valence and EmolexIntensity-JOY also vary across classes dimensions

Table 4: Summary of feature groups used in our model. To the best of our knowledge, those marked with (*) have not been previously studied to model any of the three affects: Frustration, Formality, and Politeness. This list is the set of features that were finally used in our model. A larger list of explored features is provided as supplementary material.

Features	Feature list
Lexical	Average Word Length, Average Words per Sentence, # of Upper Case Words, # Ellipses, # Exclamation marks, # Question Mark, # Multiple Question Marks, # Words, # Lower Case words, First word upper case, # NonAlphaChars, # Punctuation Chars
Syntactic	# BlankLines, NER-Person, NER-Location, NER-PersonLength, NER-Organization, TextDensity
Derived	# Contractions, ReadabilityScore- FKgrade, FirstPerson, Hedge, Subjectivity, Sentiment, ThirdPerson, SignOff
Affect*	ANEW-arousal, ANEW-dominance, ANEW-valence, EmolexIntensity-anger, EmolexIntensity-fear, EmolexIntensity-joy, EmolexIntensity-sadness, Emolex-anger, Emolex-anticipation, Emolex-disgust, Emolex-fear, Emolex-joy, Emolex-negative, Emolex-positive, Emolex-sadness, Emolex-surprise, Emolex-trust, Perma-NEG-A, Perma-NEG-E, Perma-NEG-M, Perma-NEG-P, Perma-NEG-R, Perma-POS-A, Perma-POS-E, Perma-POS-M, Perma-POS-P, Perma-POS-R
Formal Words	formal-words, informal-words (Brooke et al., 2010)

NRC lexicon (EMOLEX) (Mohammad et al., 2013) which provides a measure for the existence of the emotion as well as the intensity of the detected emotion.

3. **PERMA Model (Seligman, 2011):** The PERMA model is a scale to measure positivity and well–being in humans (Seligman, 2012). This model defines the 5 dimensions: Positive Emotions, Engagement, Relationships, Meaning, and Accomplishments as quantifiers and indicators of positivity and well–being. Schwartz et al. (Schwartz et al., 2013) published a PERMA lexicon. We use this lexicon in our work. Frustration is considered as an important measure in the study of Positive Psychology. Hence, we leverage the PERMA model for our features.

4. **Formality Lists**: Brooke et al. (Brooke et al., 2010) provide a list of words that usually indicate formality or informality in text. We use these lists for our experiments.

4.2.1 ENRON–embeddings

We train a Word2Vec CBOW model (Mikolov et al., 2013) on raw $517,400$ emails from the ENRON email dataset to obtain the word embeddings. We keep the embedding size as 50 and a window of 5, taking a mean of all the context words to obtain the context representation. For optimization, we use negative sampling, drawing 5 noisy samples at each instance. An aggregate of these embeddings (see ENRON–trained embeddings in table 5) is considered as a feature set for one of our experiments.

81

5 Experiments

This section describes experiments associated with this work. All experiments report the accuracy against the ground-truth dataset described earlier.

Tone Prediction - Can you predict Frustration? This section reports the results for predicting frustration on a held out test dataset. Table 5 reports the mean squared error for different regression models with varying feature sets. We also report results for formality and politeness against the same settings. **Ridge regression** with lexical, syntactic, and affect features is the best performing model for frustration. The politeness baseline is the best performing model for both formality and politeness prediction. We also report MSE values using the 50-dimensional ENRON–trained embeddings as features. Even though these features are trained on the large EN-RON dataset($500,000$ emails), they underperform as against the affect features. We conclude that the psycholinguistic features(i.e. affect features) are more predictive for such subjective tasks.

Classification: To understand whether one can differentiate between the positive and the negative class for *tone* dimensions such as frustration, we also model the problem as a 2–class classification problem. Neutral tags are considered a part of the negative class. Hence, the classification model predicts where the text has frustration (or formality, or politeness) or not. Table 6 shows the performance of different classification models across different feature groups where the positive class is oversampled to compensate for the class imbalance [Frustration: 249 (positive class), 731 (negative class); Formality: 455 (positive class), 525 (negative class); Politeness: 423 (positive class), 557 (negative class)]. Note that this experiment is done on the same dataset with 3 annotation/email as against 10 annotations. **Random Forest** (10 trees) is the best performing model with an accuracy of 0.86. Random Forest is the best predictor for Frustration while Logistic Regression has the highest accuracies for Formality and Politeness prediction.

Feature Importance: Which features help to predict Frustration? Figure 3 shows the relative feature importances of top few features across the three affect dimensions. PERMA-

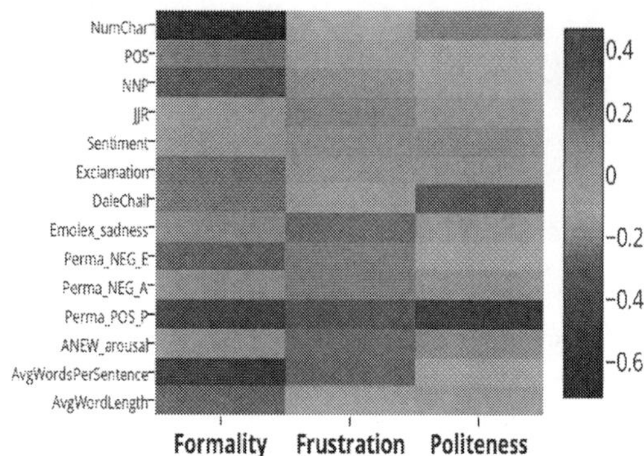

Figure 3: Figure shows the relative feature importance of top few features across all three dimensions. The importance is calculated based on results of logistic regression. PERMA-positivity has very negative correlation with frustration but is negatively correlated with politeness.

positivity has very negative correlation with frustration but is moderately negatively correlated with politeness. This confirms the hypothesis of contribution from affect features. Frustration is best predicted with affect features, formality and politeness are not.

6 Discussion

- **Comparing Frustration with Formality and Politeness:** Table 7 shows the pairwise Pearson's correlation coefficient across the *tone* dimensions. Both politeness and formality are negatively correlated with frustration. Hence, more formal you are, less frustration might be detected in the text. While the correlations are negative, no concrete relationship across these dimensions can be stated due to the subjectivity.

- **Analysis of Affect Features:** Three types of affect features used in our model follow different properties. To understand the contribution of each of them, we further study the feature importance of these features. To identify the most predictive features, we report the p–values calculated for the F-scores reported against the F-regression tests for each of the *tone* dimensions. F–test reports the p–values indicating the importance of the regression. As seen in the table 8 PERMA and ANEW

Table 5: MSE for Prediction of Frustration, Formality, and Politeness in a Regression setting. Ridge Regression out performs all other models. The Feature set with Lexical, Syntactic, and Affect features performs best for all dimensions. Values denote the MSE across 10–fold cross validation.

Model	Lex+ Syn	Lex + Syn + Derived	Lex + Syn + Affect	All	ENRON–trained Embeddings	Baseline-Formality[7] (Pavlick and Tetreault, 2016)	Baseline-Politeness[8] (Danescu-Niculescu-Mizil et al., 2013)
Frustration							
Linear Regression	0.02954	0.02823	0.02935	0.02872	0.02653	1.5356e+13	0.0655
Lasso Regression	0.02433	0.02433	0.02433	0.02433	0.02433	0.0245	0.0253
Ridge Regression	**0.02283**	**0.02231**	**0.02157**	**0.02121**	0.0265	0.0249	0.0373
SVR Regression	0.02958	0.02887	0.02633	0.0263	0.02483	–	0.0219
Formality							
Linear Regression	0.0289	0.02847	0.02803	0.02805	0.03542	2.0708e+14	0.0808
Lasso Regression	0.02807	0.02807	0.02807	0.02807	0.03756	**0.0279**	0.0429
Ridge Regression	**0.01817**	**0.01794**	**0.0176**	**0.01745**	0.0354	0.0232	0.0372
SVR Regression	0.02375	0.0242	0.02288	0.02296	0.03247	–	0.0182
Politeness							
Linear Regression	0.02082	0.01934	0.01966	0.0189	0.01922	1.6484e+14	0.0575
Lasso Regression	0.02041	0.02041	0.02041	0.0204	0.02062	0.0202	0.0218
Ridge Regression	**0.01771**	**0.01671**	**0.0161**	**0.01556**	0.01921	0.01561	0.0266
SVR Regression	0.02119	0.02035	0.02007	0.02058	0.01909	–	**0.0130**

Table 6: Accuracy for Frustration prediction when modeled as a 2-class classification problem. The positive class is oversampled to correct for class imbalance. Random forest is the best performing classifier with a precision= 0.88, recall= 0.85, and F1-Score= 0.85. The Affect features contribute more to the accuracy as compared to the derived features. All values are reported for the experimental setup with a 80–20 train-test split with 10 fold cross validation.

Model	Lex + Syn	Lex + Syn + Derived	Lex + Syn + Affect	All	Baseline-Formality	Baseline-Politeness
Logistic Regression	0.62	0.61	0.67	0.66	0.72	**0.72**
SVC	0.66	0.69	0.62	0.64	–	–
Linear SVC	0.56	0.55	0.58	0.57	0.68	0.68
Random Forest	**0.85**	**0.85**	**0.86**	**0.86**	0.73	0.70
Nearest Neighbors	0.64	0.62	0.65	0.62	**0.72**	0.71

Table 7: Pearson's Coefficients for pair–wise affects. Interestingly, the affects are negatively correlated. Being formal may make individuals less frustrated at the cost of politeness!

Affects	Formality	Politeness	Frustration
Formality	1	-0.129	-0.183
Politeness	-0.129	1	-0.252
Frustration	-0.183	-0.129	1

Table 8: p–values for top affect features using a F–Regression Test. Low values show high predictability.

Features	Formality	Politeness	Frustration
Perma-POS-R	2.43e-08	1.22e-22	0.61
Perma-NEG-M	4.31e-13	2.26e-06	2.63e-15
Perma-NEG-A	5.75e-19	0.03	4.09e-14
ANEW-arousal	4.07e-05	0.01	0.08
ANEW-dominance	0.09	5.14e-10	0.17
Emolex Intensity Sadness	0.02	0.25	5.24e-11

features report a very low p–value showing the significance of the corresponding features for regression.

- **Does the *Tone* in text change with topics?**
Figure 4 shows the affect distribution across different topics. These topics are derived based on topic modeling using Latent Dirichlet Allocation followed by KMeans clustering. A given email is tagged with a single topic and the distributions are computed over these disjoint clusters. While the affect values for all topics have a similar range, they follow a different distribution. For topic 2 which denotes content about sports-related conversations.

7 Conclusion

We present a novel approach for Frustration detection in text data. Our approach proves the importance of affect based features for this task and our traditional regression as well as classification models outperform the baselines and the word-

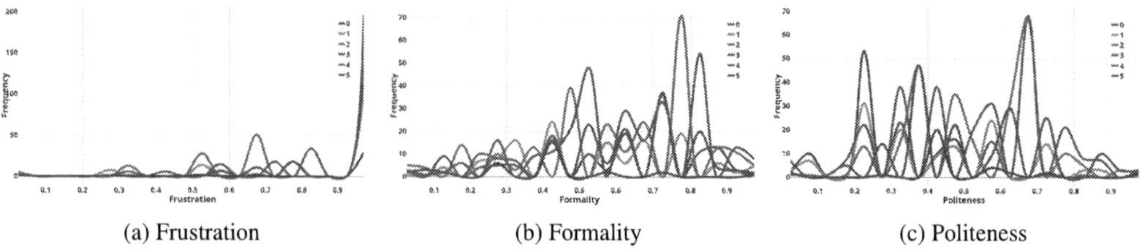

(a) Frustration   (b) Formality   (c) Politeness

Figure 4: Topics and Tone: Graph shows how the different text tone dimensions vary for different topics. Topic 2 which is content about sport has a very different frustration distribution as compared to other topics.

embeddings-based method for frustration prediction. We also show our model does comparable to baselines for formality and politeness prediction. We plan to extend this work towards defining linguistic aspects of frustration in text. We believe, this is the very first attempt at modeling a hard dimension such as frustration.

References

Nesreen Kamel Ahmed and Ryan Anthony Rossi. 2015. Interactive visual graph analytics on the web. In *ICWSM*, pages 566–569.

I Elaine Allen and Christopher A Seaman. 2007. Likert scales and data analyses. *Quality progress*, 40(7):64.

Julian Brooke, Tong Wang, and Graeme Hirst. 2010. Automatic acquisition of lexical formality. In *Proceedings of the 23rd International Conference on Computational Linguistics: Posters*, pages 90–98. Association for Computational Linguistics.

Judee K. Burgoon and Jerold L. Hale. 1984. The fundamental topoi of relational communication. *Communication Monographs*, 51(3):193–214.

Rafael A Calvo and Sidney D'Mello. 2010. Affect detection: An interdisciplinary review of models, methods, and their applications. *IEEE Transactions on affective computing*, 1(1):18–37.

Anurat Chapanond, Mukkai S Krishnamoorthy, and Bülent Yener. 2005. Graph theoretic and spectral analysis of enron email data. *Computational & Mathematical Organization Theory*, 11(3):265–281.

Leon Ciechanowski, Aleksandra Przegalinska, and Krzysztof Wegner. 2018. *The Necessity of New Paradigms in Measuring Human-Chatbot Interaction*. Springer International Publishing, Cham.

William W Cohen. 2009. Enron email dataset.

Cristina Conati and Heather Maclaren. 2009. Empirically building and evaluating a probabilistic model of user affect. *User Modeling and User-Adapted Interaction*, 19(3):267–303.

Rachel Cotterill. 2013. Using stylistic features for social power modeling. *Computación y Sistemas*, 17(2).

Cristian Danescu-Niculescu-Mizil, Moritz Sudhof, Dan Jurafsky, Jure Leskovec, and Christopher Potts. 2013. A computational approach to politeness with application to social factors. *arXiv preprint arXiv:1306.6078*.

Sufal Das and Hemanta Kumar Kalita. 2017. Sentiment analysis for web-based big data: A survey. *International Journal*, 8(5).

Jana Diesner and Craig S Evans. 2015. Little bad concerns: Using sentiment analysis to assess structural balance in communication networks. In *Advances in Social Networks Analysis and Mining (ASONAM), 2015 IEEE/ACM International Conference on*, pages 342–348. IEEE.

Jana Diesner, Terrill L Frantz, and Kathleen M Carley. 2005. Communication networks from the enron email corpus it's always about the people. enron is no different. *Computational & Mathematical Organization Theory*, 11(3):201–228.

Sidney K. D'Mello, Scotty D. Craig, Amy Witherspoon, Bethany McDaniel, and Arthur Graesser. 2008. Automatic detection of learner's affect from conversational cues. *User Modeling and User-Adapted Interaction*, 18(1):45–80.

Paul Ekman. 1992. An argument for basic emotions. *Cognition & Emotion*, 6(3-4):169–200.

Sanaz Jabbari, Ben Allison, David Guthrie, and Louise Guthrie. 2006. Towards the orwellian nightmare: separation of business and personal emails. In *Proceedings of the COLING/ACL on Main conference poster sessions*, pages 407–411. Association for Computational Linguistics.

Rohit J Kate, Xiaoqiang Luo, Siddharth Patwardhan, Martin Franz, Radu Florian, Raymond J Mooney, Salim Roukos, and Chris Welty. 2010. Learning to predict readability using diverse linguistic features.

84

In *Proceedings of the 23rd International Conference on Computational Linguistics*, pages 546–554. Association for Computational Linguistics.

Jasleen Kaur and Jatinderkumar R Saini. 2014. Emotion detection and sentiment analysis in text corpus: a differential study with informal and formal writing styles. *International Journal of Computer Applications*, 101(9).

Shibamouli Lahiri. 2015. SQUINKY! A Corpus of Sentence-level Formality, Informativeness, and Implicature. *CoRR*, abs/1506.02306.

Sisi Liu and Ickjai Lee. 2015. A hybrid sentiment analysis framework for large email data. In *Intelligent Systems and Knowledge Engineering (ISKE), 2015 10th International Conference on*, pages 324–330. IEEE.

Scott W. McQuiggan, Sunyoung Lee, and James C. Lester. 2007. *Early Prediction of Student Frustration*. Springer Berlin Heidelberg, Berlin, Heidelberg.

Albert Mehrabian. 1980. Basic dimensions for a general psychological theory implications for personality, social, environmental, and developmental studies.

Tomas Mikolov, Kai Chen, Greg Corrado, and Jeffrey Dean. 2013. Efficient estimation of word representations in vector space. *arXiv preprint arXiv:1301.3781*.

Christopher A Miller and Jeffrey Rye. 2012. Power and politeness in interactions: Admire-a tool for deriving the former from the latter. In *Social Informatics (SocialInformatics), 2012 International Conference on*, pages 177–184. IEEE.

R Miller and EYA Charles. 2016. A psychological based analysis of marketing email subject lines. In *Advances in ICT for Emerging Regions (ICTer), 2016 Sixteenth International Conference on*, pages 58–65. IEEE.

Saif M Mohammad, Svetlana Kiritchenko, and Xiaodan Zhu. 2013. Nrc-canada: Building the state-of-the-art in sentiment analysis of tweets. *arXiv preprint arXiv:1308.6242*.

Saif M Mohammad and Tony Wenda Yang. 2011. Tracking sentiment in mail: How genders differ on emotional axes. In *Proceedings of the 2nd workshop on computational approaches to subjectivity and sentiment analysis*, pages 70–79. Association for Computational Linguistics.

Myriam D Munezero, Calkin Suero Montero, Erkki Sutinen, and John Pajunen. 2014. Are they different? affect, feeling, emotion, sentiment, and opinion detection in text. *IEEE transactions on affective computing*, 5(2):101–111.

Brandon Oselio, Alex Kulesza, and Alfred O Hero. 2014. Multi-layer graph analysis for dynamic social networks. *IEEE Journal of Selected Topics in Signal Processing*, 8(4):514–523.

Ellie Pavlick and Joel Tetreault. 2016. An empirical analysis of formality in online communication. *Transactions of the Association for Computational Linguistics*, 4:61–74.

Kelly Peterson, Matt Hohensee, and Fei Xia. 2011. Email formality in the workplace: A case study on the enron corpus. In *Proceedings of the Workshop on Languages in Social Media*, pages 86–95. Association for Computational Linguistics.

Vinodkumar Prabhakaran, Huzaifa Neralwala, Owen Rambow, and Mona T Diab. 2012. Annotations for power relations on email threads. In *LREC*, pages 806–811.

Jennifer Sabourin, Bradford Mott, and James C. Lester. 2011. *Modeling Learner Affect with Theoretically Grounded Dynamic Bayesian Networks*. Springer Berlin Heidelberg, Berlin, Heidelberg.

H Andrew Schwartz, Johannes C Eichstaedt, Margaret L Kern, Lukasz Dziurzynski, Stephanie M Ramones, Megha Agrawal, Achal Shah, Michal Kosinski, David Stillwell, Martin EP Seligman, et al. 2013. Personality, gender, and age in the language of social media: The open-vocabulary approach. *PloS one*, 8(9):e73791.

Martin EP Seligman. 2011. Flourish: a visionary new understanding of happiness and well-being. *Policy*, 27(3):60–1.

Martin EP Seligman. 2012. *Flourish: A visionary new understanding of happiness and well-being*. Simon and Schuster.

Jitesh Shetty and Jafar Adibi. 2005. Discovering important nodes through graph entropy the case of enron email database. In *Proceedings of the 3rd international workshop on Link discovery*, pages 74–81. ACM.

Robert J Sigley. 1997. Text categories and where you can stick them: a crude formality index. *International Journal of Corpus Linguistics*, 2(2):199–237.

Lisa M Vizer, Lina Zhou, and Andrew Sears. 2009. Automated stress detection using keystroke and linguistic features: An exploratory study. *International Journal of Human-Computer Studies*, 67(10):870–886.

Hua Wang, Helmut Prendinger, and Takeo Igarashi. 2004. Communicating emotions in online chat using physiological sensors and animated text. In *CHI '04 Extended Abstracts on Human Factors in Computing Systems*, CHI EA '04, pages 1171–1174, New York, NY, USA. ACM.

Amy Beth Warriner, Victor Kuperman, and Marc Brysbaert. 2013. Norms of valence, arousal, and dominance for 13,915 english lemmas. *Behavior Research Methods*, 45(4):1191–1207.

Yingjie Zhou, Kenneth R Fleischmann, and William A Wallace. 2010. Automatic text analysis of values in the enron email dataset: Clustering a social network using the value patterns of actors. In *System Sciences (HICSS), 2010 43rd Hawaii International Conference on*, pages 1–10. IEEE.

Reddit: A Gold Mine for Personality Prediction

Matej Gjurković and **Jan Šnajder**
University of Zagreb, Faculty of Electrical Engineering and Computing
Text Analysis and Knowledge Engineering Lab
Unska 3, 10000 Zagreb, Croatia
`{matej.gjurkovic,jan.snajder}@fer.hr`

Abstract

Automated personality prediction from social media is gaining increasing attention in natural language processing and social sciences communities. However, due to high labeling costs and privacy issues, the few publicly available datasets are of limited size and low topic diversity. We address this problem by introducing a large-scale dataset derived from Reddit, a source so far overlooked for personality prediction. The dataset is labeled with Myers-Briggs Type Indicators (MBTI) and comes with a rich set of features for more than 9k users. We carry out a preliminary feature analysis, revealing marked differences between the MBTI dimensions and poles. Furthermore, we use the dataset to train and evaluate benchmark personality prediction models, achieving macro F1-scores between 67% and 82% on the individual dimensions and 82% accuracy for exact or one-off accurate type prediction. These results are encouraging and comparable with the reliability of standardized tests.

1 Introduction

Personality refers to individual and stable differences in characteristic patterns of thinking, feeling, and behaving (Corr and Matthews, 2009). There has been an increasing interest in automated personality prediction from social media from both the natural language processing and social science communities (Nguyen et al., 2016). In contrast to traditional personality tests – whose use so far has mostly been limited to human resource management, counseling, and clinical psychology – automated personality prediction from social media has a far wider applicability, such as in social media marketing (Matz et al., 2017) and dating web-sites and applications (Finkel et al., 2012).

Most work on personality prediction rests on one of the two widely used personality models: Big Five and MBTI. The Big Five (Goldberg, 1990) is a well-established model which classifies personality traits along five dimensions: extraversion, agreeableness, conscientiousness, neuroticism, and openness. In contrast, the Myers-Briggs Type Indicator model (MBTI) (Myers et al., 1990) recognizes 16 personality types spanned by four dimensions: Introversion/Extraversion (how one gains energy), Sensing/iNtuition (how one processes information), Thinking/Feeling (how one makes decisions), and Judging/Perceiving (how one presents herself or himself to the outside world). Despite some controversy regarding test validity and reliability (Barbuto Jr, 1997), the MBTI model has found numerous applications, especially in the industry[1] and for self-discovery. Although the Big Five and MBTI models are built on different theoretical perspectives, studies have shown their dimensions to be correlated (McCrae and Costa, 1989; Furnham, 1996).

The perennial problem of personality prediction from social media is the lack of labeled datasets. This can be traced back to privacy issues (e.g., on Facebook) and prohibitively high labeling costs. The few existing datasets suffer from other shortcomings related to non-anonymity (which makes the users more reluctant to express their true personality), limited expressivity (e.g., on Twitter), low topic diversity, or a heavy bias toward personality-related topics (e.g., on personality forums). Specifically for MBTI, the only available datasets are the ones derived from Twitter (Verhoeven et al., 2016), essays (Luyckx and Daelemans, 2008), and personality forums.[2] Clearly, the lack of adequate benchmark datasets hinders the development of personality prediction models for social media.

In this paper we aim to address this problem by introducing MBTI9k, a new personality prediction dataset labeled with MBTI types. The dataset is

---

[1] http://www.cpp.com
[2] http://www.kaggle.com/datasnaek/mbti-type

Proceedings of the Second Workshop on Computational Modeling of People's Opinions, Personality, and Emotions in Social Media, pages 87–97
New Orleans, Louisiana, June 6, 2018. ©2018 Association for Computational Linguistics

derived from the popular discussion website Reddit, the sixth largest website in the world and also one with the longest time-on-site.[3] What makes Reddit particularly suitable is that its content is publicly available and that many users provide self-reported MBTI personality types. Furthermore, the comments and posts are anonymous and cover a remarkably diverse range of topics, structured into more than a million discussion groups.[4] Altogether, the MBTI9k dataset derived from Reddit addresses all the abovementioned shortcomings of the existing personality prediction datasets.

We use the MBTI9k dataset to carry out two studies. In the first, we extract a number of linguistic and user activity features and perform a preliminary feature analysis across the MBTI dimensions. Our analysis reveals that there are marked differences in the values of these features for the different poles of each MBTI dimension. In the second study, we frame personality prediction as a supervised machine learning task and evaluate a number of benchmark models, obtaining promising results considerably above the baselines.

In sum, the contributions of our paper are threefold: (1) we introduce a new, large-scale dataset labeled with MBTI types, (2) we extract and analyze a rich set of features from this dataset, and (3) we train and evaluate benchmark models for personality prediction. We make the MBTI9k dataset and the extracted features publicly available in the hope that it will help stimulate further research in personality prediction.

The rest of the paper is structured as follows. The next section briefly reviews related work. Section 3 describes the acquisition of the MBTI9k dataset. In Section 4 we describe and analyze the features, while in Section 5 we evaluate the prediction models and discuss the results. Section 6 concludes the paper and outlines future work.

2 Background and Related Work

Personality and language are closely related – as a matter of fact, the Big Five model emerged from a statistical analysis of the English lexicon (Digman, 1990). Ensuing research in psychology attempted to establish links between personality and language use (Pennebaker and King, 1999), setting the ground for research on automated personality prediction. Most early studies in personality prediction relied on small datasets derived from essays (Argamon et al., 2005; Mairesse et al., 2007), e-mails (Oberlander and Gill, 2006), conversations extracted from electronically activated recorders (Mehl et al., 2001; Mairesse et al., 2007), blogs (Iacobelli et al., 2011), or Twitter (Quercia et al., 2011; Golbeck et al., 2011).

In contrast, MyPersonality (Kosinski et al., 2015) was the first project that made use of a large, user-generated content from social media, with over 7.5 million Facebook user profiles labeled with Big Five types. A subsequent study by Kosinski et al. (2013) on this dataset found the users' digital traces in the form of likes to be a very good predictor of personality. Schwartz et al. (2013) used the MyPersonality database in a first large-scale personality prediction study based on text messages. Over 15.4 million of Facebook statuses collected from 75 thousand volunteers were analyzed using both closed- and open-vocabulary approaches. The study found that the latter yields better results when more data is available, which was later also confirmed on other social media sites, such as Twitter (Arnoux et al., 2017).

The growing interest in personality prediction gave rise to two shared tasks (Celli et al., 2013; Rangel et al., 2015), which relied on benchmark datasets labeled with Big Five types. The overarching conclusion was that the personality prediction is a challenging task because there are no strongly predictive features. However, the results suggested that n-gram based models consistently yield good performance across the different languages.

Presumably due to its controversy, the MBTI model has thus far been less used for personality prediction. This has changed, however, with the work of Plank and Hovy (2015), who made use of the MBTI popularity among general public and collected a dataset of over 1.2 million status updates on Twitter and leveraged users' self-reported personality types (Plank and Hovy, 2015). Soon thereafter, Verhoeven et al. (2016) published a multilingual dataset TwiSty.

Our personality prediction dataset is derived from Reddit. Reddit has previously been used as a source of data for various studies. De Choudhury and De (2014) studied mental health discourse and concluded that Reddit users openly share their experiences and challenges with mental illnesses in their personal and professional lives. Schrading et al. (2015) studied domestic abuse and found that

---

[3]http://www.alexa.com/topsites
[4]http://redditmetrics.com

abuse-related discussion groups have more tight-knit communities, longer posts and comments, and less discourse than non-abusive groups. Wallace et al. (2014) tackled irony detection and concluded that Reddit provides a lot of context, which can help in dealing with the ambiguous cases. Shen and Rudzicz (2017) achieved good results in anxiety classification using the Linguistic Inquiry and Word Count (LIWC) dictionary (Pennebaker et al., 2003), n-grams, and topic modeling. To the best of our knowledge, ours it the first work on using Reddit as a source of data for personality prediction.

3 Dataset

3.1 Description

Discussions on Reddit are structured into user-created discussion groups, the so-called *subreddits*, each focusing on one topic. Each subreddit consists of user posts, which may contain text, links, video, or image content. Users can comment on other users' posts, as well as upvote or downvote them. The posts in each subreddit are ranked by the number of comments, so that the most commented posts appear at the top. Apart from being moderated, many subreddits come with their own discussion ground rules, which generally improve the discussion quality. The database of Reddit posts and comments is available on Google Big Query and covers the period from 2005 till the end of 2017, currently totaling more than 3 billion comments and increasing at the rate of 85 million comments per month.

3.2 Flairs

One distinctive feature of Reddit are the special user descriptors called *flairs*. A flair is an icon or text that appears next to a username. It is specific to each subreddit, and in some subreddits users use flairs to introduce themselves. Specifically, in subreddits devoted to MBTI discussions, such as *reddit.com/r/MBTI* and *reddit.com/r/INTP*, users typically use flairs to report their MBTI types. In addition to the MBTI type, many users also provide information about their age, gender, personality types of their partners, marital status, medical diagnoses (e.g., "*Aspie*", to indicate a person with Asperger's syndrome), other personality theories' types (Enneagram, Socionics), and even stereotypes such as "*Dumb Emotional Sensor*" (meant to indicate the sensing-feeling MBTI types).

A problem with flairs is that they are worded in different, often ambiguous ways. In some cases it may be difficult to determine whether the flair refers to a personality type. For example, "*KentJude*" is not an MBTI type even though it contains the ENTJ acronym, a clue being that it is not written in all caps. In other cases, determining the type requires some inference. For instance, from "*INTP-T (MBTI) INTP (KTS) INTj (Socionics)*" one can infer that the user took the 16personalities test,[5] which maps Big Five's neuroticism to Assertive/Turbulent dimension, and that the user's MBTI type is INTP and not INTj, because INTj is a Socionics type, for which the last letter is written in lowercase. A more contrived example is the flair "*to Infjnity and Beyond...*", meant to indicate the INFJ MBTI type.

3.3 Acquisition

Our idea was to use the self-reported MBTI type from the user's flair as that user's personality type label. We make a sensible assumption that, if a user provides his or her MBTI type in the flair, in most cases this will be because she took at least one personality test. The assumption is born out by our analysis of users' comments, which revealed that most users with self-reported MBTI types report on taking multiple personality tests, and many of them even demonstrate a good knowledge of the MBTI theory.

The acquisition of the dataset aimed for high precision at the expense of recall, in the sense that we prefer to have fewer users with reliable MBTI labels rather than more users with uncertain MBTI labels. The acquisition proceeded in five steps:

1. First, we acquired a list of all users who have any mention of an MBTI type in their flair field, and compiled a list of flairs for all users. Many of the so-obtained flairs were false positives, for the reasons outlined above;

2. We next used regex-based pattern matching to (1) identify the flairs that refer to MBTI types, (2) tag ambiguous flairs, and (3) filter out the remaining flairs;

3. We examined the ambiguous flairs and discarded those we could not resolve (e.g., *XNFJ*, indicating extravert/introvert indefinity). We grouped the remaining flairs by users and checked for consistency of MBTI types (users may change their flairs and may have different

---

[5] http://www.kaggle.com/datasnaek/mbti-type

flairs for different subreddits), removing all users with a non-unique MBTI type;

4. At this point, some MBTI types turned out to be heavily underrepresented (e.g., merely 16 ESFJ and 23 ESTJ users), so we decided to compensate for this by complementing the dataset as follows. For each underrepresented type, we performed a full-text search over MBTI subreddit comments (not the flairs), searching for user's self-declaration of that specific type using a handful of simple but strict patterns (*"I am (an) $\langle type \rangle$"* and variants thereof). We then manually inspected the comments and filtered out the false positives, adding the remaining users to the dataset;

5. Lastly, we acquired all posts and comments of the users shortlisted in steps 3 and 4 above, dating from January 2015 to November 2017.

While the above procedure yields a high-precision labeled dataset, we acknowledge the presence of a selection bias in our dataset. More concretely, our dataset includes only the users who are acquainted with MBTI and who participated in MBTI-related subreddits, who know what a flair is and decided to use it to disclose their MBTI type, and who have written at least one comment. Moreover, additional bias is likely to be introduced by steps 2 and 4 above. The terms "Reddit user" and "Redditor" should be interpreted with these limitations in mind.

The resulting dataset consists of 22,934,193 comments (totaling 583,385,564 words) from 36,676 subreddits posted by 13,631 unique users and 354,996 posts (totaling 921,269 words) from 20,149 subreddits posted by 9,872 unique users. The dataset contains more than eight times more words than used in the aforementioned large-scale research by Schwartz et al. (2013), making it the largest available personality-labeled dataset in terms of the number of words.

3.4   Analysis

Our dataset offers many exciting possibilities for analysis, some of which we hope will be pursued in follow-up work. As a first step, we provide a basic descriptive analysis of the dataset, followed by some more interesting analyses in Section 4 meant to showcase the potential utility of the dataset.

Table 1 shows the distribution of Redditors across MBTI types and across the individual MBTI dimensions. For comparison, the first column

shows the distribution estimated for the US population.[6] The data reveal that Redditors are predominantly of introverted, intuitive, thinking, and perceiving types. Incidentally, this distribution bears similarity to the distribution of gifted adolescents (Sak, 2004), and is also aligned with the data that shows that Reddit visitors are more educated than the average Internet user.[7]

Table 2 offers a different perspective on the data: the number of subreddits broken down by the number of distinct MBTI types of the users that participated in these subreddits. Interestingly, the majority (almost 47%) of subreddits attract users of the same type. Conversely, there are only 534 subreddits (1.45%) in which all 16 types participated; while this is a small fraction of the dataset, we believe it might still be sufficient for a comparative analysis between the types.

Another interesting and important aspect of the dataset is the language used for posts and comments. We ran the langid[8] language identification tool on all comments and posts of each of the user. The results suggest that the majority of users write more than 97% of their comments in English. This is in line with the web traffic data, according to which 76.4% of Reddit visitors come from native English-speaking countries.[7]

We make two versions of the dataset available: (1) a dataset of all comments and posts, each annotated with the MBTI type of the author, and (2) a subset of this dataset, referred to as MBTI9k dataset, which contains the comments of all users who contributed with more than 1000 words. Moreover, to remove the topic bias, we expunged from the MBTI9k dataset all comments from 122 subreddits that revolve around MBTI-related topics (making up 7.1% of all comments) and replaced all explicit mentions of MBTI types (and related terminology, such as cognitive functions (Mascarenas, 2016)) with placeholders. Besides comments, for each user we provide the MBTI type and a set of precomputed features (cf. Section 4). We make both datasets publicly available,[9] and use MBTI9k for the subsequent analyses.

---

[6]https://www.capt.org/products/examples/20025HO.pdf
[7]https://www.alexa.com/siteinfo/reddit.com
[8]https://github.com/saffsd/langid.py
[9]http://takelab.fer.hr/data/mbti

Type	% USA	% comm	% post	% MBTI9k
INTP	3.3	22.3	26.8	25.3
INTJ	2.1	17.2	20.6	20.0
INFJ	1.5	11.2	12.9	11.1
INFP	4.4	11.0	13.3	11.6
ENFP	8.1	6.1	7.4	6.6
ENTP	3.2	6.1	7.4	6.7
ENTJ	1.8	5.3	2.8	3.9
ISTP	5.4	5.2	3.7	4.8
ISTJ	11.6	3.4	1.3	2.4
ENFJ	2.5	3.3	1.1	2.3
ISFJ	13.8	2.4	0.7	1.3
ISFP	8.8	2.3	0.7	1.6
ESTP	4.3	1.2	0.5	0.9
ESFP	8.5	1.1	0.3	0.7
ESTJ	8.7	1.0	0.3	0.5
ESFJ	12.3	0.8	0.2	0.4
Dimension				
Introverted	50.7	75.1	80.0	78.1
Extroverted	49.3	24.9	20.0	21.9
Sensing	73.3	17.4	7.7	12.6
Intuitive	26.7	82.6	93.3	87.4
Thinking	40.2	61.7	63.4	64.4
Feeling	59.8	38.3	36.6	35.6
Judging	54.1	44.6	39.9	41.8
Perceiving	45.9	55.4	61.1	58.2

Table 1: Distributions of MBTI types and dimensions in US general public and on Reddit

# types	# subred.	%	# types	# subred.	%
1	17222	46.96	9	729	1.99
2	5632	15.36	10	640	1.75
3	3105	8.47	11	567	1.55
4	2034	5.55	12	512	1.4
5	1540	4.2	13	443	1.21
6	1217	3.32	14	377	1.03
7	964	2.63	15	362	0.99
8	798	2.18	16	534	1.46

Table 2: Distribution of subreddits by the number of distinct MBTI types of participating users

4 Feature Extraction and Analysis

4.1 Feature Extraction

For each of the 9,111 Reddit users from the MBTI9k dataset we extracted a set of features. These can be divided into two main groups: linguistic features (extracted from user's comments) and user activity features. Next we describe these features in more detail, followed by a preliminary feature analysis.

Linguistic features. The linguistic features include both content- and style-based features. The simplest of them are tf- and tf-idf-weighed character n-grams (lengths 2–3) and word n-grams (lengths 1–3), stemmed with Porter's stemmer. The total number of n-gram features is 11,140. For each user we also compute the type-token ratio, the ratio of comments in English, and the ratio of British English vs. American English words.

We used LIWC (Pennebaker et al., 2015), a widely used NLP tool in personality prediction, to extract 93 features. These range from part-of-speech (e.g., pronouns, articles) to topical preferences (e.g., bodily functions, family) and different psychological categories (e.g., emotions, cognitive processes). Complementary to LIWC, we used a number of psycholinguistic words lists, including perceived happiness, affective norms (e.g., valence, arousal, and dominance), imageability, and sensory experience, described in Preoţiuc-Pietro et al. (2017), as well as two lists of word meaningfulness ratings from the MRC Psycholinguistic Database (Coltheart, 1981). For each user, we calculated the average ratings for every word from these dictionaries, which gave us 26 features, denoted PSYCH.

User activity features. User activity features were extracted from comment and post metadata. The *global* features include the number of comments (all comments and comments on MBTI-related subreddits) and the number of subreddits commented in. The *posts* features include the overall post score (difference between the number of up and down votes), number of posts on "over 18" subreddits, the number of "self posts" (posts linking to other Reddit posts), and the number of gilded posts (posts awarded with money by other users).

Another group of features are topical affinity features. We computed comment counts for the user across subreddits and encoded these as a a a single vector, together with the entropy of the corresponding distribution. In addition, we derive topic distributions from user's comments (1) using LDA models with 50 and 100 topics (2) by manually grouping top-200 subreddits into 35 semantic categories, and encode these as 50-, 100-, and 35-dimensional vectors, respectively.

We speculate that the temporal aspect of one's activities might be relevant for personality type prediction. We therefore include the time intervals between comment timestamps (the mean, median, and maximum delay), as well as daily, weekly, and monthly distributions of comments, encoded as vectors of corresponding lengths.

Feature group	E/I	S/N	T/F	J/P
char_tf	29.03	45.16	35.48	51.61
word_tf	35.48	25.81	12.9	32.26
liwc	19.35	0.0	25.81	9.68
lda100	6.45	0.0	9.68	3.23
psy	3.23	0.0	12.9	0.0
word	3.23	9.68	0.0	0.0
char	0.0	12.9	0.0	0.0
posts	0.0	6.45	0.0	3.23

Table 3: Percentage of each feature group in top-30 relevant features for each dimension

4.2 Feature Analysis

Feature relevance. We estimate the relevance of each feature for each MBTI dimension using a t-test: feature relevance is inversely proportional to the p-value under the null hypothesis of no difference in feature values for the two classes. Table 3 shows the proportion of features from each feature group in the set of top-30 most relevant features for each MBTI dimension. For instance, tf-weighted character n-grams (char_tf) account for about 29% of top-30 most relevant features in the extravert-introvert (E/I) dimension. The main observation is that different features are relevant for different dimensions. Generally, tf-idf-weighted character n-grams are the most relevant features for all dimensions except for E/I, for which tf-idf-weighted word n-grams are most relevant. However, while LIWC, PSYCH, and LDA100 account for 48% of top-30 most relevant features for the T/F dimension, they have no relevance for the S/N dimension. Post features seem to be relevant only for S/N and J/P dimensions.

Table 4 offers a complementary view on feature relevance: it shows the proportion of highly relevant features (p-value < 0.001) from each of the feature groups for each dimension. The global, PSYCH, and LIWC features are used in substantial (>50%) proportions for one or more dimensions. The relevance of PSYCH and LIWC features is not surprising, given that these were tailored to model psycholinguistic processes. They seem most indicative for the T/F dimension and, unlike post features, the least relevant for the S/N dimension.

Temporal features. While day-of-week distribution turned out to be a good predictor for T/F and J/P dimensions, posting time differences are relevant only for S/N dimension. Day-of-week proportion of 100% for J/P basically means that all points in the distribution are indicative for that particular

Feature group	E/I	S/N	T/F	J/P
global	33.33	33.33	100.0	66.67
psy	25.0	41.67	70.83	41.67
liwc	40.86	29.03	62.37	39.78
day_of_week	0.0	0.0	28.57	100.0
word_an_tf	28.22	32.07	38.17	27.3
char_an_tf	19.28	27.06	36.26	21.47
word_an	7.4	19.58	27.28	24.72
char_an	4.45	14.4	30.3	8.82
meaning	0.0	0.0	50.0	0.0
lda100	9.0	12.0	15.0	9.0
posts	5.0	20.0	5.0	10.0
char	0.12	0.88	28.99	0.24
month	0.0	25.0	0.0	0.0
word	0.16	1.23	21.67	1.12
time_diffs	0.0	16.67	0.0	0.0
subcat	0.0	2.86	8.57	0.0
lda50	0.0	6.0	4.0	0.0
hour	0.0	0.0	0.0	4.17
sub	0.04	0.48	0.14	0.0

Table 4: Percentage of highly relevant features (p<0.001) in total number of features per feature group and dimension

dimension. In contrast, the monthly distribution proportion of 25% suggests that only four months in a year are relevant for the S/N dimension. More insight is given by Fig. 1a, which shows the distribution of comments across days of week for the J/P and S/N dimensions. Perceiving types tend to comment more on Tuesdays and Sundays, while judging types comment more on other days. The intuitive types are more active during April and May, while sensing types prefer to comment during January and July.

Word usage. The use of specific words or word classes is known to correlate well with personality traits. Extraversion is characterized by the use of social- and family-related words (Schwartz et al., 2013) and the use of exclamation marks. This is consistent with the most relevant word features for the E/I dimension in our dataset: *Friend, Social, comm_mbti, only, i'm an extrovert, fri, at least, drivers, Affiliation, Exclam, origin, !!* (word classes from LIWC and PSYCH are shown capitalized). The most relevant words for the S/N dimension are also somewhat expected: *Is_self_mean, Is_self_median, –, i, ', is a, my_, it, "a, Avg_img, my, _he, cliché, Sixltr, exist.* By definition, sensing types are more concrete while intuitives are more abstract, which seems to be reflected in the image-ability feature (e.g., *Avg_img*). Intuitives tend to use more rare (*e.g., cliché*), more complex, and longer words (as signaled, e.g., by the *Sixltr* fea-

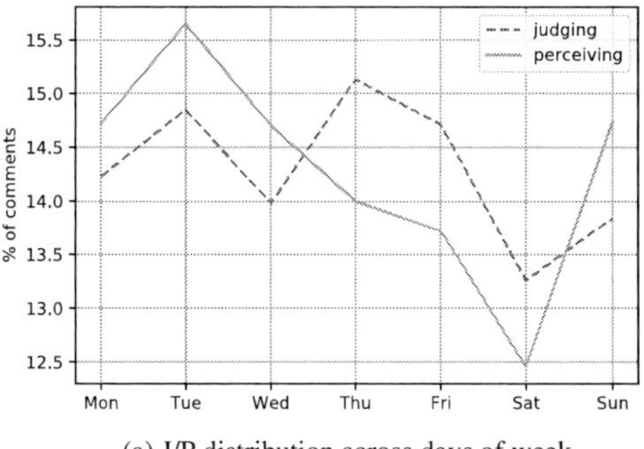

(a) J/P distribution across days of week

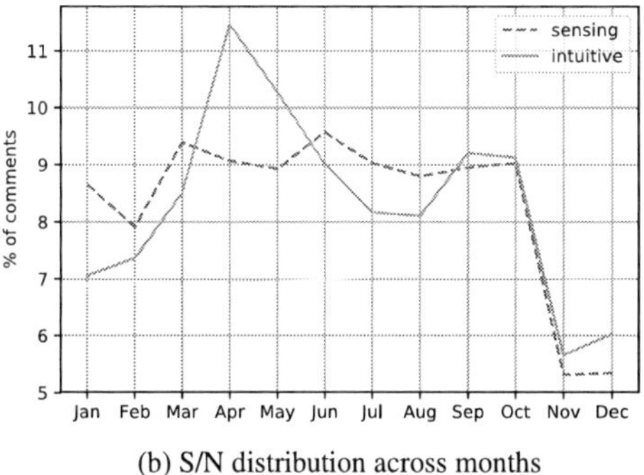

(b) S/N distribution across months

Figure 1: Temporal distribution of comments

ture: words with more than six characters). Sensing types also seem to share posts with content they found outside Reddit more than intuitives (e.g., *Is_self* features). The feelers tend to use more words about love, feelings, and emotions. They also use more social and affectionate words as well as pronouns and exclamations, as evidenced by the most relevant words for the T/F dimension: *love, Feel, Posemo, valence, Emotion, happy, i, polarity, !, i love, Ppron, SOCIAL, Exclaim, Affect, Pronoun, _so, e!. i* The most relevant words for J/P also seem to reflect the common stereotypes, such as that judgers are more plan, work, and family oriented: *Work, husband, Home, help, for, plan, sit, hit, joke, fo.* We leave a more detailed analysis for future work.

5 Personality Prediction

In line with standard practice, we frame the MBTI personality prediction task as four independent binary classification problems, one for each MBTI dimension. In addition, we consider the 16-way multiclass task of predicting the MBTI type, which we accomplish simply by combining together the predictions for the four individual dimensions.

5.1 Experimental Setup

We experiment with three different classifiers: a support vector machine (SVM), ℓ_2-regularized logistic regression (LR), and a three-layer multilayer perceptron (MLP). We use nested stratified cross-validation with five folds in the outer loop and 10 (for LR) or 5 (for SVM) folds in the inner loop; the inner loop is used for model selection with macro F1-score as the evaluation criterion. To investigate the merit of the different features, we (1) train all models with features selected using the t-test and (2) the LR model with each of the feature group separately. Feature selection and standard scaling are applied on training set only, separately for each of the cross-validation folds, and the number of features is also being optimized. Class weighting is used to account for class imbalance. A majority class classifier (MCC) is used as baseline. We use the implementation from Scikit-learn (Pedregosa et al., 2011) for all models.

5.2 Results

Per-dimension prediction. Table 5 shows prediction results for each dimension in terms of the macro F1-score, averaged across the five folds. Although we are using relatively simple models, we achieve surprisingly good results which are well above the baseline. Models using a combination of all features (LR_all and MLP_all) achieve the best results across all dimensions.

Looking into the individual dimensions, the best model for the E/I dimension is MLP_all, but its score is only slightly above the LR word n-gram model. Character n-grams and, to some extent, LIWC and PYSCH were also predictive for the E/I dimension. Models based on topical and user-activity based features did not achieve results above the baseline. Results are similar for the S/N dimension, where MLP_all again outperforms other models, while word-ngram features seem to perform rather well. The overall lowest results are for the T/F dimension, which is consistent with the findings of Capraro and Capraro (2002). Here, n-gram based features perform only slightly better than dictionary-based (LIWC, PSYCH) and topic-based (LDA) features, but overall the differences in model scores are lower. Lastly, for the J/P dimension, the best-performing model is LR_all, well above all models that use a single feature group.

As personality traits are in fact manifested on a continuous scale along each dimension, it makes

Model	Dimensions				Type
	E/I	S/N	T/F	J/P	
LR all	81.6	77.0	**67.2**	**74.8**	40.8
MLP all	**82.8**	**79.2**	64.4	74.0	**41.7**
SVM all	79.6	75.6	64.8	72.6	37.0
LR w_ng	81.0	73.6	66.4	71.8	38.0
LR chr_ng	62.2	64.0	66.4	65.8	26.5
LR liwc	55.0	49.8	65.0	57.4	14.2
LR psych	52.0	48.2	64.0	57.0	12.5
LR lda100	50.0	48.2	62.4	56.2	13.9
LR posts	49.4	53.2	48.0	51.8	9.5
LR subtf	49.6	49.6	50.4	50.2	13.2
MCC	50.04	50.04	50.0	50.02	25.2

Table 5: Macro F1-scores for per-dimension prediction and accuracy of type-level prediction for models with all features, LR models with a single feature group, and the MCC baseline

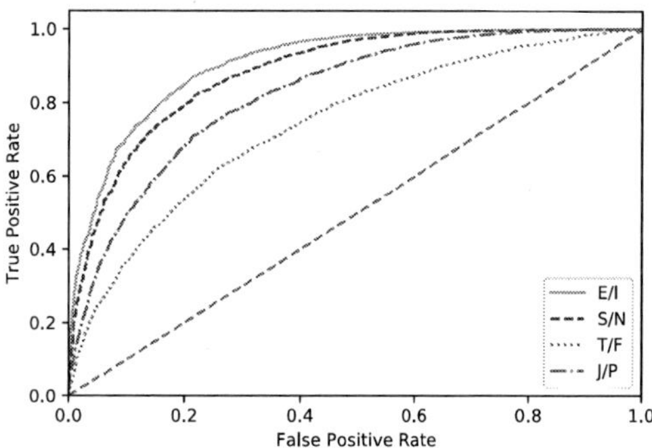

Figure 2: ROC curves for the LR_all model

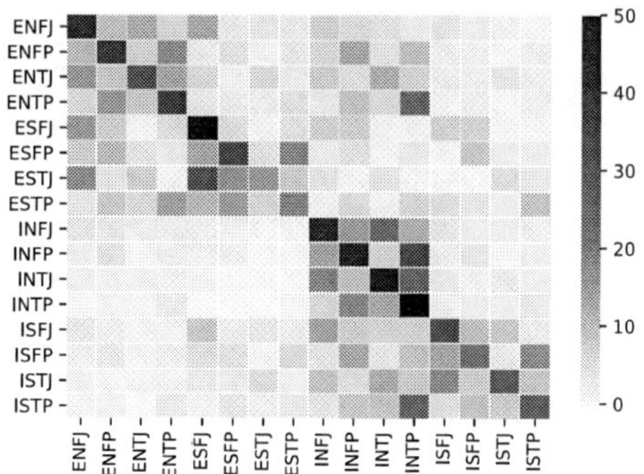

Figure 3: Heatmap of the type prediction confusion matrix

	# mismatches				
	0	1	2	3	4
Count	3757	3715	1384	240	15
%	40.83	40.77	15.61	2.63	0.16

Table 6: The number and percentage of mismatched dimensions between predicted and actual types

sense to evaluate type prediction as a confidence-rated classification task using ROC curves. Results are shown on Figure 2. The ROC curve shows the true positive rate (recall) as a function of the false positive rate (fall-out), both of which increase as the classification threshold increases. For instance, the ROC curve for the T/F dimensions tells us that we can detect about 70% of T cases with a fall-out of about 40%.

Type-level prediction. For MBTI type prediction, we concatenated the outputs of the binary models for each individual dimension. Prediction accuracy is shown in the last column of Table 5. The best result is achieved by the MLP_all model, with an accuracy of 42%, while the baseline performs at only 25%. Further insight can be gleaned from Table 6, which shows the breakdown of incorrect predictions for the LR_all model by the number of mismatched dimensions. In 82% of cases, the model predicts either the correct type or errs on one dimension, while in more than 97% of cases the model predicts two or more dimensions correctly. The likely mismatches are shown on Fig. 3, showing a heatmap of the type prediction confusion matrix for the LR_all model. The confusion matrix shows that types which are similar in the MBTI theory tend to get grouped together. For example, introverted intuitives tend to be similar and even for people it is often difficult to distinguish between INTP and INTJ. At the same time, INTJ is more similar to INFJ, while INTP is more similar to INFP. The confusion matrix shows that the model was able to capture these nuances.

6 Conclusion

We described MBTI9k, a new, large-scale dataset for personality detection acquired from Reddit. The dataset addresses the shortcomings of the existing datasets, primarily those of user non-anonymity and low topic diversity, and comes with MBTI types and precomputed sets of features for more than 9000 Reddit users.

We carried out two studies on the MBTI9k. In the first, we extracted and analyzed a number of linguistic and user-activity features, demonstrating that there are marked differences in feature values between the different MBTI poles and dimensions. We then used these features to train several benchmark models for personality prediction. The models scored considerably higher than the baseline, ranging from 67% macro F1-score for the T/F dimension to 82% for the S/N dimension. Type-level prediction reaches accuracy of 41% for exact match and 82% for exact or one-off match, which is comparable to the reliability of standardized tests (Lawrence and Martin, 2001). We also found that models using only word n-gram features also perform remarkably well, presumably due to the large size of the dataset.

We envision several directions for future work. First, the dataset could be improved in a number of ways. It could be enlarged with older posts dating back to year 2005, or by increasing the number of users by searching for MBTI declarations in comment texts rather than only the flairs. The same technique could be used to amended the dataset with self-reported demographic data, including age, gender, and location.

On the modeling side, taking into account the success of word-based features and the size of the dataset, using deep learning models for personality might be a reasonable next step. The T/F dimension might, however, require more sophisticated features, judging by the modest performance of the benchmark models on that particular dimension.

In perspective, we believe that Reddit has a lot to offer as a source of data for personality prediction and – more generally – author profiling. A large number of users and comments, highly diverse subcommunities, and the numerous interactions between users are a true gold mine for researchers from both natural language processing and social science communities.

References

Shlomo Argamon, Sushant Dhawle, Moshe Koppel, and James Pennebaker. 2005. Lexical predictors of personality type. In *Proceedings of the Joint Annual Meeting of the Interface and the Classification Society*. pages 1–16.

Pierre-Hadrien Arnoux, Anbang Xu, Neil Boyette, Jalal Mahmud, Rama Akkiraju, and Vibha Sinha. 2017. 25 tweets to know you: A new model to predict personality with social media. In *Proceedings of the Eleventh International AAAI Conference on Web and Social Media*. pages 472–475.

John E. Barbuto Jr. 1997. A critique of the Myers-Briggs Type Indicator and its operationalization of Carl Jung's psychological types. *Psychological Reports* 80(2):611–625.

Robert M. Capraro and Mary Margaret Capraro. 2002. Myers-Briggs type indicator score reliability across: Studies a meta-analytic reliability generalization study. *Educational and Psychological Measurement* 62(4):590–602.

Fabio Celli, Fabio Pianesi, David Stillwell, and Michal Kosinski. 2013. Workshop on computational personality recognition: Shared task. In *Proceedings of the AAAI Workshop on Computational Personality Recognition*. pages 2–5.

Max Coltheart. 1981. The MRC psycholinguistic database. *The Quarterly Journal of Experimental Psychology Section A* 33(4):497–505.

Philip J. Corr and Gerald Matthews. 2009. *The Cambridge handbook of personality psychology*. Cambridge University Press, Cambridge.

Munmun De Choudhury and Sushovan De. 2014. Mental health discourse on Reddit: Self-disclosure, social support, and anonymity. In *Eighth International AAAI Conference on Weblogs and Social Media*. pages 71–80.

John M. Digman. 1990. Personality structure: Emergence of the five-factor model. *Annual review of psychology* 41(1):417–440.

Eli J. Finkel, Paul W. Eastwick, Benjamin R. Karney, Harry T. Reis, and Susan Sprecher. 2012. Online dating: A critical analysis from the perspective of psychological science. *Psychological Science in the Public Interest* 13(1):3–66.

Adrian Furnham. 1996. The big five versus the big four: the relationship between the Myers-Briggs Type Indicator (MBTI) and NEO-PI five factor model of personality. *Personality and Individual Differences* 21(2):303–307.

Jennifer Golbeck, Cristina Robles, Michon Edmondson, and Karen Turner. 2011. Predicting personality from Twitter. In *Proceedings of 2011 IEEE International Conference on Privacy, Security, Risk and Trust (PASSAT) and IEEE International Conference on Social Computing (SocialCom)*. pages 149–156.

Lewis R. Goldberg. 1990. An alternative "description of personality": The big-five factor structure. *Journal of personality and social psychology* 59(6):1216.

Francisco Iacobelli, Alastair J. Gill, Scott Nowson, and Jon Oberlander. 2011. Large scale personality classification of bloggers. In *Affective computing and intelligent interaction*, Springer, pages 568–577.

Michal Kosinski, Sandra C. Matz, Samuel D. Gosling, Vesselin Popov, and David Stillwell. 2015. Facebook as a research tool for the social sciences: Opportunities, challenges, ethical considerations, and practical guidelines. *American Psychologist* 70(6):543.

Michal Kosinski, David Stillwell, and Thore Graepel. 2013. Private traits and attributes are predictable from digital records of human behavior. *Proceedings of the National Academy of Sciences* 110(15):5802–5805. https://doi.org/10.1073/pnas.1218772110.

Gordon Lawrence and Charles R. Martin. 2001. *Building people, building programs: A practitioner's guide for introducing the MBTI to individuals and organizations.* Center for Applications of Psychological Type.

Kim Luyckx and Walter Daelemans. 2008. Personae: A corpus for author and personality prediction from text. In *Proceedings of the Sixth International Conference on Language Resources and Evaluation (LREC'08).* pages 2981–2987.

François Mairesse, Marilyn A. Walker, Matthias R. Mehl, and Roger K. Moore. 2007. Using linguistic cues for the automatic recognition of personality in conversation and text. *Journal of artificial intelligence research* 30:457–500.

David Mascarenas. 2016. A Jungian based framework for artificial personality synthesis. In *Proceedings of the Fourth Workshop on Emotions and Personality in Personalized Systems (EMPIRE).* pages 48–54.

S. C. Matz, M. Kosinski, G. Nave, and D. J. Stillwell. 2017. Psychological targeting as an effective approach to digital mass persuasion. *Proceedings of the National Academy of Sciences* 114(48):12714–12719. https://doi.org/10.1073/pnas.1710966114.

Robert R. McCrae and Paul T. Costa. 1989. Reinterpreting the Myers-Briggs type indicator from the perspective of the five-factor model of personality. *Journal of personality* 57(1):17–40.

Matthias R. Mehl, James W. Pennebaker, D. Michael Crow, James Dabbs, and John H. Price. 2001. The electronically activated recorder (EAR): A device for sampling naturalistic daily activities and conversations. *Behavior Research Methods, Instruments, & Computers* 33(4):517–523.

Isabel Briggs Myers, Mary H. McCaulley, and Allen L. Hammer. 1990. *Introduction to Type: A description of the theory and applications of the Myers-Briggs type indicator.* Consulting Psychologists Press.

Dong Nguyen, A. Seza Doğruöz, Carolyn P. Rosé, and Franciska de Jong. 2016. Computational sociolinguistics: A survey. *Computational Linguistics* 42(3):537–593.

Jon Oberlander and Alastair J. Gill. 2006. Language with character: A stratified corpus comparison of individual differences in e-mail communication. *Discourse Processes* 42(3):239–270.

F. Pedregosa, G. Varoquaux, A. Gramfort, V. Michel, B. Thirion, O. Grisel, M. Blondel, P. Prettenhofer, R. Weiss, V. Dubourg, J. Vanderplas, A. Passos, D. Cournapeau, M. Brucher, M. Perrot, and E. Duchesnay. 2011. Scikit-learn: Machine learning in Python. *Journal of Machine Learning Research* 12:2825–2830.

James W. Pennebaker, Ryan L. Boyd, Kayla Jordan, and Kate Blackburn. 2015. The development and psychometric properties of LIWC2015. Technical report.

James W. Pennebaker and Laura A. King. 1999. Linguistic styles: Language use as an individual difference. *Journal of personality and social psychology* 77(6):1296.

James W. Pennebaker, Matthias R. Mehl, and Kate G. Niederhoffer. 2003. Psychological aspects of natural language use: Our words, our selves. *Annual review of psychology* 54(1):547–577.

Barbara Plank and Dirk Hovy. 2015. Personality traits on Twitter –or– how to get 1,500 personality tests in a week. In *Proceedings of the 6th Workshop on Computational Approaches to Subjectivity, Sentiment and Social Media Analysis (WASSA 2015).* pages 92–98. http://www.aclweb.org/anthology/W15-2913.

Daniel Preoțiuc-Pietro, Jordan Carpenter, and Lyle Ungar. 2017. Personality driven differences in paraphrase preference. In *Proceedings of the Second Workshop on NLP and Computational Social Science.* Association for Computational Linguistics, pages 17–26. https://doi.org/http://dx.doi.org/10.18653/v1/W17-2903.

Daniele Quercia, Michal Kosinski, David Stillwell, and Jon Crowcroft. 2011. Our Twitter profiles, our selves: Predicting personality with Twitter. In *Proceedings of 2011 IEEE International Conference on Privacy, Security, Risk and Trust (PASSAT) and IEEE International Conference on Social Computing (SocialCom).* pages 180–185.

Francisco Rangel, Paolo Rosso, Martin Potthast, Benno Stein, and Walter Daelemans. 2015. Overview of the 3rd author profiling task at PAN 2015. In *CLEF 2015 labs and workshops, notebook papers, CEUR Workshop Proceedings.* volume 1391.

Ugur Sak. 2004. A synthesis of research on psychological types of gifted adolescents. *Journal of Secondary Gifted Education* 15(2):70–79.

Nicolas Schrading, Cecilia Ovesdotter Alm, Ray Ptucha, and Christopher Homan. 2015. An analysis of domestic abuse discourse on Reddit. In *Proceedings of the 2015 Conference on Empirical Methods in Natural Language Processing.* pages 2577–2583. https://doi.org/10.18653/v1/D15-1309.

Andrew H. Schwartz, Johannes C. Eichstaedt, Margaret L. Kern, Lukasz Dziurzynski, Stephanie M. Ramones, Megha Agrawal, Achal Shah, Michal Kosinski, David Stillwell, Martin E.P. Seligman, et al. 2013. Personality, gender, and age in the language of social media: The open-vocabulary approach. *PloS one* 8(9):e73791. https://doi.org/10.1371/journal.pone.0073791.

Judy Hanwen Shen and Frank Rudzicz. 2017. Detecting anxiety through Reddit. In *Proceedings of the Fourth Workshop on Computational Linguistics and Clinical Psychology – From Linguistic Signal to Clinical Reality*. Association for Computational Linguistics, pages 58–65. http://aclweb.org/anthology/W17-3107.

Ben Verhoeven, Walter Daelemans, and Barbara Plank. 2016. TwiSty: A multilingual Twitter stylometry corpus for gender and personality profiling. In *Proceedings of the Tenth International Conference on Language Resources and Evaluation (LREC 2016)*. pages 1632–1637.

Byron C. Wallace, Laura Kertz, and Eugene Charniak. 2014. Humans require context to infer ironic intent (so computers probably do, too). In *Proceedings of the 52nd Annual Meeting of the Association for Computational Linguistics (Short Papers)*. pages 512–516. http://www.aclweb.org/anthology/P14-2084.

Predicting Authorship and Author Traits from Keystroke Dynamics

Barbara Plank

IT University of Copenhagen
Department of Computer Science
Rued Langgaards Vej 7, 2300 Copenhagen S, Denmark
`bapl@itu.dk`

Abstract

Written text transmits a good deal of non-verbal information related to the author's identity and social factors, such as age, gender and personality. However, it is less known to what extent *behavioral biometric traces* transmit such information. We use typist data to study the predictiveness of authorship, and present first experiments on predicting both age and gender from keystroke dynamics. Our results show that the model based on keystroke features leads to significantly higher accuracies for authorship than the text-based system, while being two orders of magnitude smaller. For user attribute prediction, the best approach is to combine the two, suggesting that extra-linguistic factors are disclosed to a larger degree in written text, while author identity is better transmitted in typing behavior.

1 Introduction

Language is a social phenomenon (Nguyen et al., 2015). Whenever we speak or write we transmit a good deal of additional non-verbal information that is related to identity and social factors of an author. Early work in authorship analysis has typically been concerned with finding the author of a text, i.e., *authorship attribution* (Mosteller and Wallace, 1964; Stamatatos, 2009). In recent years, there has been a surge of interest towards the social dimension of language. Studies are interested in linking social factors with linguistic features, e.g., (Eisenstein et al., 2011; Bamman et al., 2014), studying data biases (Hovy and Søgaard, 2015) or building actual attribute prediction models from linguistic features (i.e., *author profiling*). Modeling author traits can further help to improve prediction of related attributes (Liu et al., 2016; Benton et al., 2017), help debiasing models (Hovy, 2015; Zhang et al., 2018) or can be used for a wide range of applications like customer sup-

port, healthcare and personalized machine translation (Mirkin et al., 2015; Rabinovich et al., 2017). Factors studied so far include gender, age, personality or income, to name but a few (Mairesse and Walker, 2006; Luyckx and Daelemans, 2008; Rao et al., 2010; Rosenthal and McKeown, 2011; Nguyen et al., 2011; Volkova et al., 2013; Flekova et al., 2016b; Verhoeven et al., 2016; van Dalen et al., 2017; Ljubešić et al., 2017; Emmery et al., 2017; van der Goot et al., 2018).

A key question in authorship analysis and profiling is what sorts of *evidence* might bear on determining authorship (Nerbonne, 2007) (or traits). What all prior work has in common is that it *almost exclusively focused on the written text itself.* As people read or write texts, they unconsciously produce cognitive by-product, such as gaze patterns or typist behavior. This evokes and motivates our research question: to what extent is behavioral data beyond the text predictive of authorship and author traits? In this paper we focus on *keystroke dynamics.* They concern a user's typing pattern. Keystroke logs have the distinct advantage over other cognitive modalities like brain scans or gaze, that keystroke logs are more readily available; they do not rely on special equipment beyond a keyboard. While keystrokes are known to be informative for author verification (cf. Section 5), it is less clear to what extent keystrokes are predictive of authorship, and even more so, of author traits.

Contributions a) We study the effect of keystrokes to identify authorship in two corpora of varying size. b) We investigate the predictive power of typist data for age and gender prediction. c) We compare behavioral measures to traditional stylometric features.

Proceedings of the Second Workshop on Computational Modeling of People's Opinions, Personality, and Emotions in Social Media, pages 98–104
New Orleans, Louisiana, June 6, 2018. ©2018 Association for Computational Linguistics

2 Keystroke dynamics

Keystroke logs are recordings of a user's typing dynamics. When a person types on a keyboard, the latencies between successive keystrokes and their duration reflect the typing behavior of a person. For example, Figure 2 shows the keystroke hold times (average over single letters) of two users from our dataset. In its raw form, keystroke logs contain information on which key was pressed for how long (key, time press, time release). Research on keystroke dynamics typically consider timing measures derived from *time press* and *time release* events between keystrokes, such as key hold times or interkey durations (see Figure 1).

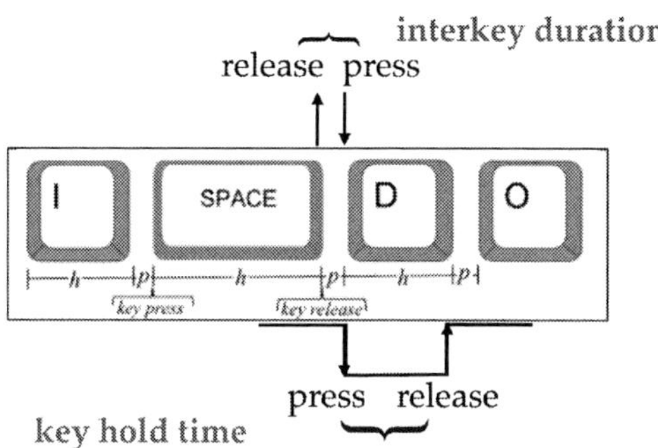

Figure 1: Keystroke logs illustrated: p are pauses between keystrokes. Figure adapted from (Goodkind and Rosenberg, 2015).

Only very recently this source has been explored as information in natural language processing, for example, to aid shallow syntactic parsing (Plank, 2016) or deception detection (Banerjee et al., 2014) (Section 5). Keystroke logs have been used in computer security for user verification, however, combining keystroke biometrics with traditional stylometry metrics has not been proven successful (Stewart et al., 2011). The authors focused on a single task and dataset only. In contrast, in this paper we examine to what extent keystroke dynamics are informative for authorship attribution *and* author profiling.

3 Experiments

Given a dataset with keystroke logs, we run two sets of experiments: a) authorship attribution, i.e., to determine *who* wrote a given piece of text; and b) authorship profiling, i.e., to determine extra-linguistic user traits, in particular age and gender.

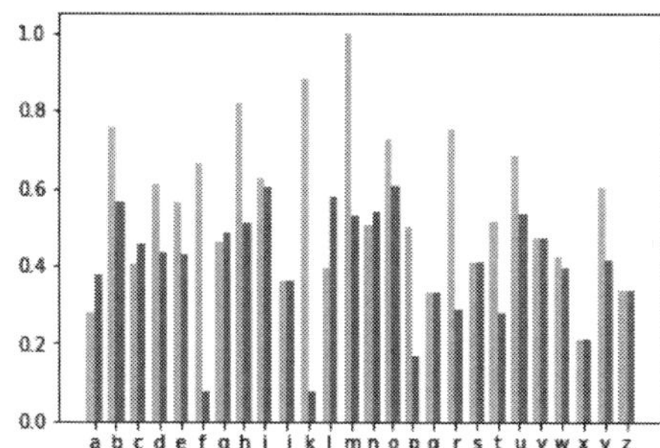

Figure 2: Keystroke basic feature set: normalized mean key hold time for two example users.

Datasets The two keystroke datasets differ in the amount of users and available meta-data. The first, STEWART, stems from students taking a test on spreadsheet modeling (Stewart et al., 2011). This dataset is not distributed with further meta-data, hence it is used for authorship attribution only. The second dataset, VILLANI (Tappert et al., 2009), is larger (144 participants) and contains demographic meta-data. Keystrokes were recorded for two tasks: free text production and a copy task (fixed text snippet). As we are interested in author attribution/profiling, we consider only the former.

Pre-processing and Features First, we remove users with fewer than 5 typing sessions, sessions shorter than 5 words, users without demographics and users that only participated in the copy task (for VILLANI). We also removed two spammers (random skribble). This resulted in a dataset with 34 and 121 users with an average of 99 and 125 tokens per session for STEWART and VILLANI, respectively. The final gender/age distribution is not balanced: 53 female/68 male users, and 56 users above/65 user below thirty. For all keystrokes, the type of key was derived: letters, numbers, punctuation etc., ignoring control keys (FN etc).

Second, we derive 218 biometric features following (Stewart et al., 2011; Tappert et al., 2010). These biometric features include duration features (mean and standard deviation) and are grouped into: i) basic keystroke features, i.e., key hold time (key press and release time) features of the 26 letters from the English alphabet (cf. Figure 2 for an illustration); and ii) extended features: key hold times over groups of keys (like digits, punctuation etc) and transition (inter-key duration) features between successive keystrokes, e.g., between letters and non-letters, or individual letters and

STEWART (34 users)	#FEATURES	F1-SCORE
Baseline (random)	–	0.4
Text	54k	50.2
Keystrokes (basic)	52	81.0
Keystrokes (extended)	218	**90.2**
Keystrokes (ext.) + Text	55k	70.2
Keystrokes (ext.) + Embeds	413	**91.4**
VILLANI (121 users)	#FEATURES	F1-SCORE
Text	46k	67.1
Keystrokes (basic)	52	2.5
Keystrokes (ext.)	218	**85.9**
Keystrokes (ext.) + Text	46k	71.1
Keystrokes (ext.) + Embeds	413	**88.1**

Table 1: Results for authorship attribution (34 users), comparison of features (text vs keystrokes), and combined models. Best result in boldface.

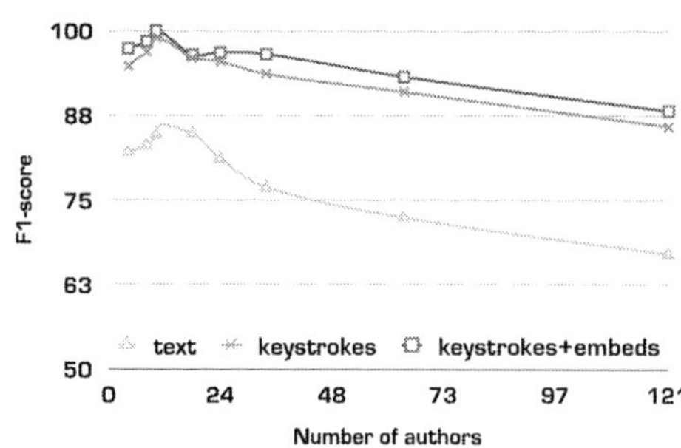

Figure 3: Results for author attribution on VILLANI for increasing number of authors. Keystroke features clearly outperform textual features.

groups of such. For these feature measurements, outlier removal and feature standardization is applied (Stewart et al., 2011).

Finally, we extract the final text from the keystroke logging data (employing revisions/backspaces were appropriate). As features we employ those used by the top performing system of the latest PAN author profiling competition (Basile et al., 2017), i.e., word n-grams and character n-grams. N-gram size is tuned on one fold on STEWART, resulting in word unigrams and character 2-3 grams. We also use word embedding features using Polyglot embeddings of 64 dimensions (Al-Rfou et al., 2013), representing text snippets as average embeddings (CBOW) over all tokens (Collobert et al., 2011), enriched with max, sum, standard deviation and embeddings coverage rate. These features worked best on dev.

Setup We use a Support Vector Machine (SVM) (Pedregosa et al., 2011) with linear kernel and ℓ_2 regularization, similar to the state-of-the-art in author profiling (Flekova et al., 2016a; Basile et al., 2017). We consider a single session of a user as a data instance, and run experiments using 5-fold cross-validation. For author profiling we ensure that all instances of an author end up in the same fold, to not confound profiling with authorship. We report results using weighted F1-score. To ease replicability, all code is released at: https://github.com/bplank/aat

4   Results

The results of training a classifier to predict the identity of an author are given in Table 1 and Fig-ure 3. The random baseline accuracy is low (0.4% F1). Biometric behavioral features work incredibly well, reaching a performance in the 80-90ies. Already the basic feature set of 52 letter duration features clearly outperforms the stylistic features, reaching 81% F1-score. In contrast, stylometric features from the text alone reach an F1 of only 50%. Note that for the dataset with more users (VILLANI, Figure 3), results for authorship are actually higher, which may be explained by the fact that the smaller dataset is more controlled by topic (exam questions). Figure 3 shows that also on the larger dataset keystroke features outperform the text-based features (word and character n-grams) for authorship, even in setups with few users. These are remarkable results. The behavioral models employ a considerably smaller feature space (cf. column 2 in Table 1). Adding stylometric features improves performance over keystrokes, but only for the embeddings setup, which results in the best setup.

The results for author profiling are given in Table 2. Baseline results (majority baseline) are higher; this task is easier. The gap between stylometric and behavioral features is smaller, but the same trend holds: biometric behavioral features are predictive of gender. To a certain extent this also holds for age (albeit to a lesser extent). Interestingly, combining biometrics with traditional token-based features consistently proves the most effective for author profiling, albeit the best way differs per trait.

Our results suggest that author identity is highly captured in keystrokes alone, while the textual signal provides complementary evidence that together proves the most effective for predicting age and gender of an author.

	GENDER	AGE	#FEATS
Baseline	33.33	38.06	–
Text	61.34	72.59	80k
Keystrokes (basic)	44.63	37.61	52
Keystrokes (ext.)	63.29	60.58	218
KS + text	60.92	**73.25**	80k
KS + embeds	**63.50**	67.12	413

Table 2: Gender and age prediction results, F1-score (age: above/below 30).

5 Related Work

Authorship attribution has a long tradition dating back to early works in the 19th century. The most influential work on authorship attribution goes back to Mosteller and Wallace (1964). For a long time approaches to authorship attribution focused on distributions of *function words*, high-frequency words that are presumably not consciously manipulated by the author (Nerbonne, 2007; Pennebaker, 2011). Recent work also includes authorship studies on microblog texts (Schwartz et al., 2013). An recent survey is Stamatatos (2009). We here study another source of information that is presumably not consciously manipulated, keystroke dynamics.

A major scientific interest in keystroke dynamics arose in writing research, where it has developed into a promising non-intrusive method for studying cognitive processes involved in writing (Sullivan et al., 2006; Nottbusch et al., 2007; Wengelin, 2006; Van Waes et al., 2009; Baaijen et al., 2012). In these studies time measurements—pauses, bursts and revisions—are considered traces of the recursive nature of the writing process. *Bursts* are defined as consecutive chunks of text produced and defined by a 2000ms time of inactivity (Wengelin, 2006). In fact, most prior work that uses keystroke logs focuses on experimental research. For example, Hanoulle et al. (2015) study whether a bilingual glossary reduces the working time of professional translators. They consider pause durations before terms extracted from keystroke logs and find that a bilingual glossary reduces the translators' workload. An analysis of users' typing behavior was studied by Baba and Suzuki (2012) to measure the impact of spelling mistakes. Goodkind and Rosenberg (2015) investigate pre-word pauses and their re-

lation to multi-word expressions. They found that within MWE pauses vary depending on the cognitive task. Banerjee et al. (2014) were the first to use keystroke patterns for deception detection.

Keystrokes were successfully used for author verification in computer security research (Stewart et al., 2011; Monaco et al., 2013; Locklear et al., 2014), as they are known to be idiosyncratic (Leggett and Williams, 1988). Our results show that keystroke biometrics are far superior over stylometry-based features in authorship attribution, and are predictive of author traits.

The study most related to ours (Stewart et al., 2011) used features from both keystrokes and linguistic stylometry for user verification in a k-nearest neighbor setup. Their study differs from ours in three aspects. First, they use a more elaborate set of stylometric features (like number of words of a certain length, and readability measures). Second, they target user authentication, thus their setup is a binary classification task (authenticated vs not-authenticated), while we here focus on a multi-class classification setup, which is a considerably more difficult task. Third, they use only a single dataset (STEWART), while we here include results on a second and larger dataset (n=121 authors). To the best of our knowledge, prior work on predicting demographics from typing behavior is typically limited to a single variable (Tsimperidis et al., 2015), except (Brizan et al., 2015), whose data is not available. Our study differs from theirs by studying age, and the focus on complementing textual with behavioral data.

Disclaimer While modeling user demographics can be seen as one step towards addressing biases in NLP it is important to be aware of potential negative side effects, both from the modeling side through potential exclusion or dual use (Hovy and Spruit, 2016), as well as the data side, when dealing with privacy sensitive data (cognitive behavioral data) or labels (e.g., mental health).

6 Conclusions

We have shown that behavioral biometrics contain highly predictive information for both authorship and author profiling. For authorship attribution, behavioral keystroke metrics significantly outperform traditional text-based features (words and character unigrams), while using a feature set which is orders of magnitude smaller (218 vs several thousands of features). In addition, we show that keystroke dynamics are also predictive for author traits (gender and age). Interestingly, for the latter task, it is most beneficial to *combine* behavioral keystroke data with traditional text-based features, suggesting that user *traits* are disclosed to a larger degree in written text while *identity* is better disclosed in typing behavior.

Acknowledgments

I would like to thank the anonymous reviewers for their valuable feedback. This research is supported by NVIDIA corporation.

References

Rami Al-Rfou, Bryan Perozzi, and Steven Skiena. 2013. *Proceedings of the Seventeenth Conference on Computational Natural Language Learning*, chapter Polyglot: Distributed Word Representations for Multilingual NLP. Association for Computational Linguistics.

Veerle M Baaijen, David Galbraith, and Kees de Glopper. 2012. Keystroke analysis: Reflections on procedures and measures. *Written Communication*.

Yukino Baba and Hisami Suzuki. 2012. How are spelling errors generated and corrected? a study of corrected and uncorrected spelling errors using keystroke logs. In *Proceedings of the 50th Annual Meeting of the Association for Computational Linguistics (Volume 2: Short Papers)*, pages 373–377. Association for Computational Linguistics.

David Bamman, Jacob Eisenstein, and Tyler Schnoebelen. 2014. Gender identity and lexical variation in social media. *Journal of Sociolinguistics*, 18(2):135–160.

Ritwik Banerjee, Song Feng, Jun Seok Kang, and Yejin Choi. 2014. Keystroke patterns as prosody in digital writings: A case study with deceptive reviews and essays. In *Proceedings of the 2014 Conference on Empirical Methods in Natural Language Processing (EMNLP)*, pages 1469–1473, Doha, Qatar. Association for Computational Linguistics.

Angelo Basile, Gareth Dwyer, Maria Medvedeva, Josine Rawee, Hessel Haagsma, and Malvina Nissim. 2017. N-gram: New groningen author-profiling model. In *Proceedings of the CLEF 2017 Evaluation Labs and Workshop – Working Notes Papers, 11-14 September, Dublin, Ireland (Sept. 2017)*.

Adrian Benton, Margaret Mitchell, and Dirk Hovy. 2017. Multi-task learning for mental health using social media text. In *Proceedings of European Chapter of Association for Computational Linguistics*. Association for Computational Linguistics.

David Guy Brizan, Adam Goodkind, Patrick Koch, Kiran Balagani, Vir V Phoha, and Andrew Rosenberg. 2015. Utilizing linguistically enhanced keystroke dynamics to predict typist cognition and demographics. *International Journal of Human-Computer Studies*, 82:57–68.

Ronan Collobert, Jason Weston, Léon Bottou, Michael Karlen, Koray Kavukcuoglu, and Pavel Kuksa. 2011. Natural language processing (almost) from scratch. *Journal of Machine Learning Research*, 12(Aug):2493–2537.

Reinder Gerard van Dalen, Léon Redmar Melein, and Barbara Plank. 2017. Profiling dutch authors on twitter: Discovering political preference and income level. *Computational Linguistics in the Netherlands Journal*, 7:79–92.

Jacob Eisenstein, Noah A Smith, and Eric P Xing. 2011. Discovering sociolinguistic associations with structured sparsity. In *Proceedings of the 49th Annual Meeting of the Association for Computational Linguistics: Human Language Technologies-Volume 1*, pages 1365–1374. Association for Computational Linguistics.

Chris Emmery, Grzegorz Chrupała, and Walter Daelemans. 2017. Simple queries as distant labels for predicting gender on twitter. In *Proceedings of the 3rd Workshop on Noisy User-generated Text*, pages 50–55, Copenhagen, Denmark. Association for Computational Linguistics.

Lucie Flekova, Jordan Carpenter, Salvatore Giorgi, Lyle Ungar, and Daniel Preoţiuc-Pietro. 2016a. Analyzing biases in human perception of user age and gender from text. In *Proceedings of the 54th Annual Meeting of the Association for Computational Linguistics (Volume 1: Long Papers)*, pages 843–854, Berlin, Germany. Association for Computational Linguistics.

Lucie Flekova, Daniel Preoţiuc-Pietro, and Lyle Ungar. 2016b. Exploring stylistic variation with age and income on twitter. In *Proceedings of the 54th Annual Meeting of the Association for Computational Linguistics (Volume 2: Short Papers)*, pages 313–319. Association for Computational Linguistics.

Adam Goodkind and Andrew Rosenberg. 2015. Muddying the multiword expression waters: How cognitive demand affects multiword expression production. In *Proceedings of the 11th Workshop on Multiword Expressions*, pages 87–95, Denver, Colorado. Association for Computational Linguistics.

Rob van der Goot, Nikola Ljubešić, Ian Matroos, Malvina Nissim, and Barbara Plank. 2018. Bleaching text: Abstract features for cross-lingual gender prediction. In *ACL*, Melbourne, Australia. Association for Computational Linguistics.

Sabien Hanoulle, Véronique Hoste, and Aline Remael. 2015. The translation of documentaries: Can domainspecific, bilingual glossaries reduce the translators workload? an experiment involving professional translators. *New Voices in Translation Studies*, 23:13.

Dirk Hovy. 2015. Demographic factors improve classification performance. In *Proceedings of the 53rd Annual Meeting of the Association for Computational Linguistics and the 7th International Joint Conference on Natural Language Processing (Volume 1: Long Papers)*, pages 752–762. Association for Computational Linguistics.

Dirk Hovy and Anders Søgaard. 2015. Tagging performance correlates with author age. In *Proceedings of the 53rd Annual Meeting of the Association for Computational Linguistics and the 7th International Joint Conference on Natural Language Processing (Volume 2: Short Papers)*, pages 483–488, Beijing, China. Association for Computational Linguistics.

Dirk Hovy and L. Shannon Spruit. 2016. The social impact of natural language processing. In *Proceedings of the 54th Annual Meeting of the Association for Computational Linguistics (Volume 2: Short Papers)*, pages 591–598. Association for Computational Linguistics.

John Leggett and Glen Williams. 1988. Verifying identity via keystroke characterstics. *International Journal of Man-Machine Studies*, 28(1):67–76.

Fei Liu, Julien Perez, and Scott Nowson. 2016. A recurrent and compositional model for personality trait recognition from short texts. In *Proceedings of the Workshop on Computational Modeling of People's Opinions, Personality, and Emotions in Social Media (PEOPLES)*, Osaka, Japan. The COLING 2016 Organizing Committee.

Nikola Ljubešić, Darja Fišer, and Tomaž Erjavec. 2017. Language-independent gender prediction on twitter. In *Proceedings of the Second Workshop on NLP and Computational Social Science*, pages 1–6, Vancouver, Canada. Association for Computational Linguistics.

Hilbert Locklear, Sathya Govindarajan, Zdenka Sitova, Adam Goodkind, David Guy Brizan, Andrew Rosenberg, Vir V Phoha, Paolo Gasti, and Kiran S Balagani. 2014. Continuous authentication with cognition-centric text production and revision features. In *Biometrics (IJCB), 2014 IEEE International Joint Conference on*.

Kim Luyckx and Walter Daelemans. 2008. Personae: a corpus for author and personality prediction from text. In *LREC 2008*.

François Mairesse and Marilyn Walker. 2006. Automatic recognition of personality in conversation. In *Proceedings of the Human Language Technology Conference of the NAACL, Companion Volume: Short Papers*.

Shachar Mirkin, Scott Nowson, Caroline Brun, and Julien Perez. 2015. Motivating personality-aware machine translation. In *Proceedings of the 2015 Conference on Empirical Methods in Natural Language Processing*, pages 1102–1108, Lisbon, Portugal. Association for Computational Linguistics.

John V Monaco, John C Stewart, Sung-Hyuk Cha, and Charles C Tappert. 2013. Behavioral biometric verification of student identity in online course assessment and authentication of authors in literary works. In *Biometrics: Theory, Applications and Systems (BTAS), 2013 IEEE Sixth International Conference on*.

Frederick Mosteller and David Wallace. 1964. *Inference and disputed authorship: The Federalist*. Addison-Wesley.

John Nerbonne. 2007. The exact analysis of text. *Foreword to the 3rd edition of Frederick Mosteller and David Wallace Inference and Disputed Authorship: The Federalist Papers CSLI: Stanford*.

Dong Nguyen, A. Seza Dogruz, Carolyn Penstein Ros, and Franciska de Jong. 2015. Computational sociolinguistics: A survey. *Compututational Linguistics*, 42(3):537–59.

Dong Nguyen, A. Noah Smith, and P. Carolyn Rosè. 2011. *Proceedings of the 5th ACL-HLT Workshop on Language Technology for Cultural Heritage, Social Sciences, and Humanities*, chapter Author Age Prediction from Text using Linear Regression. Association for Computational Linguistics.

Guido Nottbusch, Rdiger Weingarten, and Said Sahel. 2007. From written word to written sentence production. *Writing and cognition: Research and applications.*, pages 31–54.

F. Pedregosa, G. Varoquaux, A. Gramfort, V. Michel, B. Thirion, O. Grisel, M. Blondel, P. Prettenhofer, R. Weiss, V. Dubourg, J. Vanderplas, A. Passos, D. Cournapeau, M. Brucher, M. Perrot, and E. Duchesnay. 2011. Scikit-learn: Machine learning in Python. *Journal of Machine Learning Research*, 12:2825–2830.

James W Pennebaker. 2011. Using computer analyses to identify language style and aggressive intent: The secret life of function words. *Dynamics of Asymmetric Conflict*, 4(2):92–102.

Barbara Plank. 2016. Keystroke dynamics as signal for shallow syntactic parsing. In *Proceedings of COLING 2016, the 26th International Conference on Computational Linguistics: Technical Papers*, pages 609–619, Osaka, Japan. The COLING 2016 Organizing Committee.

Barbara Plank and Dirk Hovy. 2015. Personality traits on twitter–or–how to get 1,500 personality tests in a week. In *Proceedings of the 6th Workshop on*

Computational Approaches to Subjectivity, Sentiment and Social Media Analysis, pages 92–98, Lisboa, Portugal. Association for Computational Linguistics.

Ella Rabinovich, Raj Nath Patel, Shachar Mirkin, Lucia Specia, and Shuly Wintner. 2017. Personalized machine translation: Preserving original author traits. In *Proceedings of the 15th Conference of the European Chapter of the Association for Computational Linguistics: Volume 1, Long Papers*, pages 1074–1084, Valencia, Spain. Association for Computational Linguistics.

Delip Rao, David Yarowsky, Abhishek Shreevats, and Manaswi Gupta. 2010. Classifying latent user attributes in twitter. In *Proceedings of the 2nd international workshop on Search and mining user-generated contents*, pages 37–44. ACM.

Sara Rosenthal and Kathleen McKeown. 2011. Age prediction in blogs: A study of style, content, and online behavior in pre- and post-social media generations. In *Proceedings of the 49th Annual Meeting of the Association for Computational Linguistics: Human Language Technologies*, pages 763–772. Association for Computational Linguistics.

Roy Schwartz, Oren Tsur, Ari Rappoport, and Moshe Koppel. 2013. Authorship attribution of micromessages. In *Proceedings of the 2013 Conference on Empirical Methods in Natural Language Processing*, pages 1880–1891. Association for Computational Linguistics.

Efstathios Stamatatos. 2009. A survey of modern authorship attribution methods. *Journal of the American Society for information Science and Technology*, 60(3):538–556.

John C Stewart, John V Monaco, Sung-Hyuk Cha, and Charles C Tappert. 2011. An investigation of keystroke and stylometry traits for authenticating online test takers. In *Biometrics (IJCB), 2011 International Joint Conference on*.

Kirk PH Sullivan, Eva Lindgren, et al. 2006. *Computer keystroke logging and writing: Methods and applications*. Elsevier.

Charles C Tappert, Sung-Hyuk Cha, Mary Villani, and Robert S Zack. 2010. A keystroke biometric system for long-text input. *International Journal of Information Security and Privacy (IJISP)*, 4:32–60.

Charles C Tappert, Mary Villani, and Sung-Hyuk Cha. 2009. Keystroke biometric identification and authentication on long-text input. *Behavioral biometrics for human identification: Intelligent applications*, pages 342–367.

Ioannis Tsimperidis, Vasilios Katos, and Nathan Clarke. 2015. Language-independent gender identification through keystroke analysis. *Information & Computer Security*, 23(3):286–301.

Luuk Van Waes, Mariëlle Leijten, and Daphne Van Weijen. 2009. Keystroke logging in writing research: Observing writing processes with inputlog. *GFL-German as a foreign language*, 2(3):41–64.

Ben Verhoeven, Walter Daelemans, and Barbara Plank. 2016. Twisty: A multilingual twitter stylometry corpus for gender and personality profiling. In *Proceedings of the Tenth International Conference on Language Resources and Evaluation (LREC 2016)*, Paris, France. European Language Resources Association (ELRA).

Svitlana Volkova, Theresa Wilson, and David Yarowsky. 2013. Exploring demographic language variations to improve multilingual sentiment analysis in social media. In *Proceedings of the 2013 Conference on Empirical Methods in Natural Language Processing*, pages 1815–1827. Association for Computational Linguistics.

Åsa Wengelin. 2006. Examining pauses in writing: Theory, methods and empirical data. *Computer keystroke logging and writing: methods and applications (Studies in Writing)*, 18:107–130.

Brian Hu Zhang, Blake Lemoine, and Margaret Mitchell. 2018. Mitigating unwanted biases with adversarial learning. *arXiv preprint arXiv:1801.07593*.

Predicting Twitter User Demographics from Names Alone

Zach Wood-Doughty, Nicholas Andrews, Rebecca Marvin, Mark Dredze
Center for Language and Speech Processing
Johns Hopkins University, Baltimore, MD 21218
`zach@cs.jhu.edu, noa@cs.jhu.edu, becky@jhu.edu, mdredze@cs.jhu.edu`

Abstract

Social media analysis frequently requires tools that can automatically infer demographics to contextualize trends. These tools often require hundreds of user-authored messages for each user, which may be prohibitive to obtain when analyzing millions of users. We explore character-level neural models that learn a representation of a user's name and screen name to predict gender and ethnicity, allowing for demographic inference with minimal data. We release trained models[1] which may enable new demographic analyses that would otherwise require enormous amounts of data collection.

1 Introduction

Social media analysis offers new opportunities for research in numerous domains, including health (Paul and Dredze, 2011), political science (O'Connor et al., 2010), and other social sciences (Gilbert and Karahalios, 2009). Data from social media platforms such as Twitter can yield key insights into population beliefs and behaviors, complementing existing methods such as traditional surveys (Velasco et al., 2014; Dredze et al., 2015). A downside of social media sources is that they often lack traditional demographic information, such as gender, ethnicity, age, and location. Twitter is one of the most popular platforms for research, but its users rarely provide such information.

Numerous existing systems automatically infer missing demographics, such as gender, ethnicity, age and location (Mislove et al., 2011; Burger et al., 2011; Culotta et al., 2015; Pennacchiotti and Popescu, 2011; Rao et al., 2010; Jurgens et al., 2015; Dredze et al., 2013; Rout et al., 2013). Most methods rely on content authored by the user,

where words or phrases are strongly associated with specific demographic traits (Al Zamal et al., 2012). Friendship and follower relationships in social networks can also be informative (Chen et al., 2015; Volkova et al., 2014; Bergsma et al., 2013); people tend to be friends with people who live in the same geographic area (Jurgens, 2013) or tend to follow users with similar political orientations (Conover et al., 2011). Culotta et al. (2015) leveraged web traffic data to predict demographics based on who Twitter users follow, e.g. EPSN.com is popular with men, and the `@ESPN` Twitter account is mostly followed by men.

The principal drawback of these methods is their need for significant data per user, which is often time consuming or expensive to gather. When working with enormous datasets, researchers often avoid demographic analysis altogether, or use limited approaches. For example, a large-scale analysis by Mislove et al. (2011) inferred gender by simply string-matching common names, which failed to label 35.8% of the users studied. Paul and Dredze (2011) tracked flu and allergy symptoms in a dataset of 1.6 million tweets, in which 71% of users had only a single tweet and 97% had 5 or fewer. In a dataset with millions of users, obtaining sufficient content or network data for each user may require prohibitively many Twitter API calls. In production environments, a system may need to make rapid decisions based on a single message, rather than waiting until additional data can be gathered. For these reasons, methods have been proposed for inferring demographics based on the user's name and profile, such as for geolocation, gender, or social roles (Dredze et al., 2013; Osborne et al., 2014; Dredze et al., 2016; Knowles et al., 2016; Volkova et al., 2013; Burger et al., 2011; Beller et al., 2014).

---

[1] http://bitbucket.org/mdredze/demographer

Proceedings of the Second Workshop on Computational Modeling of People's Opinions, Personality, and Emotions in Social Media, pages 105–111
New Orleans, Louisiana, June 6, 2018. ©2018 Association for Computational Linguistics

We explore character-level models that learn a low-dimensional representation of a Twitter user's name and screen name, enabling demographic prediction from only a single tweet. Names are a reliable source of demographic information; the name `Sarah` or username `therealjohn` indicate gender, and names like `Carlos` and `Wei` may suggest ethnicity or race. Exact first-name matching has already been proven helpful for demographics inferring, but such methods only work when users use known names (Mislove et al., 2011; Liu and Ruths, 2013; Karimi et al., 2016). Neural models provide the flexibility to learn patterns in character sub-sequences, especially for Twitter names, which are irregular and can contain emojis or special characters. Our model produces more accurate demographic predictions than previous name-based methods, and is competitive with approaches that require more data resources.

2   Models

We hypothesize that character sequences in names are indicative of demographics, and consider models that can learn these correlations from data. Our models encode names and screen names using either convolutional (CNN) and recurrent (RNN) neural networks, which can effectively handle variable-length names. These models convert the tokens of a name into a fixed-length representation, which is then passed through two fully-connected layers to obtain a distribution over the demographic labels.

We searched over a range of model settings:

Single-sequence vs.   Multi-sequence Twitter users provide both a name and a screen name; sometimes identical and sometimes completely different. We considered as input either the name only or a concatenation of the name and screen name.

Encoder dimension and depth   We considered hidden dimensions ranging from 128 to 1024, both for the number of recurrent cells and for the number of convolutional filters. We additionally considered stacked CNN or RNN components, up to a depth of three layers.

RNN settings   Our initial experiments found a Gated Recurrent Unit (GRU) (Cho et al., 2014) cell more effective than Long-Short Term Memory (LSTM) (Hochreiter and Schmidhuber, 1997). We

considered both bidirectional and unidirectional RNNs. We evaluated both max-pooling and a learned weighted average[2] to convert the RNN output states into a fixed dimensional embedding.

CNN settings   We set the convolution filter width at either two or three. Convolutions had either the ELU activation function (Clevert et al., 2015) or no activation function. All CNN models used max-pooling to reduce the convolution outputs to a fixed dimension. The stacked CNN models used an exponentially increasing dilation rate at each layer (Yu and Koltun, 2015).

Training details   We trained all models using cross entropy loss and the Adam optimizer (Kingma and Ba, 2014), using a learning rate of 0.001 and gradients clipped at 10 (Pascanu et al., 2013). Each character in the vocabulary was embedded into a 128-dimension space. Models were implemented in Tensorflow (Abadi et al., 2016).

3   Data and evaluation

We collect data from past work to conduct experiments on gender and ethnicity prediction tasks. We consider both Twitter data and auxiliary government-provided data to train our models, but always evaluate using just Twitter data for the development and test sets. We split the Twitter data into training (60%), development (20%) and test sets (20%). For each task, we use the datasets described below to construct three types of training datasets: only auxiliary data, only Twitter data, and auxiliary plus Twitter data. When using both auxiliary and Twitter data, we train on the auxiliary data until the Twitter development accuracy begins to decline, then switch to training on the Twitter data.

Gender: We consider gender classification as a binary[3] prediction task between men and women, following past work.

Twitter: The dataset created by Burger et al. (2011) (and processed and released by Volkova et al. (2013)[4]) provides us with 58,046 users, 30,364 female and 27,682 male. These labels were

---

[2] We use the Tensorflow seq2seq implementation of Bahdanau et al. (2014) attention, to convert the sequence of RNN states to a single time-step 'sequence' for classification.

[3] A fuller consideration of of gender identity on Twitter is needed, but is outside the scope of this work.

[4] `http://cs.jhu.edu/~svitlana/data/data_emnlp2013.tar.gz`

obtained for Twitter accounts which linked to a blog in which the author included gender.

Auxiliary Data: We use gender-labeled name data from the Social Security Administration[5] which contains 68,457 unique first names and their co-occurrence with gender. We assigned each name its majority gender label.

Ethnicity: There is limited available training data for race and ethnicity. Due to the large class imbalances in available data, we consider two separate ethnicity tasks. First, we predict Caucasian vs. African-American (2-way), which offered the most data per class and a larger body of past work (Volkova and Bachrach, 2015; Pennacchiotti and Popescu, 2011). Second, we predict Caucasian vs. African-American vs. Hispanic/Latino (3-way) as a more difficult task following Culotta et al. (2015).

Twitter: From the dataset created by Culotta et al. (2015) we collect 407 of the original 770 users[6]: 215 Caucasian, 117 Hispanic/Latino, and 75 African-American. The labels were obtained by manual annotation.[7] Culotta et al. estimated inter-annotator agreement at 80%. From Volkova and Bachrach (2015) we collect 3,862 users of the original 5,000: 1,912 Caucasian, 360 Hispanic/Latino, and 1,309 African American (and 281 other). The labels were obtained by crowdsourced annotations of users' profiles, with a reported Cohen's κ of 0.71.

Auxiliary Data: We use ethnicity-labeled name data from the North Carolina Board of Elections, [8] which contains millions of names labeled with race (White, Black, and five other labels) and ethnicity (Hispanic/Latino, not, or undesignated). We combine race and ethnicity labels into our three classes (Caucasian, African-American, Hispanic/Latino).

3.1 Baselines

For each task we compare our best neural models against two baselines representing prior work: a name-only method and a user content method.

SVM: Knowles et al. (2016) predicts gender with a linear SVM trained on character n-gram features extracted from Twitter users' names. We used the authors' released implementation.

Content: Volkova and Bachrach (2015) predicts gender and ethnicity with a logistic regression classifier trained on the unigrams in the 200 most recent tweets of each user. We used our own implementation, but were unable to test on the exact same data in the original paper. When we evaluated our implementation, our AUC scores were 6-12% lower than those reported by the authors. This difference may be due to changes in the datasets as we have different tweets, fewer users, and different splits.

4 Results

Table 1 shows results on the test data for the best-performing CNN and RNN architecture on each task, with and without auxiliary data. Table 2 shows the results on dev data for each architecture, including results split by name inputs and name plus screen name inputs. We used the dev set performance to pick which architectures to evaluate on the test data, and early-stopping on dev data to get final test scores.

The (macro) F1 score is calculated as the harmonic mean of the average class precision and recall, across each class. [9] While F1 is usually quite similar to accuracy in 2-class comparisons, they diverge in the ethnicity 3-way comparison.

Our models had significantly[10] higher accuracy than the SVM baseline on both gender and ethnicity tasks. While the content baseline outperforms our best models on all tasks, it requires far more data per user.

The use of auxiliary data produced ambiguous results: it greatly helped the SVM model on the gender task, but appeared to hurt performance for all models on the ethnicity tasks. A possible explanation is that, because the SVM only considered simple n-gram features, the informative n-grams for gender are relatively consistent across Census and Twitter names. The neural models, however, learn much more complicated features, and the relevant features

---

[5] https://www.ssa.gov/OACT/babynames/names.zip

[6] Many users are no longer available on Twitter.

[7] While most accounts correspond to a single individual, some accounts represent entities for which "ethnicity" is not well-defined, but were labeled regardless.

[8] http://dl.ncsbe.gov/index.html?prefix=data/

[9] Knowles et al. (2016) defines F1 as the harmonic mean of accuracy and *coverage*, and thus our F1 scores are substantially lower.

[10] Using a two-proportion z-test, our models outperform the SVM on gender, with $p < 0.01$; on 2-way ethnicity, with $p < 0.01$; and on 3-way ethnicity, with $p < 0.02$. The content baseline is significantly better than our best models, using the same test, with at least $p < 0.0001$.

Training	Model	Gender		Ethnicity (3-way)		Ethnicity (2-way)	
		Acc	F1	Acc	F1	Acc	F1
Twitter	SVM	82.3	82.4	56.5	43.9	66.0	62.7
	CNN	83.1	83.1	**62.0**	42.5	**73.2**	**71.7**
	RNN	**84.3**	**84.3**	60.8	40.9	71.9	69.3
Twitter Auxiliary pre-train	SVM	82.9	83.2	45.9	**44.4**	58.1	60.9
	CNN	83.6	83.5	61.7	40.5	71.7	68.0
	RNN	84.1	84.1	60.2	40.1	70.5	67.3
-	Content	86.2	86.1	81.0	71.6	88.9	88.1

Table 1: Accuracy and F1 on Twitter test data. The best name-based result in each column is bolded.

Training	Model	Gender		Ethnicity (3-way)		Ethnicity (2-way)	
		Acc	F1	Acc	F1	Acc	F1
Auxiliary	SVM	77.7	77.8	44.3	42.5	59.8	60.1
	CNN: (N)	65.8	65.8	53.7	23.3	60.3	44.3
	CNN: (N+S)	64.2	64.4	53.7	23.3	58.7	56.2
	RNN: (N)	63.3	63.2	53.8	24.4	60.7	57.7
	RNN: (N+S)	63.4	63.3	53.7	23.3	60.7	67.3
Twitter	SVM	82.5	82.6	56.1	43.2	64.1	61.1
	CNN: (N)	83.3	83.2	61.9	41.9	70.5	67.2
	CNN: (N+S)	84.0	84.0	**65.9**	45.3	**73.6**	**71.7**
	RNN: (N)	83.5	83.4	60.9	38.4	69.7	63.3
	RNN: (N+S)	83.8	83.8	65.1	44.8	72.5	69.7
Twitter Auxiliary pre-train	SVM	83.6	83.8	49.8	**46.8**	62.1	63.2
	CNN: (N)	83.8	83.8	59.8	46.3	64.8	54.4
	CNN: (N+S)	82.1	82.1	64.2	44.3	71.1	67.5
	RNN: (N)	**84.1**	**84.1**	59.5	45.0	64.2	57.7
	RNN: (N+S)	83.6	83.5	63.2	42.8	70.7	67.3
-	Content	86.7	86.7	79.7	72.8	87.9	87.4

Table 2: Accuracy and F1 on Twitter development data. "N" indicates name alone, "N+S" indicates name and screen name. The best name-based result in each column is bolded.

may not transfer across domains. For the ethnicity auxiliary dataset, our model quickly overfit to the auxiliary data, learning features which did not generalize to the Twitter dataset. With either aggressive regularization or more sophisticated pre-training approaches, we might better utilize the auxiliary data when we have such a limited amount of Twitter data.

We contextualize our results with similar previous work that used other resources and datasets for similar tasks. Rao et al. (2010) reports an accuracy of 72.3% on gender prediction using n-grams and sociolinguistic features in users' tweets. Burger et al. (2011) reports a gender accuracy of 91.8% using user content and profile information, as well as a dev-set accuracy of 89.1% using the user's name field. Our SVM model reproduces the main features from their name model. Jaech and Ostendorf (2015) used character-level morphology induction to learn sub-units from OkCupid usernames, achieving a gender classification accuracy of 74.2% using only a username. Pennacchiotti and Popescu (2011) reports an F1 score of 65.5% on the 2-way

ethnicity task, using a combination of features from Twitter profiles, network, and content. In their model that used exclusively profile features, they report an F1 score of 60.9%.[11] Culotta et al. (2015) report F1 scores between 60% and 70% on the 3-way ethnicity comparison using regression and classification approaches, based on whether a user follows specific accounts associated with particular demographics. Although these are not direct comparisons on the same datasets, they demonstrate that our models achieve competitive performance on common demographics tasks while using just names.

5   Limitations

Our methods are limited by the amount of data available per category and the diversity of categories covered. Every dataset we could find was collected in a manner non-representative of Twitter in general, and had a bias towards users in the United States. Such dataset biases may

---

[11]The authors collected "users who explicitly mention their ethnicity in their profile," implying that profile features could be unfairly predictive.

affect our tool's predictions in ways that are difficult to measure, and should be a consideration in downstream analyses (Wood-Doughty et al., 2017). While the concept of race and ethnicity is a subject of study in social science research (Van den Berghe, 1978), we only consider three of the categories considered by most surveys, due to the very limited available data. To build a tool to adequately classify all widely-used race and ethnicity categories, a great deal of additional data collection and validation is required.

6 Future Work

Despite its limitations, our model improves on previous approaches that require only a single tweet per user by learning a rich representation of the user's names. While the content baseline outperforms our models, our method requires far less data and can be used in settings when it is too slow or costly to download new data. An exploratory experiment found that incorporating our name-based predictions into the content model produced a gender classification accuracy of 91.0%. That this hybrid model improves dramatically over the use of content alone indicates that the two approaches make different kinds of errors and thus could successfully complement each other(Liu and Ruths, 2013). The question of whether different predictors of Twitter user demographics have correlated errors based on user behavior is considered in Wood-Doughty et al. (2017), which offers other suggestions for more robust models.

Further work could also examine how names vary across different domains; while auxiliary government data did not consistently improve performance in our experiments, we expect that username-based features may transfer across different sites (e.g. from Twitter to Reddit) better than content-based features. In the empirical setting of datasets with a single tweet per user, there is still more information we can leverage to infer demographics; Twitter user profiles include optional fields for description, location, and a profile picture.

While extensions may make our methods more accurate or widely applicable, the present work demonstrates that neural character-level models of names can be successfully leveraged for difficult demographic predictions. We hope that these models will make possible low-resource demographic inference in varied domains. Our code and trained classifiers are available as an update to the Demographer package at `http://bitbucket.org/mdredze/demographer`.

7 Acknowledgements

This work was supported in part by the National Institute of General Medical Sciences under grant number 5R01GM114771.

References

Martin Abadi, Ashish Agarwal, Paul Barham, Eugene Brevdo, Zhifeng Chen, Craig Citro, Greg S Corrado, Andy Davis, Jeffrey Dean, Matthieu Devin, et al. 2016. Tensorflow: Large-scale machine learning on heterogeneous distributed systems. *arXiv preprint arXiv:1603.04467*.

Faiyaz Al Zamal, Wendy Liu, and Derek Ruths. 2012. Homophily and latent attribute inference: Inferring latent attributes of twitter users from neighbors. *ICWSM*, 270.

Dzmitry Bahdanau, Kyunghyun Cho, and Yoshua Bengio. 2014. Neural machine translation by jointly learning to align and translate. *arXiv preprint arXiv:1409.0473*.

Charley Beller, Rebecca Knowles, Craig Harman, Shane Bergsma, Margaret Mitchell, and Benjamin Van Durme. 2014. I'm a belieber: Social roles via self-identification and conceptual attributes. In *ACL*, pages 181–186.

Pierre L Van den Berghe. 1978. Race and ethnicity: a sociobiological perspective. *Ethnic and racial studies*, 1(4):401–411.

Shane Bergsma, Mark Dredze, Benjamin Van Durme, Theresa Wilson, and David Yarowsky. 2013. Broadly improving user classification via communication-based name and location clustering on twitter. In *HLT-NAACL*, pages 1010–1019.

John D Burger, John Henderson, George Kim, and Guido Zarrella. 2011. Discriminating gender on twitter. In *EMNLP*, pages 1301–1309. Association for Computational Linguistics.

Xin Chen, Yu Wang, Eugene Agichtein, and Fusheng Wang. 2015. A comparative study of demographic attribute inference in twitter. *ICWSM*, 15:590–593.

Kyunghyun Cho, Bart Van Merriënboer, Dzmitry Bahdanau, and Yoshua Bengio. 2014. On the properties of neural machine translation: Encoder-decoder approaches. *arXiv preprint arXiv:1409.1259*.

Djork-Arné Clevert, Thomas Unterthiner, and Sepp Hochreiter. 2015. Fast and accurate deep network learning by exponential linear units (elus). *arXiv preprint arXiv:1511.07289*.

Michael Conover, Jacob Ratkiewicz, Matthew R Francisco, Bruno Gonçalves, Filippo Menczer, and Alessandro Flammini. 2011. Political polarization on twitter. *ICWSM*, 133:89–96.

Aron Culotta, Nirmal Ravi Kumar, and Jennifer Cutler. 2015. Predicting the demographics of twitter users from website traffic data. In *AAAI*, pages 72–78.

Mark Dredze, David A. Broniatowski, Michael Smith, and Karen M. Hilyard. 2015. Understanding vaccine refusal: Why we need social media now. *American Journal of Preventive Medicine*.

Mark Dredze, Miles Osborne, and Prabhanjan Kambadur. 2016. Geolocation for twitter: Timing matters. In *NAACL*.

Mark Dredze, Michael J Paul, Shane Bergsma, and Hieu Tran. 2013. Carmen: A twitter geolocation system with applications to public health. In *AAAI Workshop on Expanding the Boundaries of Health Informatics Using AI (HIAI)*.

Eric Gilbert and Karrie Karahalios. 2009. Predicting tie strength with social media. In *Proceedings of the SIGCHI conference on human factors in computing systems*, pages 211–220. ACM.

Sepp Hochreiter and Jürgen Schmidhuber. 1997. Long short-term memory. *Neural computation*, 9(8):1735–1780.

Aaron Jaech and Mari Ostendorf. 2015. What your username says about you. In *EMNLP*.

David Jurgens. 2013. That's what friends are for: Inferring location in online social media platforms based on social relationships. *ICWSM*, 13:273–282.

David Jurgens, Tyler Finethy, James McCorriston, Yi Tian Xu, and Derek Ruths. 2015. Geolocation prediction in twitter using social networks: A critical analysis and review of current practice. In *ICWSM*, pages 188–197.

Fariba Karimi, Claudia Wagner, Florian Lemmerich, Mohsen Jadidi, and Markus Strohmaier. 2016. Inferring gender from names on the web: A comparative evaluation of gender detection methods. In *WWW*, pages 53–54. International World Wide Web Conferences Steering Committee.

Diederik Kingma and Jimmy Ba. 2014. Adam: A method for stochastic optimization. *arXiv preprint arXiv:1412.6980*.

Rebecca Knowles, Josh Carroll, and Mark Dredze. 2016. Demographer: Extremely simple name demographics. *NLP+ CSS 2016*, page 108.

Wendy Liu and Derek Ruths. 2013. What's in a name? using first names as features for gender inference in twitter. In *AAAI spring symposium: Analyzing microtext*, volume 13, page 01.

Alan Mislove, Sune Lehmann, Yong-Yeol Ahn, Jukka-Pekka Onnela, and J Niels Rosenquist. 2011. Understanding the demographics of twitter users. *ICWSM*, 11:5th.

Brendan O'Connor, Ramnath Balasubramanyan, Bryan R Routledge, and Noah A Smith. 2010. From tweets to polls: Linking text sentiment to public opinion time series. *ICWSM*, 11(122-129):1–2.

Miles Osborne, Sean Moran, Richard McCreadie, Alexander Von Lunen, Martin D Sykora, Elizabeth Cano, Neil Ireson, Craig Macdonald, Iadh Ounis, Yulan He, et al. 2014. Real-time detection, tracking, and monitoring of automatically discovered events in social media. In *ACL*.

Razvan Pascanu, Tomas Mikolov, and Yoshua Bengio. 2013. On the difficulty of training recurrent neural networks. *ICML (3)*, 28:1310–1318.

Michael J Paul and Mark Dredze. 2011. You are what you tweet: Analyzing twitter for public health. *Icwsm*, 20:265–272.

Marco Pennacchiotti and Ana-Maria Popescu. 2011. A machine learning approach to twitter user classification. *Icwsm*, 11(1):281–288.

Delip Rao, David Yarowsky, Abhishek Shreevats, and Manaswi Gupta. 2010. Classifying latent user attributes in twitter. In *Proceedings of the 2nd international workshop on Search and mining user-generated contents*, pages 37–44. ACM.

Dominic Rout, Kalina Bontcheva, Daniel Preoţiuc-Pietro, and Trevor Cohn. 2013. Where's@ wally?: a classification approach to geolocating users based on their social ties. In *Proceedings of the 24th ACM Conference on Hypertext and Social Media*, pages 11–20. ACM.

Edward Velasco, Tumacha Agheneza, Kerstin Denecke, Gan Kirchner, and Tim Eckmanns. 2014. Social media and internet-based data in global systems for public health surveillance: A systematic review. *The Milbank Quarterly*, 92(1):7–33.

Svitlana Volkova and Yoram Bachrach. 2015. On predicting sociodemographic traits and emotions from communications in social networks and their implications to online self-disclosure. *Cyberpsychology, Behavior, and Social Networking*, 18(12):726–736.

Svitlana Volkova, Glen Coppersmith, and Benjamin Van Durme. 2014. Inferring user political preferences from streaming communications. In *ACL*, pages 186–196.

Svitlana Volkova, Theresa Wilson, and David Yarowsky. 2013. Exploring demographic language variations to improve multilingual sentiment analysis in social media. In *EMNLP*.

Zach Wood-Doughty, Michael Smith, David Broniatowski, and Mark Dredze. 2017. How does twitter user behavior vary across demographic groups? In *Proceedings of the Second Workshop on NLP and Computational Social Science*, pages 83–89.

Fisher Yu and Vladlen Koltun. 2015. Multi-scale context aggregation by dilated convolutions. *arXiv preprint arXiv:1511.07122*.

Modeling Personality Traits of Filipino Twitter Users

Edward P. Tighe and Charibeth K. Cheng
Software Technology Department
De La Salle University, Manila, Philippines
edward.tighe@dlsu.edu.ph
chari.cheng@delasalle.ph

Abstract

Recent studies in the field of text-based personality recognition experiment with different languages, feature extraction techniques, and machine learning algorithms to create better and more accurate models; however, little focus is placed on exploring the language use of a group of individuals defined by nationality. Individuals of the same nationality share certain practices and communicate certain ideas that can become embedded into their natural language. Many nationals are also not limited to speaking just one language, such as how Filipinos speak Filipino and English, the two national languages of the Philippines. The addition of several regional/indigenous languages, along with the commonness of code-switching, allow for a Filipino to have a rich vocabulary. This presents an opportunity to create a text-based personality model based on how Filipinos speak, regardless of the language they use. To do so, data was collected from 250 Filipino Twitter users. Different combinations of data processing techniques were experimented upon to create personality models for each of the Big Five. The results for both regression and classification show that Conscientiousness is consistently the easiest trait to model, followed by Extraversion. Classification models for Agreeableness and Neuroticism had subpar performances, but performed better than those of Openness. An analysis on personality trait score representation showed that classifying extreme outliers generally produce better results for all traits except for Neuroticism and Openness.

1 Introduction

Personality traits aim to describe the uniqueness of an individual in terms of their interactions within themselves, with other people, and in certain environments (Friedman and Schustack, 2014; Larsen and Buss, 2008). The most common representation or model of personality traits used today is the Five Factor Model (FFM; Norman, 1963; Goldberg, 1981; McCrae and Costa Jr). The FFM, sometimes referred to as the Big Five, measures an individual's personality on five dimensions or traits, namely *Openness, Conscientiousness, Extraversion, Agreeableness*, and *Neuroticism*. It is important to note that traits vary in terms of degrees. In other words, one might be considered an extravert; however, someone could be more extraverted.

The Big Five is typically assessed by administering questionnaires such as the Big Five Inventory (BFI; John et al., 1991); however, an alternative method to assessing an individual's Big Five is through analysis of one's writing style. The way a person writes is reliably stable over a period of time (Pennebaker and King, 1999; Mehl and Pennebaker, 2003) which is similar to the stability of one's Big Five (Cobb-Clark and Schurer, 2012). Multiple studies have also shown how certain writing styles correlate to certain degrees of personality from analysis of student essays and journal abstracts (Pennebaker and King, 1999) to emails (Gill and Oberlander, 2002) to web blogs (Gill et al., 2009; Li and Chignell, 2010) to posts from social network sites (Qiu et al., 2012; Schwartz et al., 2013; Marshall et al., 2015). It is through this link between personality and writing that the field of text-based personality recognition emerged.

Although the field has taken great strides in determining state-of-the-art techniques in data processing, feature extraction, and machine learning, little focus is given to exploring language use of a group of individuals, such as those defined by nationality, in modeling personality traits. Individuals of the same nationality share practices and are exposed to certain situations that can lead to the development of certain psychological tendencies (Markus and Kitayama, 1998). Con-

Proceedings of the Second Workshop on Computational Modeling of People's Opinions, Personality, and Emotions in Social Media, pages 112–122
New Orleans, Louisiana, June 6, 2018. ©2018 Association for Computational Linguistics

versations and discussions expose individual differences and these differences eventually become embedded into natural language (Goldberg, 1981). However, many nationals are not limited to speaking just one language, such as how Filipinos speak Filipino and English, the two national languages of the Philippines. The addition of a number of regional/indigenous languages, along with the commonness of code-switching, allow for a Filipino to have a rich and diverse vocabulary. This rich vocabulary presents an opportunity to create a text-based personality model based on how Filipinos speak, regardless of the language they use. In order to do so, a web application was constructed to collect personal and Twitter data in which there were 250 Filipino participants. Raw personality scores were then experimented upon in order to determine the representation (continuous or discretized) that would best capture information. Tweets were then processed using simple language-independent natural language processing techniques. Finally, personality was modeled using both regression and classification techniques. The contributions of this paper are as follows:

- A corpus was created consisting of $610,448$ tweets from 250 Filipino participants. Each participant's personality traits were also assessed using the Big Five Inventory. Although a relatively small dataset, it serves as a source of information in which further experimentation can be performed.
- In both regression and classification, Conscientiousness is consistently the easiest personality trait to model, followed by Extraversion. Classification models for Agreeableness and Neuroticism produced subpar performances and did not fare well in regression. Lastly, models for Openness generally struggled in performance.
- In experimenting with personality score representations, results show that Neuroticism and Openness did not benefit from modeling extreme outliers ($\pm 1SD$ from the mean). Both traits were better modeled with a relaxed cut off at $\pm 0.5SD$, implying that useful information was lost when removing participants between $\pm(0.5SD - 1SD)$. As for the remaining three traits, performance was best when dealing with extreme outliers, as originally expected.

2 Related Literature

The early studies of the field mostly experimented with different feature extraction techniques on the Pennebaker and King (1999) Essay Dataset and utilized various Support Vector Machines for classification. Argamon et al. (2005) focused on determining high and low (top and bottom $\frac{1}{3}$) scoring individuals on the Extraversion and Neuroticism dimensions. Features were extracted based on a list of function words, along with other features based on Systemic Function Grammar. Their work showed that simple linguistic features contained information in determining personality traits – a task that requires "focused questions" such as those found in personality questionnaires. Soon after, multiple studies (Mairesse et al., 2007; Poria et al., 2013; Mohammad and Kiritchenko, 2013) utilized different linguistic resources in extracting information, including the Linguistic Inquire and Word Count (LIWC), MRC Psycholingusitic Database, NCR Emotion and Hashtag Lexicon, and SenticNet. Mairesse et al. (2007) conducted the first extensive study covering all five traits and treated personality recognition not just as a classification problem, but also as a regression and ranking problem as well. Their feature set is often referred to as the Mairesse baseline and consists of LIWC and MRC features. In another work, affect-related words were found to aid model performance when paired with LIWC and MRC (Mohammad and Kiritchenko, 2013). The method leading to the best improvement was where sentic computing was utilized in order to extract common sense knowledge with affective and sentiment information (Poria et al., 2013). Across the previously mentioned studies, Openness was found to be the easiest trait to model, while Agreeableness was the hardest to model.

As for studies that collected data from online sources, there was particular attention given to blogging sites. Blogs were an interesting source of data because of their personal nature. Oberlander and Nowson (2006) sourced their data from bloggers whom they administered a 41-item personality test. Classification was performed for all of the Big Five except for Openness due to nonnormal distribution of personality scores. Once again, participants were grouped according to their scores based on varying levels of standard deviation (greater than 1SD, 0.5SD, and the mean). N-gram occurrence was utilized for extracting information and various feature selection techniques were employed. Nowson and Oberlander (2007) mirrored the previous study's methodology, but experimented with both the previous dataset and a new dataset. However, Iacobelli et al. (2011) produced the most notable results using the new dataset of the previous study. Although they tested with LIWC features, they found that using boolean scoring (present or not present) performed much better. Despite utilizing a coarse questionnaire, they managed to produced the best performing models with Openness being the easiest to model and Neuroticism being the most difficult.

Other early studies that sourced online data targeted social networking sites such as Twitter and Facebook in order to dealing with enormous amounts of data. Two studies (Golbeck et al., 2011a,b) were very similar as they used LIWC to process text from Twitter and Facebook, respectively. Their main difference was the use of site-specific information, such as internal Facebook stats or Twitter usage. The later study also utilized MRC as an additional means to extract information. But most noteworthy of all was of Schwartz et al. (2013) in which the biggest study on personality modeling was conducted with a total 75,000 Facebook volunteers. They highlighted the use of Differential Language Analysis as a means to generate open topics in comparison to the closed topics – categories generated by LIWC.

More recent developments involve the shift to analyzing non-English text. This could be seen in the PAN2015 (Rangel et al., 2015), where English, Spanish, Italian, and Dutch Tweets were made available to multiple research teams. One of the top performing submissions González-Gallardo et al. (2015) extracted n-grams of characters and utilized FreeLing, a language processing tool. FreeLing had resources for each of the languages in the dataset except for Dutch, so the English module was utilized despite possibly creating more errors. In Alvarez-Carmona et al. (2015), regarded as the top performing submission, focus was given to extracting discriminative and descriptive features. This was done by applying Second Order Attributes and Latent Semantic Analysis on a Term Frequency Inverse Document Frequency matrix. Outside of the PAN2015, Peng et al. (2015) focused on predicting Extraversion by segmenting Chinese characters from Chinese Facebook users. As Chinese characters are harder to delimit than other languages, they utilized Jieba, a Chinese character tokenizer. Lastly, Xue et al. (2017) focused on the use of Label Distribution Learning as an alternative to common machine learning algorithms while processing Chinese text. They extract information from posts from Sina Weibo users with TextMind, a Chinese language psychological analysis system similar to LIWC.

Currently, trends in the field of text-based personality recognition revolve around the use of Deep Learning, as the learning algorithm, and word embedding, as the way to represent text. Studies typically do not vary from using the two techniques, but distinguish themselves through their data source, such as how Yu and Markov (2017) experiments using a small subset of Facebook status posts. Another study (Majumder et al., 2017) considered adding the Mairesse baseline to their feature set in the analysis of the Essay Dataset. Tandera et al. (2017) used two Facebook datasets, one from MyPersonality and the other manually collected. Aside from word embedding, they included features from LIWC and SPLICE, another linguistic analysis tool. Lastly, Arnoux et al. (2017), although utilizing Gausian Process regression instead of Deep Leaning, still made use of word embedding. Their results showed that it was possible to reduce a dataset significantly while still achieving comparable model performances.

3   Methodology

This research collected data and approached modeling of personality traits through different combinations of data pre-processing, feature extraction, feature reduction, and machine learning techniques. Figure 1 shows an overview of the methodology.

3.1   Data Collection

A web application was developed to interface with Twitter and administer both a personal information sheet and a personality test. The information sheet asked for information such as sex, age, and nationality, while the personality test was the Big Five Inventory (BFI; John et al., 1991, 2008), a 44-item self-report questionnaire that measures the Big Five on a 5-point scale.

Recruitment of participants was mainly performed through postings on Facebook and Twitter. Friends and colleagues were targeted first which then later expanded to their social networks by word-of-mouth. However, a majority of the re-

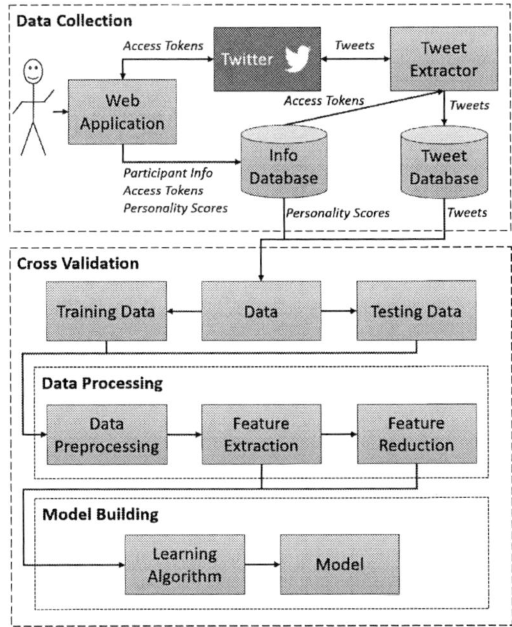

Figure 1: The methodology of this research

cruitment was focused on large Facebook groups into order to reach individuals outside of the the researcher's social network. Twitter Ads was also utilized to increase the reach of the web app, but it only resulted in a hand full of participants. Participants received no incentives for taking part in the data collection except for seeing the output of the personality test.

After recruitment, it was important to filter the participants based on their personal and Twitter account information as anyone could access the web application. Individuals were removed if they were non-Filipino or had less than 100 tweets. The filters in place ensured that the participants were at least Filipino, whether pure or mixed, and had a suitable amount of text data to process.

Each participant's Twitter account was then crawled using a Python script which retrieved up to 3,200[1] of their most recent tweets. If participants had less than 3,200 tweets, then as many tweets as possible were retrieved. Any retweets found were removed as they were not written directly by the participant. An exception was made for quoted tweets because a portion of the tweet is written by the participant. Lastly, participants

[1] The most recent 3,200 tweets is a limitation of Twitter's API; More information can be found in `https://developer.twitter.com/en/docs/tweets/timelines/api-reference/get-statuses-user_timeline`

whose tweet count fell below 100 because of the removal of retweets were removed.

After all of the filtering, a total of 250 individuals qualified as participants for this research. Table 1 shows the demographics of the participants and Table 2 shows the statistical characteristics of the participants' personality trait scores.

This research managed to collect $712,762$ tweets, but after retweets were removed, the total tweet count stood at $610,448$ with an average of $2,441.79$ tweets (SD=723.8) per participant. The participant with the lowest tweet count had 107 and the highest had $3,196$.

Table 1: Participant demographics.

Total Participant Count	250
Age	
Mean	22.34
Standard deviation	3.57
Min	19
Max	51
Sex	
Male	79
Female	169
Intersex	1
Decline to disclose	1
Nationality	
Filipino	234
Mixed-Filipino[1]	16

[1] Mixed-Filipinos are those who declared themselves Filipino and one or more nationalities

Table 2: Statistical characteristics of participants' personality trait scores.

Personality	**Mean**	**SD**	**Min**	**Max**
Openness	3.45	0.44	2.00	4.50
Conscientiousness	3.08	0.62	1.44	4.67
Extraversion	3.13	0.80	1.25	5.00
Agreeableness	3.59	0.67	1.56	5.00
Neuroticism	3.39	0.75	1.25	4.88

As this research focused on how Filipinos tweeted regardless of language, tweets in all languages were retained. 58.14% of the total tweets were labeled as English, while 31.89% were labeled as Tagalog[2]. The remaining tweets were either labeled as undefined (5.09%; unable to determine the language) or other languages (4.89%).

[2] Tagalog is a Philippine language that served as the basis for Filipino, the national language

Top among the other labels included Indonesian (1.22%) and Spanish (0.07%) – two languages that share words commonly used in Filipino. Language labels were taken from the metadata of a tweet. Table 3 shows a breakdown of the languages present in the corpus.

Table 3: The breakdown of languages present in the corpus as well as their usage per participant.

Lang	Count		Mean	SD
Eng	354889	58.14%	1419.56	585.61
Tag	194644	31.89%	778.58	516.81
Und	31062	5.09%	124.25	78.82
Oth	29853	4.89%	119.41	75.70

[Abbr] Eng - English, Tag - Tagalog, Und - Undefined, Oth - Others

3.2 Data Pre-processing

Data pre-processing is performed in order to prepare raw text and personality trait scores for classification. This research defines the Term-Document Matrix as the following:

1. Term (t): an n-gram of tokens extracted from a single tweet of a participant
2. Document (d): all terms derived from all tweets of a participant
3. Collection (C): a set of documents of all participants

3.2.1 Tokenizing

This research utilizes Tweetokenize (Suttles, 2013), a regular expression based tokenizer for Twitter, to parse each character in a tweet to properly identify words/terms and social media entities (usernames, hashtags, or emojis). The default settings were kept when processing the tweets and are as follows:

1. Uppercase letters were converted to lowercase; but tokens, where all letters are capitalized, are not converted to lowercase,
2. Repeating letters are limited to 3 (e.g. *hmmmmm* and *hmmmm* are both reduced to *hmmm*),
3. Identified usernames and urls were replaced with *USERNAME*,
4. Identified urls were replaced with *URL*,
5. Identified hashtags are not replaced with a token, and
6. Stop words are not removed.

3.2.2 N-Grams

An n-gram is a sequence of n tokens. This research experimented with only 1-grams. N-grams were extracted through the use of Natural Language Toolkit (NTLK; Bird et al., 2009).

3.2.3 Document Frequency Filtering

Document frequency filtering is applied to remove terms that are either too common or too unique. The document frequency of a term t in a collection C is defined as

$$DF(t, C) = \frac{N_{t,C}}{N_C},\qquad(1)$$

where $N_{t,C}$ is the number of documents in C wherein t occurs at least once and N_C is the total number of documents found in C. Different combinations of minimum and maximum thresholds were experimented upon, but this research limits the combinations to:

1. min: 1%, max: 99%, and
2. min: 10%, max: 70%.

3.2.4 Personality Trait Score Representation

Personality trait scores are continuous values and instantly fit as input for regression models; however, these scores must be discretized in order to perform classification. This research modifies Oberlander and Nowson (2006)'s idea of partitioning the participants based on their personality scores' mean (μ) and standard deviation (SD). Therefore, five different methods are experimented upon and are defined given a personality trait score s as

1. Continuous - refers to the natural form of personality trait scores and will be the sole trait score representation for regression
2. LAH - Stands for *Low Average High*; Groups all participants into low, average, and high; Participants nearest to a boundary between two partition have similar scores; Defined as:

$$\text{LAH}(s) = \begin{cases} high, & \text{if } s > \mu + \frac{SD}{2}; \\ low, & \text{if } s < \mu - \frac{SD}{2}; \\ average, & \text{otherwise.} \end{cases}\qquad(2)$$

3. LH - Stands for *Low High*; Groups all participants into low and high, but participants nearest to the boundary still have similar scores; Defined as:

$$\text{LH}(s) = \begin{cases} high, & \text{if } s > \mu; \\ low, & \text{if } s < \mu. \end{cases}\qquad(3)$$

4. LHNA - Stands for *Low High, No Average*; Creates distinction between high and low scorers by removing all average; Results in the removal of $\sim$38.2% of the participants; Defined as:

$$\text{LHNA}(s) = \begin{cases} high, & \text{if } s > \mu + \frac{SD}{2}; \\ low, & \text{if } s < \mu - \frac{SD}{2}; \\ \text{omit}, & \text{otherwise.} \end{cases} \quad (4)$$

5. LHNASD - Stands for *Low High, No Average, whole Standard Deviation*; Creates the most distinction between high and low scorers by increasing the threshold to $\pm 1SD$; Results in the removal of $\sim$68.2% of the participants; Defined as:

$$\text{LHNASD}(s) = \begin{cases} high, & \text{if } s > \mu + SD; \\ low, & \text{if } s < \mu - SD; \\ \text{omit}, & \text{otherwise.} \end{cases} \quad (5)$$

A visualization of the different representations can be seen in Figure 2

3.3 Feature Extraction

In order to extract information from raw text, two feature extraction techniques are used in this research: Term Frequency Inverse Document Frequency (TFIDF) and Term Occurrence (TO). Language independent approaches are preferred due to the presence of English and Filipino, among other langauges.

3.3.1 TFIDF

Term Frequency Inverse Document Frequency (TFIDF) captures the frequency of use of a term in a given document, while factoring the importance of the term in relation to the overall collection of documents. TFIDF was computed for each term in each document to construct a TFIDF word-matrix. All values were then normalized. The features in TFIDF dataset consists of the terms that appear throughout the entire collection of Twitter users.

TFIDF is computed by multiplying the Term Frequency (TF) with the Inverse Document Frequency (IDF). Given a term t of a document d of a collection C, TFIDF is defined as:

$$TFIDF(t, d, C) = \frac{N_{t,d}}{N_d} \cdot \frac{N_C}{N_{t,C}}, \quad (6)$$

where $N_{t,d}$ is the number of t in d, N_d is the total number of terms in d, N_c is the total number of documents in C, and $N_{t,C}$ is the number of documents in C wherein t occurs at least once.

3.3.2 Term Occurrence

Term occurrence (TO) is a binary representation of whether a particular term was used or not – occurred or not occurred. The TO of a term t given a document d can be defined as:

$$TO(t, d) = \begin{cases} 1, & \text{if } N_{t,d} > 0; \\ 0, & \text{otherwise,} \end{cases} \quad (7)$$

where the output is 1 if where $N_{t,d}$, the number of t in d, is greater than 0, and 0 if otherwise.

3.4 Feature Reduction

Even with the utilization of document frequency filtering, there would still be a good number of features that could contain both relevant and irrelevant information. Feature reduction would reduce a dataset, while retaining the most relevant features. Therefore, reduction is applied on the training set and would consist of the top 20% of the results of univariate linear regression test for regression and chi-square (χ^2) for classification. Experiments were performed with and without feature reduction in order to properly observe the effects.

3.5 Machine Learning Algorithms

Multiple learning algorithms were experimented upon, but this research highlights the following algorithms:

1. Linear Regression (LIN),
2. Ridge Regression (RID),
3. Support Vector Machines (linear SVM), and
4. Logistic Regression (LOG).

The algorithms were highlighted because they performed better than other the algorithms during the experiments of this research. Those that produced subpar models were not reported. The algorithms were implemented using Scikit-Learn (Pedregosa et al., 2011), a general purpose machine learning Python library. All settings were kept to Scikit-Learn's default settings.

3.6 Model Evaluation

Data was split into training (60%) and testing (40%) sets in order to have enough data for learning, while having enough data remaining for testing. As the sample count for the classes was not balanced, 10-fold stratified cross validation was performed to ensure that each class was well represented in each fold. For classification models, both F_1 score and kappa statistic are observed in

Continuous			
LAH	L	A	H
LH	L		H
LHNA	L		H
LHNASD	L		H

Figure 2: The different ways personality trait scores are represented in this research. Boxes filled with color represent partitions of participants.

evaluating a model's performance. For regression models, Mean Squared Error (MSE), Mean Absolute Error (MAE), and R^2 are observed.

4 Results and Discussion

A total of 600 models were created based on the different combinations of pre-processing, feature extraction, feature reduction, and ML techniques. All combinations were experiment on and only the best models are reported. To determine the best models per trait, goodness of fit was prioritized over minimizing error; therefore, R^2 is the basis for regression models and kappa statistic is the basis for classification. Table 4 and Table 5 shows the best regression and classification models, respectively. Each of the best performing models is compared against a baseline model of the same configuration and can be seen in Figure 3 for regression and Figure 4 for classification. Additionally, the effects of discretizing trait scores in relation to the performance of personality models is analyzed. The best classification models per personality score representation are found in Table 6.

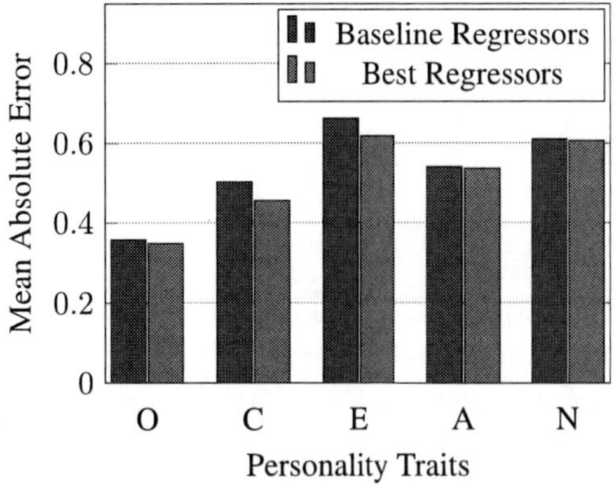

Figure 3: A comparison of the MAE between baseline mean regressors and the best regression models (as found in Table 4) per personality trait

General Findings. Out of all the Big Five, Conscientiousness is the easiest to model. Both

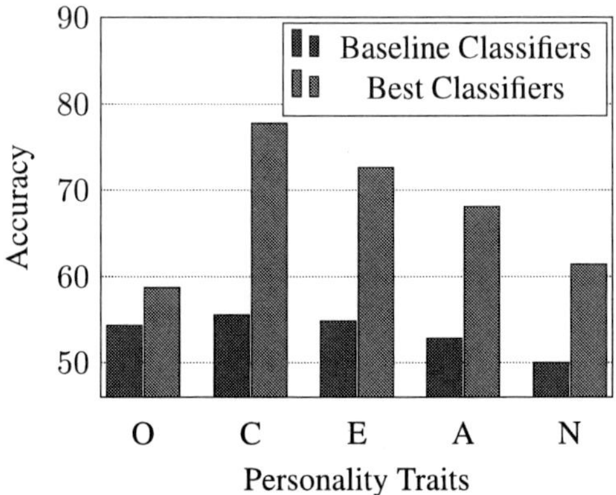

Figure 4: A comparison of the accuracies between baseline majority classifiers and the best classification models (as found in Table 5) per personality trait

in regression and classification, Conscientiousness had models with the best R^2 (0.1523) and kappa (0.5516), respectively. Extraversion came in second, again both in regression and classifications, with its R^2 of 0.1035 and a kappa of 0.4376. Results for both Conscientiousness and Extraversion indicate that simple TFIDF or TO features were able to extract useful information from a corpus of Filipino and English tweets. The remaining three traits performed poorly for regression, but Agreeableness and Neuroticism fared better in classification. The improvement in performance can mainly be attributed to excluding average scoring participants and looking for patterns in how the outliers generally tweet.

As for Openness, it can be considered the hardest trait to model, particularly because it performed worst in classification ($F_1 = 0.5669$ and $\kappa = 0.1438$). Models for openness are seen to utilize the softer document frequency filter (min=1%;max=99%) more often than in other traits. This indicates that strong patterns are not present and that in order to make appropriate predictions, most, if not all, information is needed.

Table 4: The performance and configuration of the best performing regression models per personality trait. Models were selected based on R^2.

Trait	Features	Doc Freq	Regressor	MSE	MAE	R^2
O	TO	1%-99%	LIN	0.1890	0.3493	0.0143
C	TFIDF	1%-99%	LIN	0.3174	0.4572	0.1523
E	TFIDF	10%-70%	LIN	0.5719	0.6190	0.1035
A	TFIDF	1%-99%	RID	0.4393	0.5374	-0.0088
N	TFIDF	1%-99%	LIN	0.5558	0.6066	-0.0031

Note: Although there were experiments with and without feature reduction, all the best performing models utilized all features; therefore, feature reduction was not included in the table.

Table 5: The performance and configuration of the best performing classification models per personality trait. Models were selected based on kappa statistic.

Trait	Personality Rep	Features	Doc Freq	χ^2 Selection	Classifier	F_1	κ
O	LHNA	TO	1%-99%	top 20%	SVM	0.5669	0.1438
C	LHNASD	TFIDF	10%-70%	top 20%	LOG	0.7764	0.5516
E	LHNASD	TO	10%-70%	top 20%	LOG	0.7165	0.4376
A	LHNASD	TO	10%-70%	n/a	LOG	0.6767	0.3547
N	LHNA	TFIDF+TO	10%-70%	top 20%	LOG	0.6086	0.2281

This is also supported by the small differences in evaluation metrics found across the different personality trait score representations as seen in Table 6. In other words, retaining extreme outliers (LHNSSD) did not help in classification of Openness and actually performed slightly worse than having all participants presents across 3 trait groupings (LAH).

Configurations in Regression Models. The best regression models, as seen in Table 4, indicate that there are no relatively strong features in the prediction of an individual's trait score. Four traits utilized the softer document frequency filter (min=1%;max=99%) with Extraversion using the harsher one. In terms of features, TFIDF values are preferred over TO. And interestingly, none of the best models utilized feature reduction. However, despite the generally low performances, the findings show that simple TFIDF values contain some information about one's personality, at least for Conscientiousness and Extraversion. TFIDF values can be considered shallow information, so further investigation using more in-depth feature extraction techniques could yield better results.

Configurations in Classification Models. All of the best classification models, as seen in Table 5, utilized personality representations that removed average scoring users and focused on out-moved average scoring users and focused on outliers - LHNASD and LHNA. As for features, TO was more useful than TFIDF as it was used in four out of the five traits; however, TFIDF was utilized by Conscientiousness, the best overall performing model. The features remaining after the harsher document frequency filter (min=10%;max=70%) proved to be more useful than the softer filter in all traits, except for Openness. This indicates that patterns indeed emerge when comparing individuals on the opposite ends of a personality dimension. Lastly, unlike in regression, feature selection was more useful than simply allowing the ML algorithms find patterns in the data.

Personality Trait Representation. As personality trait questionnaires typically output a numerical value, it is important to look at different ways to represent the scores – whether in continuous or discrete form. Continuous values provide the best coverage as they match the raw values output by questionnaires (e.g. 1.0 to 5.0 for the Big Five Inventory) and include all participants for testing and training purposes. Problems arise as features may not be highly correlated to the whole personality dimension or possible be correlated to a subset of individuals. On the other hand, discrete values allow for the grouping of individuals based on the mean and standard deviation of their scores. Grouping individuals makes classification possi-

Table 6: The F1 scores and kappa of the best performing classifiers per personality score representation.

Traits	LAH		LH		LHNA		LHNASD	
	F_1	κ	F_1	κ	F_1	κ	F_1	κ
O	0.4176	0.1233	0.5691	0.1388	0.5669	**0.1438**	0.5530	0.1222
C	0.4505	0.1693	0.6646	0.3295	0.7497	0.5010	0.7764	**0.5516**
E	0.4526	0.1680	0.6178	0.2359	0.6492	0.3033	0.7165	**0.4376**
A	0.3796	0.0743	0.5635	0.1298	0.5595	0.1329	0.6767	**0.3547**
N	0.3651	0.0475	0.5347	0.0711	0.6086	**0.2281**	0.5707	0.1469

ble, but problems can arise with individuals nearest to the boundary of a group as they would have similar scores to individuals in the groups next to them. A solution to this would be to create space in between classes; however, participants would have to be removed resulting in possible information loss. Because of the pros and cons of each method, analysis is performed on how personality scores affect personality modeling of Filipino Twitter users.

As seen in Table 6, LHNASD (*Low, High, No Average, whole Standard Deviation*) produced the best performing classifiers for three out of the five traits, namely Conscientiousness, Extraversion, and Agreeableness. This was expected because useful information was most likely found when comparing extreme high and low outliers, and not when including those who scored nearer to the mean. This is apparent by the gradual increase in evaluation metrics as the classes are reduced in size and the distances between outliers expands. However, it is important to note that Neuroticism and Openness fared best when utilizing the LHNA (*Low, High, No Average*) representation – the other representation that places space between outliers. LHNA has almost double the training data than LHNASD. Training instances of LHNA range from 88 to 103 across all traits, while LHNASD ranges from 46 to 53. This implies that there isn't strong discriminative information between extreme outliers and that the removal of participants also removed information useful for Neuroticism and Openness. Interestingly, models for Openness do not vary so much in terms of kappa statistic across all personality representation. The model for LAH (*Low, Average, High*), the hardest representation to predict because it has three class, has a kappa of (0.1233), while the model of LHNA has a kappa of 0.1438. In fact, LAH actually has better agreement than that of LHNASD (0.1222) indicating that the outliers of Openness are not easily distinguishable, at least with respect to the features extracted.

5 Conclusion and Recommendations

This research was able to collect text and personal data from 250 Filipino Twitter Users and use the way they tweet, regardless of language, to create personality trait models. In the process, different combinations of data processing and machine learning techniques were experimented upon to identify the best configurations and produce the best models. Findings show that Conscientiousness is an easy trait to model, directly followed by Extraversion. On the other hand, Openness is the hardest trait to model. Experiments in regression did not produce suitable models, but at least indicated that simple TFIDF values contain some information for Conscientiousness and Extraversion. Classification models had better results and generally benefited from modeling the outliers instead of classifying all of the participants. Lastly, Neuroticism and Openness also did not benefit from modeling of extreme outliers ($\pm 1SD$ from the mean) implying that outliers for the trait are not easily distinguishable.

As the participants were all Filipinos, further analysis of the content could provide insights into how personality traits manifest through the language use of Filipino Twitter users. The addition of more in-depth feature extraction techniques, such as topic modeling or the integration of multiple language-specific resources, might also help in improving the models' performances. Lastly, creating specific models of groups of individuals defined by demographics – such as by age, gender, or nationality – regardless of the number of languages used, proves to be a useful approach in personality modeling and can serve as a starting point for understanding their linguistic style.

References

Miguel A Alvarez-Carmona, A Pastor López-Monroy, Manuel Montes-y Gómez, Luis Villasenor-Pineda, and Hugo Jair Escalante. 2015. Inaoes participation at pan15: Author profiling task. *Working Notes Papers of the CLEF.*

Shlomo Argamon, Sushant Dhawle, Moshe Koppel, and James Pennebaker. 2005. Lexical predictors of personality type.

Pierre Arnoux, Anbang Xu, Neil Boyette, Jalal Mahmud, Rama Akkiraju, and Vibha Sinha. 2017. 25 tweets to know you: A new model to predict personality with social media. In *Proceedings of the Eleventh International Conference on Web and Social Media, ICWSM 2017.*

Steven Bird, Ewan Klein, and Edward Loper. 2009. *Natural language processing with Python: analyzing text with the natural language toolkit.* "O'Reilly Media, Inc.".

Deborah A Cobb-Clark and Stefanie Schurer. 2012. The stability of big-five personality traits. *Economics Letters*, 115(1):11–15.

Howard S. Friedman and Miriam W. Schustack. 2014. *Personality: Classic theories and modern research.* Pearson.

Alastair J Gill, Scott Nowson, and Jon Oberlander. 2009. What are they blogging about? personality, topic and motivation in blogs. In *ICWSM.*

Alastair J Gill and Jon Oberlander. 2002. Taking care of the linguistic features of extraversion. In *Proceedings of the Annual Meeting of the Cognitive Science Society*, volume 24.

Jennifer Golbeck, Cristina Robles, Michon Edmondson, and Karen Turner. 2011a. Predicting personality from twitter. In *Privacy, Security, Risk and Trust (PASSAT) and 2011 IEEE Third Inernational Conference on Social Computing (SocialCom), 2011 IEEE Third International Conference on*, pages 149–156. IEEE.

Jennifer Golbeck, Cristina Robles, and Karen Turner. 2011b. Predicting personality with social media. In *CHI'11 extended abstracts on human factors in computing systems*, pages 253–262. ACM.

Lewis R Goldberg. 1981. Language and individual differences: The search for universals in personality lexicons. *Review of personality and social psychology*, 2(1):141–165.

Carlos E González-Gallardo, Azucena Montes, Gerardo Sierra, J Antonio Núñez-Juárez, Adolfo Jonathan Salinas-López, and Juan Ek. 2015. Tweets classification using corpus dependent tags, character and pos n-grams. In *CLEF (Working Notes).*

Francisco Iacobelli, Alastair J Gill, Scott Nowson, and Jon Oberlander. 2011. Large scale personality classification of bloggers. In *Affective computing and intelligent interaction*, pages 568–577. Springer.

Oliver P John, Eileen M Donahue, and Robert L Kentle. 1991. The big five inventoryversions 4a and 54.

Oliver P John, Laura P Naumann, and Christopher J Soto. 2008. Paradigm shift to the integrative big five trait taxonomy. *Handbook of personality: Theory and research*, 3(2):114–158.

Randy J. Larsen and David M. Buss. 2008. *Personality psychology: Domains of knowledge about human nature.* McGraw Hill Education.

Jamy Li and Mark Chignell. 2010. Birds of a feather: How personality influences blog writing and reading. *International Journal of Human-Computer Studies*, 68(9):589–602.

François Mairesse, Marilyn A Walker, Matthias R Mehl, and Roger K Moore. 2007. Using linguistic cues for the automatic recognition of personality in conversation and text. *Journal of artificial intelligence research*, 30:457–500.

Navonil Majumder, Soujanya Poria, Alexander Gelbukh, and Erik Cambria. 2017. Deep learning-based document modeling for personality detection from text. *IEEE Intelligent Systems*, 32(2):74–79.

Hazel Rose Markus and Shinobu Kitayama. 1998. The cultural psychology of personality. *Journal of cross-cultural psychology*, 29(1):63–87.

Tara C Marshall, Katharina Lefringhausen, and Nelli Ferenczi. 2015. The big five, self-esteem, and narcissism as predictors of the topics people write about in facebook status updates. *Personality and Individual Differences*, 85:35–40.

Robert R McCrae and Paul T Costa Jr. A five-factor theory of personality. In Lawrence A. Pervin and Oliver P. John, editors, *Handbook of Personality: Theory and Research.* The Guilford Press, New York, NY.

Matthias R Mehl and James W Pennebaker. 2003. The sounds of social life: A psychometric analysis of students' daily social environments and natural conversations. *Journal of personality and social psychology*, 84(4):857.

Saif M Mohammad and Svetlana Kiritchenko. 2013. Using nuances of emotion to identify personality. *Proceedings of ICWSM.*

Warren T Norman. 1963. Toward an adequate taxonomy of personality attributes: Replicated factor structure in peer nomination personality ratings. *The Journal of Abnormal and Social Psychology*, 66(6):574.

Scott Nowson and Jon Oberlander. 2007. Identifying more bloggers. *Proceedings of ICWSM.*

Jon Oberlander and Scott Nowson. 2006. Whose thumb is it anyway?: classifying author personality from weblog text. In *Proceedings of the COLING/ACL on Main conference poster sessions*, pages 627–634. Association for Computational Linguistics.

Fabian Pedregosa, Gaël Varoquaux, Alexandre Gramfort, Vincent Michel, Bertrand Thirion, Olivier Grisel, Mathieu Blondel, Peter Prettenhofer, Ron Weiss, Vincent Dubourg, et al. 2011. Scikit-learn: Machine learning in python. *Journal of machine learning research*, 12(Oct):2825–2830.

Kuei-Hsiang Peng, Li-Heng Liou, Cheng-Shang Chang, and Duan-Shin Lee. 2015. Predicting personality traits of chinese users based on facebook wall posts. In *Wireless and Optical Communication Conference (WOCC), 2015 24th*, pages 9–14. IEEE.

James W Pennebaker and Laura A King. 1999. Linguistic styles: Language use as an individual difference. *Journal of personality and social psychology*, 77(6):1296.

Soujanya Poria, Alexandar Gelbukh, Basant Agarwal, Erik Cambria, and Newton Howard. 2013. Common sense knowledge based personality recognition from text. In *Mexican International Conference on Artificial Intelligence*, pages 484–496. Springer.

Lin Qiu, Han Lin, Jonathan Ramsay, and Fang Yang. 2012. You are what you tweet: Personality expression and perception on twitter. *Journal of Research in Personality*, 46(6):710–718.

Francisco Rangel, Paolo Rosso, Martin Potthast, Benno Stein, and Walter Daelemans. 2015. Overview of the 3rd author profiling task at pan 2015. In *CLEF*, page 2015. sn.

H Andrew Schwartz, Johannes C Eichstaedt, Margaret L Kern, Lukasz Dziurzynski, Stephanie M Ramones, Megha Agrawal, Achal Shah, Michal Kosinski, David Stillwell, Martin EP Seligman, et al. 2013. Personality, gender, and age in the language of social media: The open-vocabulary approach. *PloS one*, 8(9):e73791.

Jared Suttles. 2013. Tweetokenize. `https://github.com/jaredks/tweetokenize`.

Tommy Tandera, Derwin Suhartono, Rini Wongso, Yen Lina Prasetio, et al. 2017. Personality prediction system from facebook users. *Procedia Computer Science*, 116:604–611.

Di Xue, Zheng Hong, Shize Guo, Liang Gao, Lifa Wu, Jinghua Zheng, and Nan Zhao. 2017. Personality recognition on social media with label distribution learning. *IEEE Access*, 5:13478–13488.

Jianguo Yu and Konstantin Markov. 2017. Deep learning based personality recognition from facebook status updates. In *Proceedings of 8th International Conference on Awareness Science and Technology (iCAST)*, pages 383–387. IEEE.

Grounding the Semantics of Part-of-Day Nouns Worldwide using Twitter

David Vilares
Universidade da Coruña
FASTPARSE Lab, LyS Group
Departamento de Computación
Campus de A Elviña s/n, 15071
A Coruña, Spain
david.vilares@udc.es

Carlos Gómez-Rodríguez
Universidade da Coruña
FASTPARSE Lab, LyS Group
Departamento de Computación
Campus de A Elviña s/n, 15071
A Coruña, Spain
carlos.gomez@udc.es

Abstract

The usage of part-of-day nouns, such as 'night', and their time-specific greetings ('good night'), varies across languages and cultures. We show the possibilities that Twitter offers for studying the semantics of these terms and its variability between countries. We mine a worldwide sample of multilingual tweets with temporal greetings, and study how their frequencies vary in relation with local time. The results provide insights into the semantics of these temporal expressions and the cultural and sociological factors influencing their usage.

1 Introduction

Human languages are intertwined with their cultures and societies, having evolved together, reflecting them and in turn shaping them (Ottenheimer, 2013; Dediu et al., 2013). Part-of-day nouns (e.g. 'morning' or 'night') are an example of this, as their meaning depends on how each language's speakers organize their daily schedule. For example, while the morning in English-speaking countries is assumed to end at noon, the Spanish term ('mañana') is understood to span until lunch time, which normally takes place between 13:00 and 15:00 in Spain. It is fair to relate this difference to cultural (lunch being the main meal of the day in Spain, as opposed to countries like the UK, and therefore being a milestone in the daily timetable) and sociopolitical factors (the late lunch time being influenced by work schedules and the displacement of the Spanish time zones with respect to solar time). Similar differences have been noted for different pairs of languages (Jäkel, 2003) and for cultures using the same language (Sekyi-Baidoo and Koranteng, 2008), based on manual study, field research and interviews with natives. Work on automatically extracting the semantics of part-of-day nouns is scarce, as

classic corpora are not timestamped. Reiter and Sripada (2003); Sripada et al. (2003) overcome it by analyzing weather forecasts and aligning them to timestamped simulations, giving approximate groundings for time-of-day nouns and showing idiolectal variation on the term 'evening', but the work is limited to English.

The relation between language and sociocultural factors implies that the semantics of part-of-day nouns (e.g. 'end of the morning') cannot be studied in isolation from social habits (e.g. 'typical lunch time'). A relevant study of such habits is done by Walch et al. (2016), who develop an app to collect sleep habits from users worldwide. While they do not study the meaning of words, their insights are used for validation.

We propose a new approach to study the semantics of part-of-day nouns by exploiting Twitter and the time-specific greetings (e.g. 'good morning') used in different cultures. By mining tweets with these greetings, we obtain a large, worldwide sample of their usage. Since many tweets come with time and geolocation metadata, we can know the local time and country at which each one was emitted. The main contribution of the paper is to show how it is possible to learn the semantics of these terms in a much more extensive way than previous work, at a global scale, with less effort and allowing statistical testing of differences in usage between terms, countries and languages.

2 Materials and methods

To ground the semantics of greetings we used 5 terms as seeds: 'good morning', 'good afternoon', 'good evening', 'good night' and 'hello' (a time-unspecific greeting used for comparison). We translated them to 53 languages and variants using Bing translator.[1] We use *italics* to refer to greet-

---

[1] We used the mstranslator API for the Bing translator.

Proceedings of the Second Workshop on Computational Modeling of People's Opinions, Personality, and Emotions in Social Media, pages 123–128
New Orleans, Louisiana, June 6, 2018. ©2018 Association for Computational Linguistics

ings irrespective of the language. 172,802,620 tweets were collected from Sept. 2 to Dec. 7 2016.

For some languages (e.g. Spanish), there is no differentiation between 'good evening' and 'good night', and they both are translated to the same expression. For some others, some expressions cannot be considered equivalent, e.g. 'good morning' is translated to 'bonjour' in French, which is however commonly used as 'hello', or simply as 'good day'.

Text preprocessing is not necessary: we rely on metadata, not on the tweet itself, and only the seed words are needed to categorize tweets within a part of day. To clean up the data, we removed retweets, as they last for hours, biasing the temporal analysis. Duplicate tweets were kept, as similar messages from different days and users (e.g. 'good night!') are needed for the task at hand. Tweets need to be associated with a timestamp and country-level geolocation. Tweets have a creation time, composed of a UTC time and a UTC offset that varies depending on the time zone. However, most tweets are not geolocated and we must rely on the data provided by the user. This may be fake or incomplete, e.g. specifying only a village. We used fine-grained databases[2] to do the mapping to the country level location and performed a sanity check, comparing the Twitter offset to the valid set of offsets for that country[3], to reduce the amount of wrongly geolocated tweets.[4] Comparing the solar and standard time could provide more insights, but this requires a fine-grained geolocation of the tweets. We obtained a dataset of 10,523,349 elements, available at https://github.com/aghie/peoples2018_grounding: 4,503,077 *good morning*'s, 599,586 *good afternoon*'s, 214,231 *good evening*'s, 880,003 *good night*'s and 4,359,797 *hello*'s.[5]

3 Results and validation

Given a country, some of the tweets are written in foreign languages for reasons like tourism or immigration. This paper refers to tweets written in official or *de facto* languages, unless otherwise specified. Also, analyzing differences according

Country$_{lang}$	morning	afternoon	night	hello
Philippines$_{en}$	08:02:49	13:39:52	00:13:42	14:27:20
Japan$_{ja}$	08:07:28	15:46:50	01:04:19	*6
South Africa$_{en}$	08:10:07	14:50:52	22:51:48	13:40:19
Germany$_{de}$	08:16:41	13:15:18	23:29:38	14:35:06
Indonesia$_{in}$	08:17:18	16:25:11	19:02:09	13:55:00
Netherlands$_{nl}$	08:25:42	14:28:09	23:44:56	14:10:13
Ecuador$_{es}$	08:32:54	15:03:22	22:10:59	14:37:10
United States$_{en}$	08:33:23	13:26:25	21:06:00	13:33:13
Nigeria$_{en}$	08:34:37	14:11:49	17:19:19	13:40:23
Venezuela$_{es}$	08:37:03	15:04:00	21:18:05	14:11:07
Malaysia$_{en}$	08:39:17	13:31:41	01:02:33	13:56:49
Chile$_{es}$	08:39:38	15:06:52	00:10:43	14:11:56
Colombia$_{es}$	08:40:19	15:13:16	21:10:57	14:42:58
Canada$_{en}$	08:40:30	13:19:33	21:10:57	13:47:40
Mexico$_{es}$	08:51:04	15:26:35	21:58:24	14:25:37
India$_{en}$	08:51:24	13:40:00	00:03:12	14:12:54
United Kingdom$_{en}$	09:06:33	14:30:45	19:49:17	14:13:03
Turkey$_{tr}$	09:16:40	13:12:23	00:41:08	13:56:42
Australia$_{en}$	09:17:43	15:15:38	20:33:47	13:48:28
Brazil$_{pt}$	09:18:20	14:47:51	23:31:34	14:26:07
Pakistan$_{en}$	09:29:12	13:29:28	01:23:05	13:43:58
Russian Federation$_{ru}$	09:36:17	13:44:42	23:51:49	14:14:44
Spain$_{es}$	09:42:41	16:43:57	00:24:28	14:26:33
Argentina$_{es}$	09:43:47	16:20:05	00:26:55	14:02:03
Greece$_{el}$	09:46:11	17:12:35	23:28:56	15:01:05
Kenya$_{en}$	09:57:39	14:15:33	21:44:26	14:07:03
Portugal$_{pt}$	10:10:22	15:27:35	23:05:25	14:57:34
France$_{fr}$	12:37:09	*7	00:41:08	14:41:07

Table 1: Average local time for the greetings coming from the countries with most data, sorted by the average time for the greeting *good morning*. *Hello* was used as sanity check.

to criteria such as gender or solar time can be relevant. As determining the impact of all those is a challenge on its own, we focus on the primary research question: *can we learn semantics of the part-of-day nouns from simple analysis of tweets?* To verify data quality, *good morning* tweets were revised: out of 1 000 random tweets from the USA, 97.9% were legitimate greetings and among the rest, some reflected somehow that the user just started the day (e.g 'Didn't get any good morning SMS'). We did the same for Spain (98,1% legitimate), Brazil (97.8%) and India (99.6%).

Existing work and dated events are used to ratify the results presented below.

3.1 Worldwide average greeting times

Table 1 shows the average greeting times for the countries from which we collected more data.

---

[2] http://download.geonames.org/export/dump/

[3] http://timezonedb.com

[4] Free geolocation API's have rate limits and their use is unfeasible with a large amount of tweets.

[5] The dataset does not contain tweets from the first two weeks of October due to logistic issues.

[6] Hello translated to 'Konnichiwa', as good afternoon.

[7] The French term for afternoon (après-midi) is not commonly used as part of a greeting.

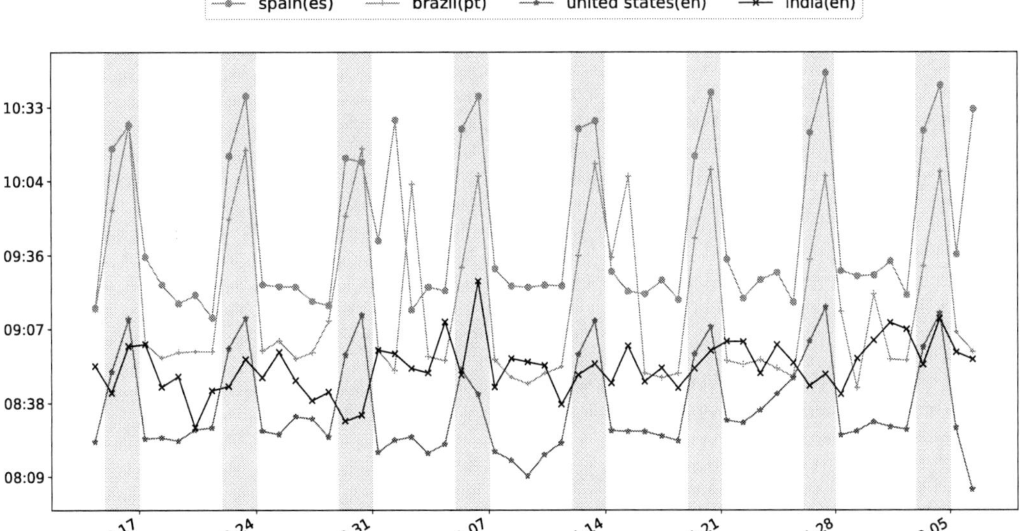

Figure 1: Average day time for the greeting *good morning* in different countries (USA, Brazil, Spain and India) for a period from mid October to early December, 2016. Weekends are shaded in gray.

Asian, African and American countries tend to begin the day earlier than Europe (with exceptions, e.g. Germany). The table reflects that countries in southern Europe (e.g. Spain, Portugal or Greece) start the day later than the northern ones (the Netherlands or UK). For some countries, e.g. France, this information is known to be biased, as *good morning* ('bonjour') is used all along the day. A validation at a fine-grained scale is unfeasible, but the results at the country level are in line with Figure 3 of Walch et al. (2016), e.g., they state that Japan, the USA or Germany have earlier wake up times than Spain, Brazil or Turkey.

The average greeting times for *good afternoon* reveal insights that may stem from cultural differences (e.g. lunch break time). Anglo-Saxon and South Asian countries have the earliest afternoon (with averages between 13:00 and 14:00), while in Mediterranean countries the morning lasts longer (average greeting times for *good afternoon* around 15:00 or 16:00). A number of countries under the influence of the United Kingdom, such as the United States, Pakistan or India show earlier *afternoon* times. The opposite happens in South America, historically influenced by Portuguese and Spanish colonialism during the Early modern period, which exhibits later *afternoon* times.

This poses interesting questions for future work, such as whether there is a particular reason that could justify this behavior, like having more similar cuisine practices. In this context, the adoption of food practices in colonialism has been already studied by anthropologists and historians (Earle, 2010). Trigg (2004) points out how in the early period of the Spanish colonialism in the Americas, they 'civilized' the Indigenous community by making them adopt manners, dress and customs. She points that the role of food was specially relevant due to its large social component, and was not limited to the way the food was eaten, but also prepared, served and consumed.

Twitter also reflects differences between countries regarding night life. On the one hand, Anglo-Saxon countries wish *good night* earlier (from 19:49 in the UK to 21:10 in Canada) than other societies. On the other hand, southern European countries go to bed later, and some of them even wish a *good night* after midnight (e.g. Spain). Comparing to Walch et al. (2016), we find similar tendencies. For example, in their study Spain, Turkey or Brazil use the smartphone until later than Canada, the USA or the UK, and therefore they go later to bed. Our Twitter approach also captures the particular case of Japanese mentioned by Walch et al.: they wake up very early, but use the smartphone until late in the night, suggesting a later bed time.

A fine-grained analysis shows how Twitter captures other cultural and working differences. Figure 1 charts the average day time for *good morning* for the USA, Brazil, Spain and India during part of the polling period. The time peaks in the weekends for many of the countries, showing that Twitter captures how business and work are reduced during holidays, resulting in later wake up times.

However, this is not visible in some countries where working conditions are sometimes questioned (Mosse et al., 2002): for India the weekend peak is less pronounced, which can be considered as an indicator that a significant part of its population does not enjoy work-free weekends.

The usage of part-of-day expressions can be helpful to understand more complex issues, such as how foreigners integrate into a country and adapt to its daily schedule. We take the USA as example, as it has a large foreign community of Spanish speakers, mainly from Mexico (and in a smaller proportion from other Latin American countries). If we calculate the average day time for the Spanish form of 'good morning' ('buenos días') in the USA, we obtain that the result is 08:09, while the corresponding English greeting's average time is 08:33. This is reinforced by Figure 2, where 'buenos días' average day time is consistently lower than 'good morning'.[8] This would be in line to their presence in low-wage jobs that require to wake up earlier, e.g. waiter, cleaning or construction work (Flippen, 2012; Liu, 2013).

It is worth noting that, assuming that these 'buenos días' greetings come from latinos, those in the USA wake up even earlier than in their countries of origin (see Table 1).

Figure 1 also shows how national holidays influence societies. For example, Nov. 2 (Day of the Dead) and Nov. 15 (Proclamation of the Republic) are holidays in Brazil, producing a peak in that country's graph similar to the behavior in the weekends. Similarly, Nov. 1 (All Saints' Day) and Dec. 6 (Constitution Day) are holidays in Spain and similar peaks are observed too. From Figure 2 we can see how Thanksgiving (Nov. 24 in 2016) reflects a four-day weekend in the USA: many businesses allow employees to take this holiday from Thursday, resulting into a gradual and increasing peak that spans until Sunday. This is cap-

---

⁸The peak occurring on 29th October for the Spanish tweets is due to a case of spam that could not be avoided according to the procedure described in §2.

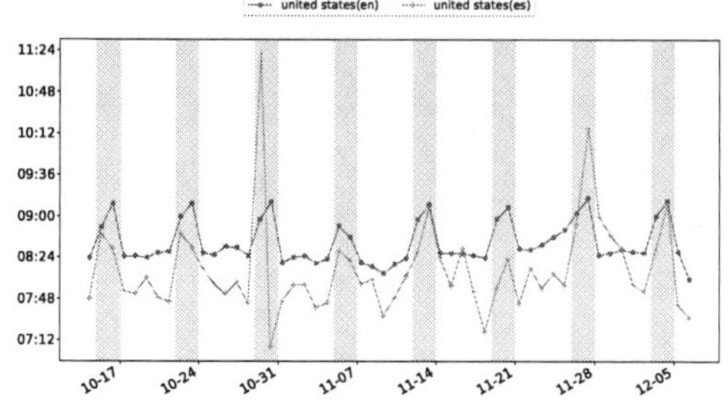

Figure 2: Average day time for the greeting 'good morning' and its Spanish form in the USA.

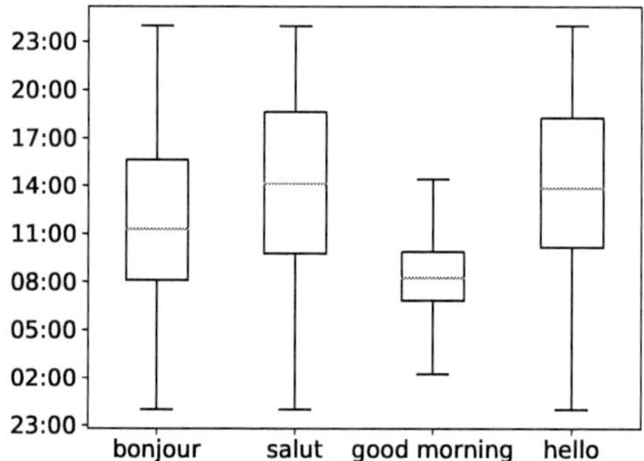

Figure 3: Box & whisker plot for the French and English *good morning*'s and *hello*'s in Canada.

tured by the English *good morning*s, but not by the Spanish ones. The day after the USA 2016 elections (Nov. 9), a valley occurs on the *good morning* time for the States (Figure 1). The winner was not known until 03:00, suggesting that the distribution of greetings reflects social behaviors in other special events.

3.2 Daily analysis

Twitter can be used to do a time-of-day analysis, e.g., as said in §3.1, 'bonjour' is assumed to be used all along the day. To test this, we take Canada, where French and English are official languages. Figure 3 shows how 'bonjour' and 'salut' ('hello') are used all along the day, while 'good morning' is used in the morning hours. English and French *hello*'s share a similar distribution.

Figure 4 shows a greeting area chart for the USA, showing how 'good evening' and 'good afternoon' are well differentiated, with the transition happening over 16:30. This contrasts to countries such as Spain (Figure 5), where the language has a single word ('tarde') for 'evening' and 'afternoon', whose greeting spans from over 14:00, as the morning ends late (see §1), to 21:00.

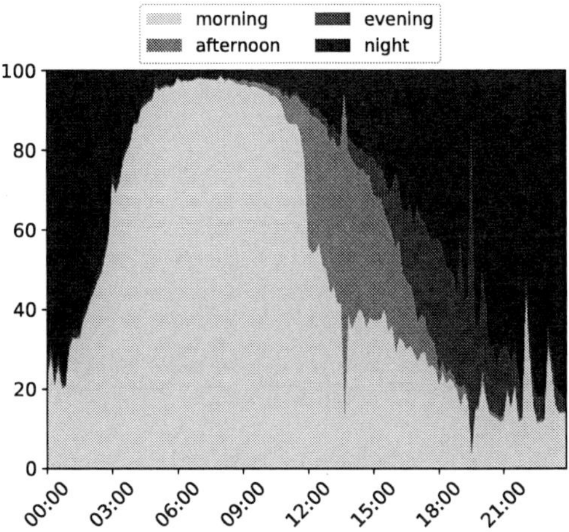

Figure 4: Stacked area chart for the greetings in the USA: % (y axis) vs time (x axis).

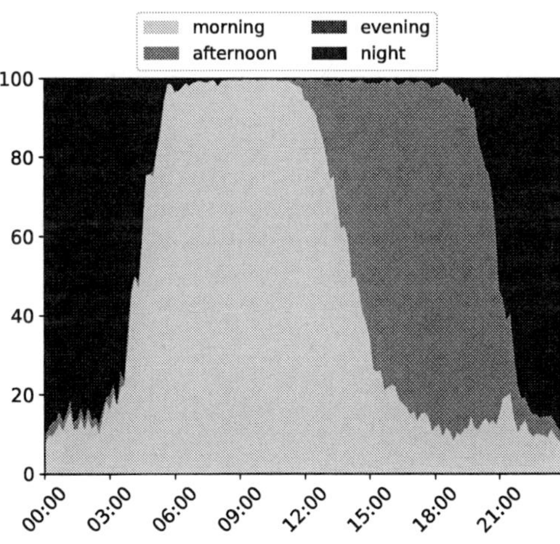

Figure 5: Same as Figure 4, but for Spain.

Area plots like these give a clear picture of the semantics of part-of-day nouns, as they depict the exact times when they are used. The precise semantics can be grounded more rigorously using statistical testing to know the exact time intervals at which people significantly use a specific greeting.

For example, to know when to switch from *good morning* to *good afternoon* in Spanish, we can: (1) group the number of 'buenos días' ('good morning') and 'buenas tardes' ('good afternoon') by in-tervals of 10 minutes, and (2) apply a binomial test to each interval, to determine if one of the greetings is significantly more likely to occur than the other (assuming equal probability of occurrence). For example, for Spain, we obtain that the morning ends at 14:00 (p-value=2×10^{-8} at 14:00, 0.09 at 14:10) and the afternoon starts at 14:40 (p-value becomes statistically significant again with 4×10^{-7}, showing a significant majority of *good afternoon*).

4   Conclusion

We crawled Twitter to study the semantics of part-of-day nouns in different countries and societies, showed examples from the polled period and ratified them against existing research and dated events. For space reasons we cannot show insights for all scenarios, but full results are at `https://github.com/aghie/peoples2018_grounding`.

Acknowledgments

DV and CGR receive funding from the European Research Council (ERC), under the European Union's Horizon 2020 research and innovation programme (FASTPARSE, grant agreement No 714150), from the TELEPARES-UDC project (FFI2014-51978-C2-2-R) and the ANSWER-ASAP project (TIN2017-85160-C2-1-R) from MINECO, and from Xunta de Galicia (ED431B 2017/01).

References

Dan Dediu, Michael Cysouw, Stephen C. Levinson, Andrea Baronchelli, Morten H. Christiansen, William Croft, Nicholas Evans, Simon Garrod, Russell D. Gray, Anne Kandler, and Elena Lieven. 2013. Cultural evolution of language. In Peter J. Richerson and Morten H. Christiansen, editors, *Cultural Evolution: Society, Technology, Language, and Religion*, volume 12 of *Strüngmann Forum Reports*, pages 303–332. MIT Press, Cambridge, MA.

Rebecca Earle. 2010. "if you eat their food …": Diets and bodies in early colonial spanish americarebecca earle"if you eat their food …". *The American Historical Review*, 115(3):688–713.

Chenoa A Flippen. 2012. Laboring underground: The employment patterns of hispanic immigrant men in Durham, NC. *Social Problems*, 59(1):21–42.

Olaf Jäkel. 2003. 'Morning, noon and night': Denotational incongruencies between English and German.

In Cornelia Zelinsky-Wibbelt, editor, *Text, Context, Concepts*, pages 159–178. Mouton de Gruyter, Berlin/New York.

Cathy Yang Liu. 2013. Latino immigration and the low-skill urban labor market: The case of Atlanta. *Social Science Quarterly*, 94(1):131–157.

David Mosse, Sanjeev Gupta, Mona Mehta, Vidya Shah, Julia fnms Rees, and KRIBP Project Team. 2002. Brokered livelihoods: Debt, Labour Migration and Development in Tribal Western India. *The Journal of Development Studies*, 38(5):59–88.

Harriet Joseph Ottenheimer. 2013. *The Anthropology of Language: An Introduction to Linguistic Anthropology*, 3rd edition. Wadsworth, Cengage Learning, Englewood Cliffs, NJ.

Ehud Reiter and Somayajulu G. Sripada. 2003. Learning the meaning and usage of time phrases from a parallel text-data corpus. In *Proceedings of the HLT-NAACL 2003 Workshop on Learning Word Meaning from Non-Linguistic Data*, pages 78–85.

Yaw Sekyi-Baidoo and Louisa A. Koranteng. 2008. English general greetings in the Ghanaian sociolinguistic context. *The International Journal of Language, Society and Culture*, pages 113–126.

Somayajulu G. Sripada, Ehud Reiter, Jim Hunter, and Jin Yu. 2003. Exploiting a parallel text-data corpus. In *Proceedings of Corpus Linguistics 2003*, pages 734–743.

Heather Trigg. 2004. Food choice and social identity in early colonial new mexico. *Journal of the Southwest*, pages 223–252.

Olivia J Walch, Amy Cochran, and Daniel B Forger. 2016. A global quantification of "normal" sleep schedules using smartphone data. *Science advances*, 2(5):e1501705.

Author Index

Association for Computational Linguistics
209 N. Eighth Street
Stroudsburg, Pennsylvania 18360

ISBN 978-1-5108-6360-6